Beyond the Blue Horizon

Also by Brian Fagan

Beyond the Blue Horizon

How the Earliest Mariners Unlocked the Secrets of the Oceans

Brian Fagan

BLOOMSBURY PRESS
NEW YORK · LONDON · NEW DELHI · SYDNEY

Published by Bloomsbury Press, New York

All papers used by Bloomsbury Press are natural, recyclable products made from wood grown in well-managed forests. The manufacturing processes conform to the environmental regulations of the country of origin.

LIBRARY OF CONGRESS CATALOGING-IN-PUBLICATION DATA

Fagan, Brian M.
Beyond the blue horizon : how the earliest mariners unlocked
the secrets of the oceans / Brian Fagan.—1st ed.
p.   cm.
Includes bibliographical references and index.
ISBN 978-1-60819-005-8 (hardback)
1. Navigation, Prehistoric. 2. Sea peoples—History.
3. Ocean travel—History. I. Title.
GN799.N3F33 2012
910.4'5—dc23
2011045758

First published by Bloomsbury Press in 2012
This edition published in 2013

Paperback ISBN: 978-1-60819-403-2

1   3   5   7   9   10   8   6   4   2

Typeset by Westchester Book Group
Printed and bound in the U.S.A. by Thomson-Shore Inc., Dexter, Michigan

To

Peter and Pete

With gratitude for friendship and perceptive diagnosis

They seek only a view of the sea, what Jefferson called the water prospect without termination. Somehow that openness, at least to people usually "pent up in lath and plaster," opens something else, certainly reverie, possibly looming as seamen know it, a glimpse over the horizon.

—Herman Melville, *Moby-Dick*

Under the insistence of steam, and the Hydrographic Office, old concepts of sea, seafaring, and seascape must change.

The Century Magazine, September 1899

Contents

THE PACIFIC TO THE WEST

Preface

I LEARNED TO SAIL on the English Channel when I was eight years old, pushing seven decades ago. We sailed not in a gleaming fiberglass yacht or a high-tech racing dinghy, but in a heavy fishing boat with faded tan sails. When the wind dropped, we rowed, standing to our oars, for we were too small to sit and row from the thwarts. No engine, no electronic instruments, but we shipped out with a skipper who knew his home waters backwards. He measured the state of the tide by looking at exposed rocks, gauged the wind by feeling it on his weathered cheek, and knew almost as much about the local seabed as he did about the Dorset coastline where he fished. To sail with the first of my seafaring mentors was to step back into a working boat from Victorian times, when men like him lived off the sea by oar and sail, as his father and grandfather had done.

My childhood friends and I learned the basics of rowing and sailing the hard way—nothing sophisticated, but enough to hoist and trim a sail, to pull an oar correctly, and to steer a course on a familiar landmark. But what we learned above all else was a feel for the sea and its moods, a way of looking at the ocean with a mixture of caution and respect that has remained with me for a lifetime of sailing.

A Dorset fishing boat was one thread in my sailing life. Another was literary—the works of Arthur Ransome, an English journalist turned children's book author who wrote classic sailing tales between the 1930s and 1950s that are still devoured by generations of British young. They tell of the Swallows and the Amazons, two families of children who had believable sailing adventures in England's Lake District, among the mudflats and shallows of Suffolk, and on the North Sea. Adventures on dinghies and small cruising boats—the stories were so believable that I yearned to emulate them, and I'm glad to say that I have. Teenage adventures in traditional converted fishing boats, dinghies, rented yachts, and then in boats of my own: my seafaring life has been a kaleidoscope of truly memorable experiences. And some very nasty ones: lying hove to in a North Sea gale and being becalmed for two days in the middle of the Mediterranean in a bumpy sea cannot be described as anything but indelibly unpleasant experiences.

Beyond the Blue Horizon had its birth in my sailing life, with all its varied adventures and mishaps, in decades of striving to complete voyages happily and safely. Most of the time, I've succeeded, but there have been many times when I've contemplated my mortality in the face of the seemingly inexorable forces of the ocean. Wherever I've sailed, the past has lurked in the background—an anchorage off the shrines at Delos, in the heart of the Aegean Sea; burial mounds on the skyline in Denmark; the gray soils of shell middens on Southern California's Channel Islands. Such lurkings bring out the archaeological side of me, the ghosts of long-vanished seafarers going about their business far from the spotlight of history. Inevitably, sailing fast in rough seas, I've wondered how our forebears plucked up the courage to sail across open water to unexplored coastlines or to take passage beyond the horizon toward land that may not exist at all, with seemingly effortless panache. Making my way on a compass course across a seemingly featureless seascape, I've thought of our ancestors paddling, rowing, and sailing across the same waters without any of the blandishments of modern technology or a reliable diesel engine belowdecks, let alone a compass. Then I start wondering: How do you cross oceans without charts, a compass, a sextant, or satellite navigation? How do you decipher the inconspicuous clues of impending foul weather or discern with certainty that land lies over the horizon? Then there's the question of questions: Why did our forebears go to sea at all? What compelling forces sent them into deepwater paddling or rowing on rafts, in dugouts and planked open boats, and, eventually under sail in much more sophisticated watercraft?

In my professional life, I'm an archaeologist. My colleagues and I study ancient human societies as they change and develop over immensely long periods of time. The harsh realities of preservation mean that we reconstruct ancient cultures from durable, usually unspectacular clues such as stone tools, pottery fragments, and house foundations. Only rarely can we look beyond the artifacts at the intangibles of human existence—our cosmology, ritual beliefs, and social relationships. Perhaps hardest of all, how do we gain an understanding of how ancient people perceived the land- and seascapes around them—and how did they decipher them?

Beyond the Blue Horizon is not a narrative of shipwrecks and watercraft, although these are important components in the story. It's about events both afloat and ashore. As the pioneering underwater archaeologist George Bass once forcibly reminded me, shipwrecks, however important, tell us more about societies ashore than they do about what survives on the seabed. Excavating shipwrecks can be glamorous, the stuff of which *National Geographic* is made, but the most important questions generated by such discoveries lie on land. This book looks at the wider context of ancient seafaring, at the human societies that pioneered voyaging on open water. Why did they take to hitherto unexplored inshore or offshore waters? What compelled a few members of these societies to search for new lands? Was it land hunger, factional quarreling at home, a search for prestige and trading opportunities, or simply a deeply felt restlessness and curiosity? Of course, we will never know the whole story, but generations of archaeological and historical research, especially in recent years, allow us to tell at least an incomplete tale.

This is not a tale of galleons and famed European navigators like Christopher Columbus, Ferdinand Magellan, and James Cook. Our story ends before Columbus landed in the Bahamas in 1492 or Cook observed the transit of Venus on Tahiti in 1769 and revealed the seductive delights of Polynesia to an entranced Europe. These are well-trodden historical events. Ours is an earlier world of anonymous, mostly nonliterate people who formed part of the backdrop of history. Kings might rise and fall, empires come to prominence then fade into obscurity, but the timeless routine of cabotage (coasting) along quiet shorelines, of canoe voyages between Pacific Islands and trading ventures in monsoon seas or across the North Sea and farther afield continued—quiet events as predictable as the passage of the seasons. The humble folks on these voyages were the people who decoded most of the world's oceans, not out of any overwhelming ambition to "serve God and to get rich," as with the Spanish conquistadores who conquered Aztec Mexico, but simply as part of their existence in the heart of an intricate, often spiritually charged cosmos.

Nor do I explore claims of very early seafaring, long before the deliberate seagoing of more recent history. No question, a few humans may have floated across open straits to islands like Flores, in Southeast Asia, and from mainland Greece to Crete hundreds of thousands of years ago. Fascinating as these assertions may be, they are irrelevant here. We're concerned not with putative accidental journeys, with the reality that people can stay afloat on buoyant logs, but with deliberate journeys on the water. Why did people take to the sea, then paddle, row, and sail on it as a regular part of daily life?

Many early seafaring societies held powerful supernatural beliefs about the ocean. This is a story about ventures afloat that may seem amazing through the magnifying glass of history, but to those who undertook them they were often merely an extension of lives lived at the edge of the ocean. *Beyond the Blue Horizon* is a celebration of human ingenuity and often brilliant adaptation to ever-changing environments, and of the compelling restlessness that drove so much of human history. I have this sense of restlessness myself, which is why I've woven some of my own experiences into the story. They say that history repeats itself. Time and time again, far from land or in narrow waters, in fair weather and foul, I've sensed an ancient skipper from the same waters looking over my shoulder and been reassured that they must have felt much the same way as I did. And this is why I wrote this book.

BEYOND THE BLUE HORIZON defies neat chronological organization, for it's a book with many narratives, one that covers enormous tracts of the world's oceans and a bewildering array of human societies. Most history books follow a chronological gradient, and with good reason, for such a timescale provides a convenient framework for, say, an account of

someone's life, an unfolding diplomatic crisis leading to war, or something like the Medieval Warm Period of a thousand years ago. I always
find myself reading such books as stories passing through time, on the
general principle established by the King in *Alice in Wonderland*: "Begin
at the beginning, and go on till you come to the end: then stop." An admirable piece of advice for most books, to be sure, but I'm uncertain as
to whether *Blue Horizon* is best read that way. With the diffuse narratives
in these pages, you have options.

For this reason, I've organized the story in sequences of chapters that
describe early seafaring in different regions of the world. Chapter 1, "'The
Sands and Flats Are Discovered,'" sets the stage and makes the point
that the skills acquired while skirting coasts are little different from
those used offshore. This book revolves around the close relationships
between ancient seafarers and the ocean. Here I draw on my own experience in small boats of all kinds to discuss some of the mind-sets that
one needs to pilot small vessels close to the shoreline and far offshore.
(There are, of course, some chapters not enhanced by personal experience: I have not sailed everywhere!) I also introduce another major
thread: the complex relationships our forebears enjoyed with seascapes
beset by uncontrollable forces, waters where powerful beasts and deities, as well as the ancestors, dwelt. Chapters 2 to 4 describe the earliest
deliberate seafaring, which began off the Southeast Asian mainland
more than 50,000 years ago, then trace the remarkable voyages that led
to the colonizing of the Pacific and some of the remotest islands on
earth. From the Pacific, we travel in Chapters 5 and 6 to the Mediterranean, where seafaring began in the Aegean soon after the Ice Age, by at
least 8000 B.C.E. By 2000 B.C.E., mariners were sailing regularly between
the Persian Gulf and the Indus River in what is now Pakistan. Traveling
Indian Ocean waters depended on the predictable reversals of the monsoon winds over a wide area between Southeast Asia and Africa, a phenomenon described in Chapters 7 to 9. It was no accident that the first
truly global maritime trade networks developed in the arms of the monsoon. Chapters 10 and 11 take us back to the first passages over open
water in Europe's North Sea, where, I argue, the ocean was considered

the realm of the ancestors. Thousands of years of coastal paddling and sailing culminate in the Norse voyages to Iceland, Greenland, and beyond. The next three chapters explore a different form of decoding in the Americas. The Aleutian Islands and the Northwest and California coasts, described in Chapters 12 and 13, provide fascinating examples of how inshore waters became part of the fabric of Native American societies. Chapter 14, "The Fiery Pool and the Spiny Oyster," delves into the complex relationship between the ancient Maya of Central America and the unfathomable waters of the Underworld. This complex marriage of a violent mythic world, truly a Fiery Pool, and human existence underlay not just Mesoamerican seafaring but the entire panoply of Maya civilization. Similar close relationships between the living and spiritual worlds may also have brought South American balsa rafts to Maya shores. Finally, the Epilogue draws together the many themes of the book. We end in the industrialized world, where, as recently as the early twentieth century, the magnificent technology of ocean liners and warships from the Industrial Revolution thrived alongside humble seafarers using sailing and rowing boats little changed since medieval times.

Everyone should dive into the book via Chapter 1, for it is crucial to understanding the various decodings that follow. After that, you're on your own. I'd like to give you two options to consider:

Option the first is the obvious one. Like the King, you can read the book as a linear narrative, migrating from area to area as you go along. A brief summary statement introduces each region and its chapters, to ease the transition from one part of the world to another, thus allowing you to travel long distances between chapters. There are, in general terms, chronological gradients within the area chapters, but this is not the case when you go from, say, Southeast Asia to the Mediterranean, where the time-scale winds back to the beginning again.

Option the second provides you with hierarchies of chapters, grouped by areas. By using this approach, you can concentrate on, say, the Pacific or the Americas, leaving other material aside until later. Provided you end by reading the Epilogue, you should leave both with focused narratives of areas that interest you and with a general sense of the central messages of the book. If you choose this approach, your choices are open-ended. Using the notes at the end of the book, you can then delve more deeply into the enormous literature that surrounds each chapter. No King of Wonderland peers over your shoulder here. Like the Norse with their sense of *æfintyr*, their restless curiosity, the choices for maritime exploration are yours.

Author's Note

GEOGRAPHICAL PLACE NAMES ARE spelled according to the most common usage. Archaeological and historical sites are presented as they appear most commonly in the sources I used to write this book. Some obscure locations are omitted from the maps for clarity; interested readers should consult the specialist literature.

The notes tend to emphasize sources with extensive bibliographies, to allow you to enter the more specialized literature if desired.

The B.C.E./C.E. convention is used throughout this book. "The present" by international agreement is 1950 C.E. Dates before 10,000 B.C.E. are quoted as "years ago."

A knot (a nautical mile), commonly used on charts and in sailing directions, is 1.15 statute miles (1.85 kilometers). I use it here to refer to boat speed and to the velocity of currents and tides, the usual nautical practice, where it means one nautical mile per hour. Other distances are in statute miles. I give metric equivalents for all measurements where appropriate. A fathom, once used extensively on charts and in daily nautical conversation, is 6 feet (1.83 meters).

All radiocarbon dates have been calibrated to dates in calendar years using the latest version of what is a constantly revised calibration curve. You can view the calibration curve at www.calpal.de.

Following scholarly convention, I refer to:

- Andean civilization: the area of South America in both the Andes range and along the coast where early civilizations flourished.
- Mesoamerican civilization: the area of Central America where highland and lowland civilizations came into being.

I have tried to keep nautical terms to a minimum for landlubbers. A few important ones are defined in the text, amplified by a few short boxes.

Nonsailors should note that, following common maritime convention, wind directions are described by the direction they are blowing *from*. A westerly wind blows from the west, and northeast trade winds from the northeast. Ocean currents and tides, however, are described by the direction they are flowing *toward*. Thus, a northerly current and a northerly wind move in opposite directions.

CHAPTER 1

"The Sands and Flats Are Discovered"

YOU RAISE YOUR EYES and the land falls away at your feet. I sat on the cliffs at Céide Fields, in Ireland's County Mayo, and gazed westward across a tumult of gray, windswept Atlantic toward an indistinct horizon swept by dark rain showers. Below me, precipitous cliffs battered by ocean swells tumbled into the surf with a low roar. There was nothing between North America and me except a featureless distance of tumultuous open water with unbridled power.

I sat there for more than an hour, my face buffeted by rain and wind, contemplating the immensity of the open ocean. My mind wandered, as it so often does, into the past, lulled by the endless rush of wind and sea. I became an Irish monk of 1,300 years ago, alone with a handful of companions amid towering swells in a small boat of stitched hide, just a rag of leather sail aloft on a short mast. We were rolling heavily in the rising gale with no land in sight and no idea whether land lay over the horizon. Hour after hour, we huddled in our thick, sodden cloaks deep in the boat. Only the helmsman stood watch at the steering oar, quietly chanting a Te Deum as he watched the endless procession of waves that could capsize us in a moment. We were in pursuit of a dream, of a mythic land somewhere in the western ocean, a place where the unknown began. Did such a land exist? We had no idea, just will-o'-the-wisps of sailors' tales of distant islands of the blessed where one could live in contemplative peace, close to God.

At Céide Fields, you feel as if you stand on the edge of the known world. Today, we know that Boston and New York, Greenland and

Newfoundland, lie on the invisible shores 3,000 miles (4,828 kilometers) to the west. Atlases, charts, and Google Earth delineate the extremities of what was a vast, sinister wilderness a thousand years ago. To our European forebears of that era, the western coasts of Europe were the frontiers of the earth. As I walked along the cliffs, I asked myself what compelled such men to leave familiar shores and venture into the vast, open ocean? Were they insane or desperate, or clever enough to think that they would know how to find their way home? And what did they believe lay beyond the horizon that was worth finding—only the knowledge of what was on the far side?

Irish monks were not, of course, the first people to sail beyond the horizon. Human experience of the oceans began far earlier in many parts of the world. Southeast Asian mainlanders were paddling or sailing from island to island to New Guinea and Australia by at least 50,000 years ago; their descendants were living in the Bismarck Strait region of the southwestern Pacific by 30,000 years ago. People were crisscrossing open water to Aegean islands by at least 8000 B.C.E.; Chinese fleets visited the East African coast a good century before Vasco da Gama rounded the Cape of Good Hope; raft sailors from what is now Ecuador traded with Maya lords in Central America long before 1492. In time, and in many places, the land became part of the sea, landscapes and seascapes as one. But the fundamental question remains, whatever the setting: What pushed people across the horizon, or in some cases gave them no incentive to leave familiar coastal waters? In other words, how and why did they decode the ocean?

The answer to this question comes from many sources, from written records, oral traditions, from old sailing directions and anthropological inquiries. Archaeology provides many of the clues, but, unfortunately, much of the record has long vanished. Canoes and other watercraft have long rotted away, but their crews left often transitory settlements behind them, sometimes natural rock shelters visited repeatedly over time. So archaeologists with their trowels and dental picks have prised charcoal fragments and seeds from thin occupation layers and shell heaps found in small archaeological sites that once formed coastal settlements scattered over hundreds, even thousands, of miles. From charcoal come radiocarbon dates and the chronology for early seafaring, some of it dating back more than forty millennia into the remote past.

THERE WAS NO single moment in human history when people first decoded the ocean and we then moved onward and upward toward a future in which we completely mastered the ocean. Over thousands of years, we developed extremely diverse relationships with open water, often with profound ritual undertones. It is not as if someone had invented the screwdriver or the internal combustion engine; what happened was that the sea gradually became a human environment, learned by mariners through constant observation, osmosis, and cultural memory. Traveling by sea meant, in some senses, submitting to it, or at least adapting to its rhythms and reading its most inconspicuous signals. Today, much of this intimacy with the ocean has vanished in the face of the computer and satellite navigation. A tanker or motor yacht can travel from point A to point B with utterly predictable, stunning accuracy. Even the smallest sailing vessel anywhere can fix its position within a few feet in seconds.

Apart from a permissible, and understandable, nostalgia for the days of sextants and star sights, we've lost a great deal by interposing a layer of technology between the ocean and ourselves. Before steam engines, diesels, and GPS, there was something different about those who spent their lives on or alongside the sea, wherever they sailed or paddled. The watery locales upon which they spent much of their lives—whether tropical islands surrounded by coral reefs, the windy straits of the Aegean Sea, or the harsh waters of the Aleutians in the far North Pacific—defined their character. We know little about these anonymous folk, almost people apart, for they never set their thoughts on paper and passed their experience to others by word of mouth. The Norwegian novelist Alexander Kielland knew a sailor when he met one, laconic as they almost invariably were. He wrote perceptively of them: "What the sea is for those who live on the shore, no-one may know; for they say nothing. They live their entire lives with their faces turned toward the sea. The sea is their company, their adviser, their friend and their enemy, their livelihood and their churchyard."[1] The relationship, he added, was one of few words but a watchful one that changed with the moods of the waves that broke a few yards from their houses.

Sometimes the ocean invited trust, at other times fear and apprehension, but always profound respect and the realization that one could never control its capricious whims. Kielland's remarks could apply with equal force to Maori canoe skippers, Aleutian fisherfolk, or Egyptian timber ship captains. They possessed an intimate knowledge not just of winds and waves but also of underwater landscapes of currents and tides. Of these men, anthropologist Knut Kolsrud wrote, "Since ancient times, [they have] seen the life of the sea, not a flat, grey surface with waves, but underneath, a landscape with shallows and depths, with clay, sand, stone, and vegetation, with currents and eddies and with creatures of the sea."[2] What they had learned the hard way passed from father to son in a seamless continuity through dozens of generations and was never written down. Today, these ancient skills are rapidly passing into historical oblivion in a world where we use computer keys to find out where we are, even on the summit of Mount Everest or hundreds of miles from land in the mid-Atlantic. Our task is to identify how different ancient societies developed their own portraits of the ocean and decoded its mysteries. Why did people venture into deep water when they were well aware of the dangerous winds and high seas that battered them along the coast?

SKETCHING A PORTRAIT of the sea as a human environment was a challenging task, but one made somewhat easier by my own experience at sea. Although I've been sailing since I was eight years old, I'm certainly not a man apart, like many ancient seafarers. I've spent a lifetime in small craft trying to master both coastal and deeper waters. My hard-earned skills wither alongside those of a traditional Polynesian navigator, an Arab dhow skipper, or a Norse merchant seaman in the North Atlantic. Time and time again, too, I've found myself reading about a voyage, a coasting passage, or tricky pilotage among tropical reefs and realized that I'd experienced much the same challenges and sensations at some time or another—instincts of impending danger, about being in the wrong place, the helpless feeling of a flat calm in a featureless ocean, your sails thrashing endlessly in an ocean swell hundreds of miles from land. Different boats, often different waters, to be sure, but again and again, like other sailors, I've had the sea as intimate company. Deciphering the mysteries of the ocean came easier when I invoked firsthand experience.

My early sailing mentors were so at home afloat that the ocean was part of their being. I learned the basics of sailing and seamanship—and, I realize now, of having the sea as company—from a Dorset fisherman who had spent his life working his nets and traps along the English Channel coast. He knew every nuance of local waters the subtle eddies of a rising tide on rocky shallows where lobsters could be trapped, the dappled gray skies that signaled an approaching equinoctial gale, the best spots for taking mackerel with spinner and line. But he had rarely sailed out of sight of land. "I'm a shallow-water man," he once told me. His deciphered ocean covered about 20 miles (32 kilometers) of rugged tidal coastline. Thus it has been for most sailors everywhere, who rarely stray far from local waters.

I also sailed with another shallow-water man, who never cruised farther afield than about 70 miles (113 kilometers) from home, all of it among a tapestry of tidal estuaries and sandbanks. Tom Armelagos was an elderly sailor of vast experience who sailed off eastern England in an old-fashioned, engineless barge yacht with a flat bottom and what are called leeboards—drop keels set on either side of the vessel to provide depth when beating against the wind. He had been sailing through those sandbanks and estuaries since he was a teenager in the years before World War I, always without an engine, at the mercy of fast-running tides and the wind. Tom had a compass, a pair of binoculars, and a long pole, painted with 1-foot (0.3-meter) marks to a depth of 12 feet (3.66 meters), with which he sounded the depth while sailing in very shallow water. He had infinite patience—to wait for wind, to remain at anchor when the tide was against him. Time was unimportant. Wind and tide ruled.

Tom had no electronics, just ancient skills. His faithful marked stick carried him into narrow channels, where there were perhaps 4 feet (1.2 meters) to spare on either side of the boat. On occasion, we would run up on a sandbank on a falling tide, have a leisurely lunch, and then sail off when we were afloat once more. He would anchor safely in complete shelter among sandbanks or mudflats with only 2 feet (0.6 meter) below his keel at low tide. In deeper water, he turned to another traditional artifact, used by ancient seamen of many stripes: hour after hour, I would man the side and cast a lead weight on a tagged line marked in fathoms. (A fathom is 6 feet, or 1.83 meters.) I would cast ahead, then note the mark at the surface and call it out: "Two fathoms deep" meant more than 12 feet (3.66 meters). "By the mark, five" meant exactly 30 feet (9 meters). We used a terminology redolent of the nineteenth century and Admiral Lord Nelson's navy, and we navigated like medieval cargo ships—by feel. On one occasion, we approached the coast of south-

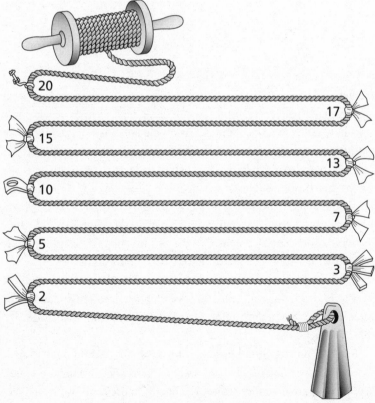

Figure 1.1 *A lead and line.*

eastern England, where the ocean is deep until close to shore. The Admiralty chart displayed clearly defined five- and ten-fathom lines close offshore, together with cabalistic symbols such as "sh," for *shell*, or "snd," for *sand*. Tom took a chunk of heavy grease and packed it into a cavity in the bottom of the lead weight. I cast the line, called out the sounding, and then pulled in the line and looked at the residue from the bottom trapped in the grease. An expert like my skipper knew the seated deposits so well, he could tell roughly where he was. In this way, we felt our way inshore on a day when the visibility was less than a mile, using the five- and ten-fathom lines and the samples from the bottom as our guides.

As a teenager, I spent time sailing on a converted, engineless fishing boat under a retired naval officer of mercurial temper who had learned his seamanship on one of the last naval square-riggers before World War I. Day after day, our taskmaster reminded the crew that all boats without engines relied on sails and people power alone. The three weeks were a brutal experience in the hard school of seafaring, but the lessons have been with me ever since. "You're on your own out there," he told us. "Use your eyes and never stop learning." Your mind-set was what mattered, the way you looked at the ocean.

I finally realized what he meant when I discovered Danish church towers. I was thoroughly lost on a hazy gray day. The monotonous terrain carved by retreating Ice Age glaciers went on for mile after mile. Thoroughly bemused, I turned to the British Admiralty's *Baltic Pilot*, navigational scripture compiled by long-forgotten nineteenth-century naval surveyors.

The surveyors were intrepid young officers, let loose with compass, lead, and line in small sailing boats to survey remote coasts. As I turned the *Pilot*'s pages, I thought of such a boat rowing a mile offshore against a chill wind. Like me, the midshipman or lieutenant would be peering at the shore, searching for distinctive landmarks that would tell them where they were. Most of these youths—they were little more—would have been at sea since their early teens. They knew how to sail and row in all kinds of weather, how to spot a safe landing from outside the breakers. They camped for days on windy promontories, took refuge from gales on uninhabited beaches. These young surveyors were cartographers and navigators, but, above all, they defined the seascape by landmarks—conspicuous headlands, distinctively colored cliffs, prominent houses or fortifications, even groves of trees. Their task revolved around a simple question: How could a sailor venturing along an unfamiliar coast find his way safely? The *Admiralty Pilots*, compiled originally during the Age of Sail, are a lasting monument to the surveyors' skill. In the older editions, written for small coasters and sailing vessels, the authors' calm, dispassionate voices resonate down the generations: "Mariners are advised to exercise extreme caution when sailing during spring tides in this vicinity," or "Anchorage may be obtained in 10 fathoms [18 meters] off the beach in SW winds."[3]

They delivered with the church towers. The archipelago coast had few distinguishing landmarks, just a low ridgeline and brown, sandy cliffs. The *Baltic Pilot* surveyor knew well that the shore was featureless, but as he peered ashore, he noticed something that I had ignored: the church towers belonging to the small villages on the ridge. Each was different—some spires, others square towers, a few lattice-like. The *Baltic Pilot* described the height and distinguishing features of each church. There were no photographs in those days, so the surveyor penned a small sketch instead. (Naval officers were taught to sketch for this very reason.) I riffled through the *Pilot* until a sketch matched the approaching tower off the bow. The villages were about a couple of miles apart, so it became a matter of following the churches until we came to our destination, which lay beyond a narrow channel between two islands. Here again the surveyor had done his homework. We picked up a gap between two cliffs, identified an approach beacon that was already in place in the mid-nineteenth century, and came safely to port. That day in Denmark was a navigational epiphany. Thanks to Victorian surveyors, I'd learned how to decipher a small part of the ocean.

Everywhere, the ocean has a language of its own. You soon learn that each shoal has its own dialect, each coastline has the equivalent of the Danish churches, especially in shallow tropical waters.

I remember approaching an anonymous island among the Exumas of the southern Bahamas on a brilliant, hot day. The wind, such as it was, was behind us, the pellucid water so clear that I could see ripples in the sand 12 feet (3.7 meters) below the keel. We slipped along peacefully with just enough steerageway (speed over the bottom) to keep moving, with the rising tide pushing us along slowly. Occasionally, a large ray glided under the bow, a fleeting profile against the white sand. Then the water color changed abruptly and we went on alert. I went into the bow, looking for the narrow channel of darker, deeper water that led inshore. After ten somewhat anxious minutes, I spotted a belt of darker water close ahead. Standing on the bow and grasping a stay, I conned the ship through the narrows. "Steer small," I cried as the shallower water lightened to brilliant turquoise just to the right. We moved slightly to the left; the water darkened, but only briefly, for more turquoise lay close on the other side. The channel narrowed, the water lightened ominously. A few dozen yards astern, turquoise shallows and dark rocks lurked below the surface. We slowed still more. Suddenly the deeper water widened out behind the sandbanks on either side, with no sign of any further shallowing. I gestured to the right, toward what appeared to be a wider pool quite close to the beach. We turned head to wind, barely moving, dropped the anchor, and dug it firmly into the bottom. "What's the depth?" I called. "Eight feet [2.4 meters]" was the answer. Not much water lay beneath our keel, but enough at low tide. I sighed with relief. I'd managed to bring us to anchor by observing the changing colors of the bottom, an essential survival skill for skippers sailing among tropical islands.

As the days passed, I developed an eye for the bottom, which enabled me to tell the depth of the water at a glance within a foot (0.3 meter) or so. I learned how tropical waters set among shallow lagoons and protected by coral reefs have their own language of colors and telltale clues that allow one to judge water depth and to pass safely through deepwater channels—if you set a close lookout and arrive with an oblique sun and in calm enough conditions to decipher the messages of water color. It's an arcane skill, in which experience and judgment are everything.

The language of coastal waters is what you learn first, and that's how all travel by water first began. You steer from landmark to landmark with the shore on one side, a process known as coasting, or you employ line-of-sight navigation, steering toward a conspicuous landmark visible on the horizon offshore. The signpost might be a steep headland with yellow cliffs or a peak on an island hovering offshore, but whatever it is, the point of reference is a clearly visible marker that is easily identified not only by you but also by others. The Santa Barbara Channel, in Southern California, is my base. Here, mountainous Santa Cruz Island lies about 24 miles (39 kilometers) offshore. To sail from the mainland to the island is navigational simplicity itself, a matter of steering for the highest or lowest point on the island until you can discern beaches and coves at sea level. At about 7 miles' (11.3 kilometers') distance, your eyes focus on flickers of white sandy beaches or indentations in the steep cliffs. Still in deep water, you identify your anchorage and steer accordingly. This is classic line-of-sight navigation, a passage that I've made hundreds of times. Along the way, I've learned some of the local ocean's moods and the strategies for accommodating them.

The late Alan Villiers, expert sailor and student of traditional sailing vessels, spent time on Arab dhows and in the Indian Ocean immediately before World War II. Villiers took passage with a Red Sea mariner on a cargo vessel coasting along desolate shores. He "never took bearings . . . he kept his eyes open, he knew his ship, and his life had been spent in the Red Sea . . . to him as familiar as a well-lit street on a citizen's homeward journey."[4] Not that the skipper was doing anything out of the ordinary. His coast hugging was second nature, something learned at his father's knee. Coasting and line-of-sight navigation decoded all but completely open maritime landscapes.

A WELL-LIT STREET: the essence of coasting is experience and close familiarity, but what about finding your way and sailing over the horizon, out of sight of land? It's a big mental jump for a neophyte sailor to take the next step, to skipper his or her own boat out of sight of shore to a landfall beyond the horizon—even if he or she knows what land, what harbors, lie at the other end. The feeling of apprehension can be absolutely overwhelming. Imagine doing this for the first time, truly venturing into the unknown like an astronaut landing on the moon, where no one has gone before. Deciding to sail into featureless, open water requires a powerful economic, political, or social motive, complete confidence in one's own skills, or deep-felt religious faith, like that of medieval Irish monks seeking solitude in Iceland, or perhaps just a profound restless curiosity, a quality so distinctive that the ancient Norse gave it a name: *æfintyr*. The reasons for going offshore, for exploring the unknown, are as important as the intricacies of finding one's way around, which most pilots knew anyhow before they set out.

Contrary to popular belief, sailing offshore is much easier than making a passage close to land. Close inshore, a vessel under paddle or sail faces numerous hidden dangers, especially when tides run strong, or in poor visibility or bad weather when approaching land with a wind behind you. Under such conditions, the land forms what a sailor calls a lee shore; it lies downwind, so that the wind tends to blow you ashore. Once there, you will find it hard to claw your way to safety, clear of menacing cliffs and shallow water, under sail or human power. Unless you can reach a completely sheltered anchorage and have good anchors, you are helpless in the face of the elements.

Open water is, of course, hazardous, but it has some advantages. The first is sea room—plenty of space to maneuver, to reduce sail and lie to in storms. The ocean far from land is more predictable, in the sense that prevailing winds often blow from the same general directions for much of the time. The trade winds of the Atlantic and the Pacific are classic examples. Monsoon winds in the Indian Ocean blow relatively gently from the northeast for six months or so per year before reversing and filling in more boisterously from the southwest. Even people on land know of these predictable winds, and especially of the seasons of the year when they reverse, allowing easy sailing in the opposite direction. When ancient Polynesian navigators wanted to sail east in the face of prevailing northeasterly trades, they waited until the months between January and March, or for major El Niño years, when the wind turned to the west and the trades faltered. It was a matter of lingering patiently, then setting out at once when the wind changed. The Norse who sailed west to Iceland knew that easterly winds often prevail for weeks on end during May in that part of the Atlantic. They also knew that they could sail home later on the wings of the prevailing westerlies. Northeasterly winds are common in the English Channel and the Bay of Biscay in spring, a good season for small boats to sail westward, whereas a journey to Iceland can take weeks against the prevailing westerlies of summer.

For all the predictable winds, you fear becoming lost in a void of open water and sailing endlessly without a glimpse of your destination. Away from the land, you sail in a circle of open water, with no cliffs or mountain peaks to give you a sense of direction. When I first knew that I was going to skipper a boat across an ocean, I made myself sail off-shore, out of sight of land off the California coast, for two days. The familiar landmarks vanished astern; night fell, then a new dawn; nothing, not even a ship, was in sight. As I gazed over the featureless gray ocean at first light, a mindless fear, a moment's panic, even, descended on me. Where was I? I had no sense of direction in the overcast of morning. Of course I could glance at the compass and be reassured, but what if I had not had one aboard? A modest swell was running, so I covered the binnacle and tried sailing at a constant angle to the waves. After a couple of hours, I felt much more comfortable. I soon began to learn that there are navigational clues in the open sea, which is as much a landscape as the land. With a brilliantly lit sky and bright stars above you at night, and the sun by day, predictable natural signposts abound.

Unlike me, ancient navigators served long apprenticeships with experienced pilots before they skippered a vessel offshore. They learned the moods and telltale signs of the ocean from countless passages and from meticulous oral recitations of lore acquired over many generations, just as they knew the myths and folk wisdom of the land. I possess little of the intimacy with surrounding waters that was commonplace among those who ventured out in canoes or small fishing boats. Their lives, their survival, depended on their partnership with the water. They acquired a mental closeness to the ocean that is very different from our more impersonal attitudes. I had the instruments—a compass, chronometer, and sextant—but lacked the intimacy they relied upon instead.

Crossing an ocean in a small yacht is a memorable experience for someone who spends most of his or her life looking out at the ocean from the land. Cast off from familiar landmarks such as beaches or prominent headlands, the surrounding horizon is your entire universe; your companions are the sun by day, the moon and stars at night. Day follows day in an unchanging rhythm of hours on watch, hours asleep below, the only changes being those imposed by wind and weather. If you are sailing on the Atlantic's northeast trades, you can sail for day after day without trimming a sail or altering course. In mid-ocean, I had the sense that our boat was stationary, that wind and waves were moving past, as Europe moved farther away and the Caribbean islands approached us. A soothing sense, to be sure, when you are hundreds, even thousands, of miles from land, even if you take your position with a sextant and stopwatch every day. The feeling is even more acute when you are sailing with just a compass. I've spoken to other ocean sailors about this and found it's a common sensation. Many traditional societies have similar perspectives.

The apprehension I feel today is born of cautious experience of the sea and its pitiless moods, not of ignorance. Herein lies, I think, one reason why ancient seafarers could make the voyages they did. To venture into the unknown was a logical extension of inherited skills that were already familiar. It truly was no big deal, but to us the distances seem enormous and our instruments make the journeys seem daunting. But mentally we live much more remotely from the ocean and do not have the social milieu in which voyaging in search of new land, new opportunities, is deeply ingrained in everyone's daily lives. Also ingrained in the minds of ancient voyagers was the inevitability of casualties, of canoes that never returned, a tough fatalism about foundering or shipwreck that survives among many European and American fisherfolk in modern times. Decoding every ocean was a matter of long experience and no illusions, careful navigation and close familiarity with deepwater seascapes.

ANCIENT SEAFARERS RELIED on the sights and sounds of open water to guide them—the movements of heavenly bodies, flocks of birds flying toward land, swells refracting off invisible cliffs, the vagaries of tides and currents, even the sounds of waves breaking on rocks in foggy weather. Those who used such devices tended to think of the sea in different ways. To most coastal people, land and sea were as one, so much so that some Australian Aborigines claimed well-defined territories under the waves. To cross broad straits and make longer passages required additional pilotage skills, often associated with powerful rituals and requiring long apprenticeships. But those with the knowledge passed freely from land to sea, for to them they were as one. Only occasionally have I felt really close to the ocean in comparable ways—becalmed out of sight of land in the Pacific on an absolutely flat sea colored deep red by the setting summer sun, or anchored in a remote British Columbian fjord on a pitch-black night with only a plashing waterfall for company. The great power of the ocean was quiet, and I seemed, for a brief while, to belong. I had the ocean as company.

Despite this familiarity and spiritual intimacy, our forebears treated the ocean with respect and peopled it with powerful forces. Great reservoirs of myth and oral tradition surrounded legendary canoe voyages and miraculous survival from great storms. For all the long Polynesian voyages of a thousand years ago, there was always a sense of powerlessness in the face of deep waters. In many ancient societies, the symbolic landscapes of human existence extended into deep water and beyond the horizon, into a supernatural realm of uncontrollable forces—to a place of death, where ancestors resided. Here powerful monsters and savage deities lurked, ready to seize people from canoes and carry them into the depths. Northwest Indian seafarers dreaded mythic beasts such as Komogwa, an octopuslike creature, and its familiar, the killer whale. To other societies, like the Bronze Age Europeans of three thousand years ago, the ocean was the realm of the ancestors, of death.

A sense almost of dread, but certainly of respect, for the ocean passed into Christian doctrine from earlier times. The sea was a source of life, of food and other benefits, but it was also a fearsome place, where storms could reduce people to madness. It was "the great abyss" never experienced in the Garden of Eden, a symbol of the disorder that preceded the creation. The author of the Book of Revelation envisioned a new heaven and a new earth at the end of time but stated firmly that "there was no more sea."

Ordinary travelers set sail in fear and trembling, dreading the loneliness, the dark nights, and the heaving swells. Even those sailors familiar with the ocean might dip relics in the sea or seek the intervention of the Virgin Mary. Potential hazards lurked on every side. Quite apart from navigational hazards like fog and unmarked rocks, headwinds could delay a passage for weeks. Pirates could descend without warning. Seasickness was a universal complaint, so much so that the Catalan *Customs of the Sea* ruled that agreements made at sea were invalid, because some passengers would promise a thousand marks of silver to anyone who would put them ashore.

In Europe, the apprehension of earlier times gradually gave way to more benevolent visions of the ocean. Daniel Defoe, who, while ashore, experienced the memorable Great Storm of 1703, wrote lyrically of safe bays and anchorages that were refuges in gales. "Our shores are sounded, the sands and flats are discovered, which they knew little or nothing of, and in which more danger lies." "Dreadful parts of the world" now attracted trade. The art of navigation had "made all the horribles and terribles . . . become as natural and familiar as daylight."[5] Eighteenth-century science laid the foundations for the proper study of the oceans amid a growing confidence that humans were capable of understanding the workings of creation. The monsters and sea serpents of earlier times lingered in sailors' tales, but a more benevolent view of the sea resulted. The seashore became a resort, "a stage on which the collision of the elements unfolded," a place for shipwrecks and dramatic rescues, but also for contemplating the natural world and ourselves.[6]

Industrialization, the explosive growth of cities, the advent of air travel, and the end of the days of sail have changed our vision of the oceans profoundly. Today, the sea is an impersonal presence in our lives, a place we go on holiday, live alongside, or explore aboard large cruise ships or ferries. Outside territorial waters, the oceans are open to everyone, their boundaries set, even if their depths are still little known. In earlier times, intricate cultural attitudes shaped both supernatural beliefs about the sea and the ways in which people deciphered them. We can only look back at these beliefs and values through faint historical mirrors, so our understanding of the early decodings of the oceans must, perforce, rely heavily on what we know about seafarers and their watercraft, and also about the societies that begat them. Just occasionally, the curtain of the past draws aside and we can glean a sense of the powerful supernatural pull exerted by the dark and unfathomable ocean.

Our relationship with the ocean has gone through several stages. For thousands of years we probed the ocean cautiously, sailing and paddling along its coasts, making cautious passage to islands visible on the horizon offshore. Such explorations were merely an extension of life ashore, where crossing rivers and lakes was a seamless part of daily life. These inshore explorations were the arena where the fundamental skill of pilotage, of making one's way across short passages of open water, came into play, the inconspicuous signposts of the ocean that turned featureless landscape into familiar stomping ground. Then came the defining moment when canoe skippers first ventured out of sight of land, epitomized by the restless voyages of Lapita canoes in the southwestern Pacific after 3000 B.C.E. and, much later, by mariners using the monsoon winds of the Indian Ocean to sail from the Red Sea, Arabia, and East Africa to India's Malabar Coast and beyond. These voyages came about because of restlessness, social pressures, and mercantile opportunities, but, beyond more seaworthy watercraft, they required no special pilotage skills that were not already in common use by people who were well aware of the movements of the heavenly bodies. The so-called European Age of Discovery of the fifteenth century C.E. and later brought rudimentary technology to the equation. But it was not until the invention of the steamship and, in the past three quarters of a century, computer technology that we entered a world in which the process of decoding the ocean was complete. However, even now, you can look down from the deck of a cruise ship or a motor yacht and see a fishing boat trawling under sail or a Polynesian catamaran skimming across a lagoon. The skills of the ancient sailor still survive alongside those of the Industrial Revolution.

ACROSS THE PACIFIC

> During these three months and twenty days, we sailed
> in a gulf where we made a good four thousand leagues
> across the Pacific Sea, which was rightly so named. For
> during this time we had no storm, and we saw no land
> except two small uninhabited islands, where we found
> only birds and trees.
>
> —Ferdinand Magellan, 1520[1]

WE ARE *HOMO SAPIENS*, the wise people. Our ancestors had evolved in
tropical Africa by about 200,000 years ago. By about 70,000 years before
present, we were on the move—out of Africa and into Southeast Asia,
Eurasia, Europe, and, by about 15,000 years ago, into the Americas.
Much of this great diaspora unfolded during the last Ice Age glaciation,
when huge ice sheets mantled higher latitudes in the Northern Hemisphere and global sea levels were about 300 feet (91 meters) below the
modern shoreline. An extensive continental shelf extended southward
from mainland Southeast Asia; Australia and New Guinea were as one;
only relatively narrow deepwater channels separated dry land. It was
inevitable that sooner or later, ingenious humans with all the cognitive
abilities of modern humanity would colonize hitherto uninhabited
landmasses that hovered on, or just over, the horizon. Why they did so is
a matter of guesswork, but we now know that deliberate seafaring began in these waters before 50,000 years ago.

The three chapters that follow tell the story of how and, as much as we can decipher, why the descendants of Ice Age hunters in Southeast Asia had colonized, first, New Guinea, Australia, and the Bismarck Strait area of the southwestern Pacific by at least 30,000 years ago. There the canoes paused until around 3000 B.C.E., when new generations of farmers and seafarers, known to archaeologists as the Lapita people, developed a remarkable maritime society that traveled from island to island as far east as Fiji, on the threshold of remote Polynesia. We describe some of the social mechanisms they used to maintain contacts between widely separated islands. Here the restless seafaring paused for hundreds of years, then suddenly began once again, for reasons that elude us. Then, suddenly, around 950 C.E., long-distance voyaging recommenced. Within little more than a couple of centuries, descendants of Lapita people from the west colonized the widely scattered islands of eastern Polynesia. Some of them might have sailed even farther—to South America, generations before Ferdinand Magellan, James Cook, and other European mariners found their way into the heart of Polynesia.

CHAPTER 2

—

Sunda and Sahul

MAINLAND SOUTHEAST ASIA, January, 55,000 years ago. The northwest wind blows hard across the wide coastal plain. Strong gusts from offshore whip the coastal mangrove swamps; dark riffles chase across calm inlets close inshore. Clinging thickets give way abruptly to the blue open water, a mass of seething whitecaps that reach to a low coastline on the far horizon. Among the mangroves, a raft of bamboo logs bobs gently. Long poles driven into the muddy bottom keep it in place. Three men and a woman cast fiber fishing nets into the shallows. Occasional squalls ruffle their hair and cause their fishing platform to lurch. Suddenly, a violent squall jerks the heavy logs against the anchor poles, which come loose without warning and float away. The fishers grab for them and for nearby mangrove branches, but it is too late. Their raft drifts out of control into deep water. Waves break over the logs; the crew sit helplessly, clasping their gourds of freshwater against their chests. Their companions ashore watch silently, gazing out toward the land in the distance. In minutes, the raft is but a black dot among the whitecaps.

Months later, on a hot, calm day, the fishers are once again among the mangroves on their bamboo rafts, following an age-old routine established long before human memory. The dense vegetation crowds around them; the wide ocean is invisible, although only a short distance away. Suddenly, a once familiar voice breaks the torpor of midday. The fisherfolk peer seaward, then pole their fishing platform toward open water. A bamboo raft approaches from offshore, the crew paddling hard as a gentle following wind wafts them to land. Some of the castaways have returned from the land beyond the horizon. They tell stories of their new home, a deserted, forested place where the same trees, plants, and fish are to be found. As night falls, an elder from the raft shares the watery landscape of his imagination, a realm created by ancestral beings. He recounts ancient myths, speaks of the water between the two lands as a large river, of the two lands as one place, part of a familiar world. The paddlers plan to return when the winds shift to carry the raft southward once more.

Accident or deliberate exploration: we will never know whether offshore voyages from Southeast Asia, the first long-term seafaring by humanity, began by chance or because someone decided to venture into deeper water. For sure, they were hunters and foragers, as no one had yet started cultivating their food. Their ancestors had hunted, gathered plant foods, and fished along the low-lying coasts of the mainland for tens of thousands of years. They frequented an undulating continental shelf formed by late–Ice Age sea levels far lower than those of today. Today, geologists call this the Sunda Shelf, a large, now submerged plain that once supported complex river deltas, floodplains, and mangrove swamps—facts we have learned from cores drilled into the modern seabed.[1] While some hunting bands stayed inland, others never left the shore, where shellfish abounded and fish were plentiful in the inlets and pools of the coastal mangroves. They must have had some form of simple watercraft on which to move around. To cross rivers and lakes, they could have relied on hollowed-out logs and simple bamboo rafts. Traversing relatively wide bodies of water was an integral part of daily life. For people living on the coast and fishing in mangrove swamps, land and ocean formed a seamless environment. Almost certainly, the sea and water loomed large in complex spiritual beliefs about this land- and seascape, which passed from generation to generation through chant, dance, recitation, and song.

You gaze out at open ocean from much of the Cambodian and Vietnamese coasts today, but the geography was very different during the late Ice Age. Thanks to much lower sea levels, distances from landmass to landmass were much shorter between 60,000 and 10,000 years ago. At the height of the late Ice Age, 18,000 years before the present, mainland

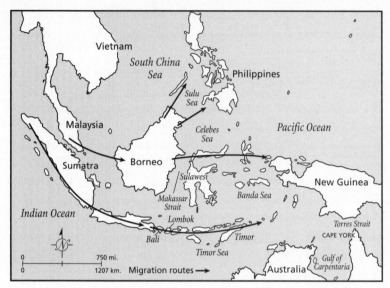

Figure 2.1 *Map showing migration routes in Southeast Asian waters.*

Asia ended at the Lombok Strait, between Bali and Indonesia. At the Makassar Strait, between Borneo and Sulawesi, only some 19 miles (30 kilometers) separated the mainland from Sulawesi and a group of nearby forested islands.[2] Today scientists call this archipelago Wallacea, after the Victorian biologist Alfred Russel Wallace. From Wallacea, only a further 62 miles (100 kilometers) or so of open water brought a canoe to the arid, low-lying shores of another, now largely vanished continental shelf, known scientifically as Sahul, which incorporated New Guinea and Australia.

Sometime around 55,000 years ago—the date is an informed guess—a raft or possibly a canoe crossed open water to Wallacea, perhaps by accident, and voyaging to what is now New Guinea and beyond began. The crossing would have been considerably longer than navigating familiar large rivers inland, but the rafts used would have certainly remained buoyant for the longer distance. The crossing was not necessarily a traumatic experience for those gifted with deep-felt beliefs and confidence in spiritual pathways across the water. But the accident, if it was one, would have led almost immediately to deliberate voyages, simply because the people knew their environment really well and were spiritually prepared for open water.

No CANOES SURVIVE from these early voyages, nor do we know much about the people who paddled them. Their history, shared through the generations by word of mouth, has long since vanished in the passing of more than 50,000 years. Only archaeology provides clues, and these are mainly from such prosaic finds as stone tools, animal bones, and shells. But understanding why people made such passages, apparently without hesitation, requires delving not only into the maritime environment but also into the realm of the intangible, into the nature of their relationship with the ocean. The only present comparisons, and they are tenuous at best, come from coastal groups in northern Australia, who still flourish in somewhat equivalent environments, exploiting inshore waters and fishing on reefs, in narrow inlets, and sometimes farther offshore.

Most associate the Australian Aborigines with deserts and arid terrain, not with mangrove swamps and coral reefs. But some bands still dwell along the coasts of the Gulf of Carpentaria and Cape York Peninsula, the part of Australia closest to New Guinea, which lies some 90 miles (145 kilometers) north across the Torres Strait.[3] Their ancestors have lived this way for at least 3,000 years, and perhaps very much longer. The Aborigines' complex and intensely spiritual relationship with the sea provides a fascinating glimpse at beliefs about the ocean that I suspect were widespread among coastal dwellers in the region for thousands of years.

The Yolngu of the western gulf believe the sea is alive like a person, with angry and placid moods, a place you respect, lest it claim you. They understand its rhythms, its tides and currents, the winds and waves that ruffle its surface. The Yolngu understand that the sea can wreak vengeance and can kill. Like hunters living far inland, they negotiate the power of their landscape, their environment, turning threat into sacred power. Their rituals invoke the strength and spiritual heft of sea creatures. The Aborigines cooperate with the ocean, just as they cooperate with one another, for they live with it every day. Its power is part of everyone's body and soul. The sea journeys of sacred beings and their teachings pass down the generations in narrative, song, and ritual. These ancient values still survive as modern-day Aboriginal fisherfolk venture into deep water or take journeys of the imagination.

The Aborigines of the northern coast dwell on land, but their creator beings hail from the saltwater world. At one location in the Gulf of Carpentaria, the sweeping movement of a tiger shark's tail created bays and inlets. It killed a porpoise, which turned into a rock. In this way, natural features in their homeland came into being and acquired spiritual potency. Another western-gulf group, the Yanyuwa, say that "we are people who originate in the sea," which means that their spiritual and cultural legacies come from the ocean. Their inheritance obliges them to respect the sea and to follow the paths and marks set across the ocean landscape by ancestral figures.

Like the Aborigines, and indeed all coastal hunters and fisherfolk, the Asian mainlanders of fifty millennia ago possessed an intimate knowledge not only of the surrounding land but also of the waters that extended to the horizon—just as they must have been familiar with fish and bird migrations, with cloud formations, even luminescence in the water. (Luminescence is a visible glow, caused by bioluminescence, light produced by living organisms.) Today their descendants use the rising of constellations such as Orion and the Pleiades to foretell seasonal wind shifts and to track when certain fish will feed close inshore. For instance, the Pleiades appear at the coldest time of the year, when the highly prized dugong moves inshore seeking warmer water. Everyone knows that Torres Strait pigeons will arrive from the northwest to feed on wild plums when the southeasters are about to die down, in about September. Their knowledge extends to seemingly minor details, such as how local currents and tidal streams form roads through inshore waters, which fishers traverse on mangrove-wood rafts to different fishing places.

Each group possesses kin-owned maritime territories that extend into the water, to reefs, nearby islands, and fishing grounds. These can reach offshore as far as the eye can discern and to the seabed, where the mythic Rainbow Serpent lives. Sea rights can extend far beyond the horizon, even to the outer fringes of the Great Barrier Reef. These rights, akin to land tenure ashore, given to them by ancestral beings and passed from one generation to the next, shape daily life along the coast. The watery territories extend into the realm of the imagination. Just as there is the Dreaming among peoples on land, here there is the Sea Dreaming, an equivalent that encompasses territories and paths on the sea. The practical day-to-day world and the spiritual realm intertwine in coastal Aboriginal existence, among people who are ingenious and highly adaptive, accustomed to maintaining connections with people living at a distance, either on land or across water. Everywhere along the coast, people live amid what one might call seascapes of memory, amid waters that are alive, at one with human actors.

Did the mainlanders of 50,000 years ago have similar seascapes of memory? If they were like any other hunters and fisherfolk, they must have, for a close knowledge of at least inshore waters could make the difference between life and death. One can imagine a sudden squall with strong winds that swamp a canoe without warning. The crew bail frantically and paddle for a small rocky outcrop where they know there is temporary shelter and shallow water free of predatory sharks. They run their canoe onto a tiny sandy beach, jump out, and bail the dugout dry. As night falls, they turn the canoe on its side and use it as a shelter for the night. Next morning, the wind has dropped and they paddle for the mainland.

INSHORE WATERS MERGED clear of mangroves and sandspits into open water. If the Aborigines are any guide, then the fishing territories of each coastal band extended into deeper waters, to offshore reefs or small islands—and beyond, even if no one ventured there except to catch the occasional deepwater fish on calm days. The same spiritual forces that governed the placid waters of estuaries and mangrove swamps must have exercised power offshore. This wider seascape was never featureless, never a physical or spiritual blank, and not necessarily a hostile place. The waters off Sunda were generally pellucid and warm, often mirror-calm, and ruffled by gentle afternoon sea breezes and soft air from the land at night, as they are today. Offshore, the prevailing trade and monsoon winds brought rougher seas, but life-threatening storms were rare. The seascape was alive, ever changing. Usually benign, it could sometimes be a fearful place, fraught with spiritual menace, so much so that Australians paddling offshore carried sacred plants in their canoes. Fortunately, the proper rituals could placate evil forces, creating mental and supernatural pathways that deciphered the mysteries of open water. With some form of spiritual guidance, to be set adrift offshore would not necessarily presage disaster. Our castaways took a mental journey through sea landscapes defined by ancestral beings, even if humans had never traveled them.

Nor were the involuntary seafarers necessarily sailing into a physical void. They must have known from telltale signs that land was out there, over the horizon—great pillars of dark smoke from natural brushfires started by lightning strikes, flocks of land birds flying toward the mainland, distinctive cloud formations that mass over higher ground. Sometimes distant shorelines could be seen hovering offshore, faintly visible through dense summer-heat haze, as much an enemy of the sailor today as it was during the late Ice Age. On brilliantly clear winter days, densely forested islands would have stood out dark against the cerulean blue of ocean and sky. Even before humans traveled offshore, the world of the mainlanders did not necessarily end in the mangrove swamps at water's edge. Along Sunda's coasts, the people knew that summer and winter brought different wind patterns, the former the southerlies associated with the monsoon, the other the northeast trade winds. Anyone carried to Wallacea on a raft knew that in due time the winds would reverse and they could return to their homeland if they wished. The marine landscape was as decipherable and predictable as that of the land, especially when you could see your destination.

Sunda and Sahul constituted an ideal seafaring environment. Currents and winds were relatively predictable, year in and year out. Chains of higher and lower islands provided landmarks for line-of-sight passage making. Safe landing places and sandy beaches, as well as sheltered mangrove inlets, abounded. The biological anthropologist Joseph Birdsell has identified two obvious crossing routes, based on island chains.

The first began in the north, taking the voyager from one intervisible island to the next. In fact, it was, and still is, possible to keep land in sight all the way from mainland Asia to the end of the Bismarck Archipelago, off eastern New Guinea. Birdsell's southern route goes closer to the northwest Australian coast. He also describes likely sub-routes, each of which contained between eight and seventeen stages. When sea levels were at their lowest, no stage was longer than about 62 miles (100 kilometers). The islands formed a progressively longer string, visited and colonized one by one. Even when sea levels rose to about 230 feet (70 meters) below modern levels, the distances between high islands would not have been much larger, although, of course, low-lying shelves would have been submerged. Birdsell wrote, "It is highly probable that there was a constant if somewhat straggling trickle of small groups of human beings over all or most of the routes."[4]

Both Birdsell routes are thoroughly viable even today. Navigating along a string of islands is much the same as coasting from one bay to the next, with the difference that you cross open water from one landmark to another. The New Zealand archaeologist Geoffrey Irwin, himself an expert small-boat sailor, has calculated the distances between the intervisible islands of Birdsell's northern route.[5] He used a 164-foot (50-meter) sea level, and radiuses of sight of visible land ahead—not necessarily lower-lying islands that cannot be seen except at close range. He notes that the distance on the first voyage from the mainland to Sulawesi was much the same as the last one to New Guinea.

Steering from one visible island to another was one means by which seafarers pressed outward from mainland Southeast Asia, but passage making was more complex than that. Knowledge of islands visible at a distance starts on land, where conditions would often have been good enough to make the presence of neighboring islands a matter of familiarity. Circumstances are different at sea. Under ideal conditions, someone in a canoe can see as far as the curvature of the earth will permit, allowing for light refraction by the atmosphere. But cloud, haze, spume, and other phenomena can obscure the horizon even on days when visibility is excellent, making the sighting of land from the ocean much harder.

The islands and sea lanes between the South China Sea and Southeast

Asia out to New Guinea, Australia, and the near islands of the southwest Pacific lie between the northern and southern tropical cyclone belts. According to the Admiralty *Pilots*, those definitive chroniclers of sea conditions throughout the world, these waters enjoy generally benign weather and long periods without gale-force winds. During the summer months, the monsoon brings northwesterly winds and currents to the waters around New Guinea, the Bismarck Strait area in the southwest Pacific, and the Sahul coastline. Thus, you could easily paddle or sail southward. North of the equator, which runs through Borneo and north of New Guinea, the northeasterly trades blow during the same period, so voyaging to lands offshore was also easy. Then winter brings the southeasterly trades and north-flowing currents, so a seafarer could return to where he came from if he so desired. These seasonal weather patterns allowed people in simple watercraft to colonize and explore coastlines and islands over an enormous area in relative safety. And, as time went on, the same seasonal patterns allowed communities on islands scattered over thousands of square miles to interact and trade freely with one another.

Irwin calls these waters a voyaging corridor, which enjoyed favorable weather conditions and, most important, predictable and relatively gentle wind shifts that allowed people to sail out to islands visible on the horizon, and also to return as the seasons changed without having to battle headwinds.[6] The waters beyond Sunda became part of the islanders' cultural landscapes, as familiar to them as a nearby grove of trees or a convenient fishing stream. This notion of all-encompassing marine and terrestrial landscapes is central to any decoding of ocean waters, whether they be off Sunda and Sahul, in the stormy North Pacific along the Aleutian Islands, or in the Mediterranean.

FOR ALL THE natural assets of the Sunda–Sahul voyaging corridor, there remains the issue of watercraft. An accidental drift on a raft is one thing; sustained voyaging over many generations is quite another, especially on longer passages when one could encounter large swells and wind waves. Going offshore for hours or even days at a time required much more durable and seaworthy vessels than lashed-up bamboo logs.

Rafts are simplicity itself. The first ones were probably no more than floating platforms for fishing in shallow water and among mangrove swamps, easily poled and secured in place when needed. Like the far more elaborate Andean rafts described in Chapter 14, some may have had projecting center logs at both ends to make it easier to pole them through narrow channels, against currents and tidal streams, and in calm water. Fiber bindings are ideal for rafts, for they don't bite into the logs as they work against one another in a seaway. One of the reasons that the Norwegian anthropologist and explorer Thor Heyerdahl was able to cross successfully from Peru to Polynesia in his balsa raft *Kon-Tiki* in 1947 was that the raft's fiber lashings never cut into the soft logs. Deeper water would have required new propulsion methods as well, for the crew had to both paddle and steer their rafts if they were to reach the land on sight on the horizon. Poles must soon have become flat-bladed paddles, which, when used by several people, would move the raft along slowly in calm conditions. Again, less a matter of invention than of necessity, for anyone who has stirred a boiling container over a fire knows that a wooden paddle does the job best. Paddles worked well in calm or moderate weather, but rough water was another matter, for flat, clumsy rafts, even when constructed of buoyant wood, were practically immovable when paddled against even moderate headwinds.

For all their disadvantages, rafts must have been widespread and easy to build, for bamboo grows naturally along the northern route south and east from Sunda and along the more westerly route as far as Java. Bamboo rafts are still used in northern Australia's Gulf of Carpentaria. Even if rafts were the usual means of crossing open water—and they had the advantage of being able to carry enough people to form founder populations—it would be naïve to think that there were not profound changes in boats over thousands of years of water crossings. Three other types of vessel come to mind—reed boats and bark and dugout canoes.[7] Reeds make for light boats, easily carried ashore, but they become waterlogged and useless within two or three days. For instance, the tule-reed canoes used by early California Indians to cross to offshore islands could be used for only about four days before they had to be dried out on the beach. Even after short journeys, their owners laid them out in the sun as often as possible, as do reed-boat users along the Peruvian coast, where such craft are used in the inshore anchovy fisheries to this day. Vietnamese fisherfolk still use high-ended reed boats, even in rough open water, but these days they waterproof them with highway asphalt. Sewn-bark canoes may well have been used on Sunda's rivers and lakes, but no traces of them survive, although they are known from parts of Australia, perhaps remnants of once widely distributed watercraft but probably never large enough to have carried truly major loads.

In their simplest forms, dugout canoes are little more than hollow tree trunks blocked at both ends—the familiar wooden trough put to other uses. Dugouts have crossed rivers and lakes since very early times and need little improvement to do so. I must confess that they terrify me, and with good reason. On numerous occasions, I crossed crocodile-infested rivers in Africa in wildly gyrating, heavily laden dugouts with the water but a couple of inches below the edge. Fortunately, only once did we go in, and that was in the shallows, when someone accidentally stepped on the edge of the canoe. Dugouts are easily hollowed out from straight tree trunks, but, inevitably, they are long and narrow. This makes even a well-built example potentially unstable, even in calm water and expert hands. With their low sides, they swamp readily in even slight waves, and in the absence of large, straight tree trunks and the axes and adzes to hollow them out, they must have been relatively small and unable to carry anything but a light load or one or two people—in smooth water. Dugouts in their most basic form paled in comparison with the raft, even if they moved faster when paddled in calm water. They would have lacked not only load-carrying capacity but also the strength and stability to survive in open water, except in the most expert hands. (Many Australian Aborigines are remarkably adept at handling dugouts in rough water.)

Swells and wind waves would have been the catalysts for significant innovation. The most pressing problem was that of stability, or "tippiness," as a sailor friend of mine once called it. The solution came with double hulls or single outriggers, either of which widened the beam of the canoe and made it much more stable—in short, a kind of platform.

Both configurations also allowed for the use of masts and sails, for in these waters, with their predictable winds, sailing must have begun very soon after seafaring.

For any ocean passage, even one of only a few miles, it's clearly desirable to cross as fast as possible, faster than one would with a clumsy raft. Poles gave way to paddles, and at some point paddles yielded to sails. After all, why work if you can set a sail to undertake the same task? Sailing modern-day fore-and-aft rigs, with their mainsails and jibs of varying sizes, requires a considerable learning curve, but to start sailing downwind is easy enough, for anyone wearing a skin cloak would have known that a strong wind blowing into the billowing garment could knock one over. Perhaps the first sails were set on rafts, then transferred to canoes. A long paddle at the stern steered the canoe or raft when the wind blew from behind. From this simple beginning, refinements like wooden spars (masts, yards), fiber ropes to control the sail and also to hoist and lower it rapidly if need be, would have been logical solutions to even a moderately experienced sailor. Speed was the greatest potential advantage of sailing. A well-handled sailing canoe with an outrigger or twin hulls can make remarkably fast passages when scudding before even a moderate breeze, which would have made crossing longer stretches of open water a viable proposition. Some of the open-water passages in the Sunda voyaging corridor were up to 62 miles (100 kilometers) long, so a vessel capable of handling waves became essential once voyaging became commonplace.[8]

TWO CANOES SKIM effortlessly across the calm sea with a gentle monsoon wind behind them. At the stern of one canoe, the oldest crew member steers with a long oar. His eyes are never still as he scans the horizon for mounting clouds and impending squalls. He steers toward the low peak poking through the heat haze far ahead. The other canoe keeps close company. Only the elder at the steering oar knows the rituals and songs that will carry them safely to shore.

The archaeological portrait is very incomplete, but the maritime expansion seems to have been impressively rapid.[9] Radiocarbon dates tell us people were fishing off the island of Timor, in Wallacea, by at least

42,000 years ago. South and southeast of Wallacea, another crossing of 62 miles (100 kilometers) across the deep Timor Trough ended on Sahul, the large, now partially submerged landmass that encompassed New Guinea, Australia, and what is now the shallow Arafura Sea. New Guinea had been settled early: by 50,000 years ago, people were living in the highlands. Some of them left stone axes on the Huon Peninsula, at the eastern end of the island, some 10,000 years later. The crude tools could have ringed trees and helped clear forest, perhaps to encourage the growth of edible plants such as wild taro and yams on forest fringes. Much of Sahul was deserted rolling, semiarid lowlands, capable of supporting few people per square mile. Human settlement soon extended far inland in search of more plentiful landscapes. We know that humans had settled deep in Australia by about 45,000 years ago, so the crossing took place at least that early.

The canoes approach land as the afternoon shadows lengthen. The gentle monsoon wind is as steady as ever, then strengthens as the outriggers sail inshore. A young man stands at the bow of each canoe, watching for telltale color changes in the water, for the lighter blue and dark patches of coral and sandbanks lurking ahead. Almost simultaneously, the lookouts gesture to the right. The helmsmen heave on their steering paddles and alter course immediately. Meanwhile, the elder looks for potential landing spots. He identifies a sheltered sandy beach, then casts around for smoke, houses, or other signs of human occupation. Everyone has their weapons close at hand. Fifty yards (46 meters) from the breakers, a word, and the crews drop the sails. They grab paddles and head cautiously for shore. Moments later, the canoes ground. The crews leap out and haul the craft clear of the surf. The beach is totally deserted. There is no one in sight.

Every landfall on an unknown shore was a potentially hazardous one. No one knew whether hostile inhabitants lurked in the dense forest or whether they would be attacked. For all the dangers, the passages continued. Within a few thousand years, the seafarers were even farther offshore. New Guinea's Huon Peninsula faces the Bismarck Strait and the islands of Near Oceania, with New Britain Island only a 30-mile (48-kilometer) journey offshore. People were catching tuna and sharks on New Ireland, slightly farther east, by at least 35,000 years before present. Once you are past the large Bismarck Archipelago islands, interisland distances increase, but that did not inhibit the seafarers. From New Ireland, it's a direct voyage of 109 miles (175 kilometers) to Buka Island, in the northern Solomons. Although there are some small, low islands on the way, these would not have been visible from any distance, so a direct journey was most likely. The inhabitants of the Kilu rock-shelter, on Buka, lived on deepwater fish a mere 5,000 years later. From there, it was an easy matter to colonize the rest of the Solomon chain, for only short distances separate the islands. Some islands remained elusive, among them more distant Manus, some 143 miles (230 kilometers) from New Ireland and 137 miles (220 kilometers) from New Guinea outliers. You cannot see the island until you are well out of sight of land astern, which may be why Ice Age seafarers never landed there.

Whichever route was used, the seafarers were rarely out of sight of land. Their voyages involved island hopping and limited open-water travel, with few days at sea. Even a drift in a raft from Timor to Australia would have taken no more than about seven days with strong following winds. The voyagers traveled down natural voyaging corridors marked both by generally favorable weather and seasonal reversals of wind and current. To make such passages would have required a degree of self-sufficiency on the part of the crews. They would have had to carry adequate water supplies for several days, and sufficient food that would keep for the duration of the trip. But there would have been fish that could be taken in deep water, especially those attracted to the shadows cast by a raft on the surface. I learned this when crossing the Atlantic and began making a beeline for any driftwood or floating weed, for fish almost invariably lurked in the shadows close under water. The same must have been true off Sunda and Sahul.

These very earliest of seafarers were likely extremely conservative when venturing offshore. They were well aware that the ocean was a dangerous, hostile place. Experience—hard-won knowledge of winds and currents, and of long calmer periods when a laden canoe or raft could paddle or sail from one island to the next—was all-important. A watchful skipper would know the telltale signs of impending rainstorms and approaching squalls, of wind shifts and fast-flowing currents close in-shore. He would have learned the landmarks visible far offshore, both ahead and astern, that guided the way to safe anchorage. This lore passed from one generation to the next by oral tradition and ritual.

We can imagine a quiet, moonlit night at sea. The canoe moves qui-etly with the wind as the elder watches the waves and feels them through his legs, detecting a slight pattern at an angle to the bow, swell deflected from invisible land some distance away. A silent gesture and the canoe alters course. Later, the older man tells of earlier voyages, of mythic be-ings that first sailed these waters long ago . . . No sailor in these waters, or in others, for that matter, ever sailed in an intellectual vacuum. Once deliberate voyaging began, he always had the benefit of those who had gone before him, in large part because every passage was undertaken with the intention of returning or, at minimum, with a high probability that the crew could return on the route by which they had come while still outward-bound.

So the voyages continued, carrying small canoeloads of settlers from one island to the next, not necessarily out of curiosity but because the natural dynamics of fishing and coastal living were never static. People were always on the move; families splintered, relatives quarreled; dis-putes over fishing territories or food shortages threatened survival. And, just as on land, the option of moving away was always there. In these instances, voyagers simply sailed away to distant islands visible from the shore. Then, eventually, after about 25,000 years ago, the voyag-ing stalled—partly, perhaps, because of the endemic malaria in the Bis-marcks and on neighboring islands but also because the islands seemed to end at the Solomons and New Caledonia. Thousands of years were to pass before new generations of voyagers traveled deeper into Pacific waters.

CHAPTER 3

"Butterfly Wings Scattered Over the Water"

THE BISMARCK ARCHIPELAGO, 20,000 years ago. The young man turns the shiny flake from end to end in his hands. The lustrous surface gleams in the sunlight. As he plays with it, a spot of reflected light shines on a nearby tree trunk. He moves it back and forth, then turns it at a friend nearby, who puts his hands in front of his eyes. Together, they test the razor-sharp edge on a palm frond, slicing through the stalk with ease. Neither of them has seen volcanic glass like this before, stone from a distant land across the water that they've never visited. A handful of flakes had arrived in a canoe from a neighboring island that morning, wrapped carefully in bark fiber, bartered for shell adze blades made locally.

Near Oceania laps at the eastern shores of New Guinea and stretches far south and west into the Pacific.[1] The heavily forested islands form a voyaging corridor with predictable winds and currents, sheltered from the tropical cyclone belts to the north and south. A canoe could sail in summer from New Ireland or New Britain down the Solomons as far as distant San Cristobal or Santa Ana, then return during the winter when the winds shifted. By 25,000 years ago, late–Ice Age seafarers had settled as far south and east as the Solomon Islands. They were hunters and fisherfolk, clinging to the islands in small camps and rock shelters. Judging from the lack of imported artifacts, each island community seems to have kept to itself as they all adapted slowly to their new homelands.[2] But this isolation may be an illusion, for about 20,000 years ago, we have clear signs of contacts with others. Small obsidian flakes now appear in settlements in the Bismarck Archipelago, toolmaking stone carried

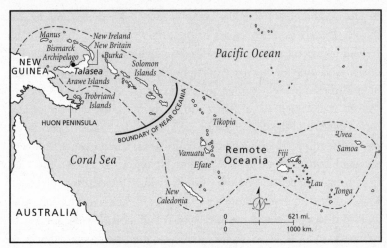

Figure 3.1 *Map of the Lapita world.*

thither from Mopir and Talasea, on New Britain. Since Talasea is a straight-line distance of at least 217 miles (350 kilometers) from the Bismarcks, it's clear that the islanders were venturing long distances to obtain useful commodities. (We know this because the distinctive trace elements of different obsidian sources can be identified with spectrographs.)

As interisland visits intensified, so did exploration. About 13,000 years ago, a canoe from either the north coast of Sahul or the northern end of New Ireland sailed 124 to 143 miles (200 to 230 kilometers) across the open Pacific to invisible Manus Island. Thirty-seven to 56 miles (60 to 90 kilometers) of the passage involved sailing out of sight of land. As the archaeologist Matthew Spriggs writes, "These would have been tense hours or days on board that first voyage and the name of the Pleistocene Columbus who led this crew will never be known."[3] This epic voyage, known only from evidence of human occupation on Manus dating to at least 13,000 years ago, leaves no doubt that late–Ice Age peoples in the southwestern Pacific were capable of long ocean voyages.

These explorers were without agriculture, but had hunted out so much island quarry that they deliberately imported game. The islanders brought the arboreal marsupial the gray cuscus (*Phalanger orientalis*) by canoe from New Guinea to islands where they were unknown. Cuscuses had arrived on New Ireland by 15,000 years ago, bandicoots on the Admiralty Islands by 12,000 years before present, and wallabies on New Ireland by 7,500 years ago. These seemingly haphazard attempts to increase food supplies on relatively impoverished islands are unique in human history: for the first time anywhere, people shifted food resources instead of moving to them. Sometime later, farming began on the islands. New Guinea and the Bismarcks were the places of origin for many tropical crops, among them such later staples as taro, sugarcane, and some forms of banana. Fruit trees were also important on the islands, with trees being cropped to improve orchard yields. Domesticated plants allowed canoe skippers to store food such as taro and yams for long voyages. Waterlogged remains of such species found on New Britain date to at least 2250 B.C.E. However, for all the voyaging, the human population of the southwest Pacific was still tiny. This may have been because of endemic malaria, for at least two species of malaria parasite had accompanied the first human settlers when they crossed from Sunda to Sahul thousands of years earlier. Only in the New Guinea highlands, above the habitats of malaria mosquitoes, did denser farming populations flourish.

Island life changed dramatically in about 1600 B.C.E., just when a massive eruption of Mount Witari, on New Britain, smothered much of the island in choking ash. The Witari cataclysm dwarfed the famous Krakatau Island explosion of 1883, in the Sunda Strait off Indonesia, and must have killed many of the island's inhabitants. Either just before or after the disaster, strangers in much larger, more powerful canoes arrived in the Bismarcks from the west.

The outriggers appear without warning, large canoes with high-peaked, woven-fiber sails that seem to move faster than the wind. Heavily laden, they come swiftly to land on a beach by a stream some distance from the hunters' camp. Men, then women and children, disembark cautiously, the males with weapons in hand. The islanders watch silently from the forest's edge as the newcomers pull their canoes clear of the breakers. They offload piles of taro roots and yam plants, axes, adzes, and large pots. Two elders approach the canoes cautiously, making gestures of friendship, chanting ritual greetings. They're puzzled to discover that the strangers speak a different, unintelligible language, but smiles and nods defuse the tension. In the days that follow, the seafarers clear forest for taro plots, plant crops, and build permanent houses, which are much more substantial than the hunters' temporary shelters. It's clear that they are here to stay. Except for some bartering of game meat for exotic shells, the contacts between hunter and farmer are sporadic at best. Within a few weeks, the hunters board their canoes and paddle away to forage elsewhere. Meanwhile, more outriggers arrive from the east and establish another village some distance away. However, some time later some of these new arrivals also restlessly sail away to the next island on the horizon, their crews as much at ease on the water as they are on the land.

We archaeologists call these newcomers the Lapita people, because a University of California at Berkeley anthropologist, Edward W. Gifford, mounted an archaeological expedition to New Caledonia, south and slightly east of the Solomon Islands, in 1952, setting to work at a site his team named Lapita, on the west coast. There he unearthed a distinctive kind of stamped pottery radiocarbon-dated to about 800 B.C.E., which was nearly identical to some exotic potsherds found on Tonga, far to the east, thirty years earlier.[4] Gifford realized that his "Lapita ware" was a marker for deep-sea voyaging in the western Pacific centuries earlier than had been assumed. Similar pottery soon turned up throughout the southwest Pacific. Some of the vessels bear intricate designs, including stylistic elaborations of human faces, perhaps intended as symbolic depictions of cultural identity at a time when Lapita people traveled over enormous distances. Today, we know of more than two hundred radiocarbon-dated Lapita sites scattered from the Bismarcks to the Solomons and far beyond into Remote Oceania—to Fiji, Tonga, and Samoa, in Polynesia.

With so many dates and this distinctive pottery, we can now track what was a rapid migration of seafarers across Near Oceania—one of the most remarkable maritime explorations in history.[5] Quite where the Lapita people originated is still a mystery, but it might have been from the northern Moluccas, in eastern Indonesia, where clay vessels of similar shapes, but without the stamped decoration, are known. The newcomers spoke an Austronesian language, one of a vast family of such tongues that spread, perhaps from Taiwan or some other location, more than half-way around the world, from Madagascar, in the Indian Ocean, to Rapa Nui (Easter Island), deep in the Pacific. By 1500 B.C.E., they had settled throughout Near Oceania. For the next two or three centuries, the canoes stayed where they were, the newcomers intermarrying with the indigenous populations.

Around 1200 B.C.E., a new chapter in long-distance voyaging began. For the first time, canoes voyaged into Remote Oceania and its uninhab-ited islands, beyond an invisible, and perhaps psychological, barrier at the southeastern end of the Solomons that had stood for about 30,000 years. They sailed first to the Santa Cruz Islands, which lie 235 miles (380 kilometers) southeast of San Cristobal. The journey from the southern Solomons to the archipelago was simply a matter of using the seasonal winds and following the east–west zenith path of the stars that passed over both island groups. This technique, latitude sailing, was the foun-dation of deepwater navigation as canoes sailed ever farther east. Be-tween about 1200 and 1100 B.C.E., other groups of Lapita people moved into the Vanuatu archipelago, then on to New Caledonia.

Still others sailed east from either Santa Cruz or Vanuatu against the prevailing trades and currents. They crossed 530 miles (850 kilometers) of unexplored ocean where there were no islands to stop and rest, until they arrived in the Fiji archipelago, in around 800 B.C.E. From Fiji came even more voyages eastward, threading through the numerous islands of the Lau archipelago and from there to Samoa and Tonga, in what is now known as western Polynesia. Without question, the Lapita colonists were the ancestors of later Polynesian navigators who were to settle Hawaii, Rapa Nui, and some of the remotest islands on earth many centuries later.

We still know little about the Lapita people or their voyages, except for the pathways left by their shell-decorated potsherds. We can only guess at the ritual exchanges, the volatile relationships—friendships and enmities—that defined their vast island world. They were farmers, so, as crews zigzagged from island to island, they carried seedlings, as well as chickens, dogs, and pigs, the first domesticated animals to arrive in the

Figure 3.2 *A Fijian canoe with the French explorer James Dumont d'Urville's ship* L'Astrolabe *on its voyage of 1826–29. M. Jules Dumont d'Urville,* Voyage de la Corvette L'Astrolabe Execute Pendant Les Années 1826–1827–1828–1829. *Paris: J. Tartu, 1833.*

southwestern Pacific. They literally carried their own landscape with them. The new foods added great flexibility to island economies that relied heavily on fish and wild plant foods and some limited hunting. Lapita crops could be stored, which tided people over from one season to the next. Above all, canoe skippers could remain at sea for much longer, the pressing limitation now being their ability to carry drinking water. A significant expansion in longer-distance trade and in settlement and exploration of hitherto uncolonized islands might have resulted. This expansion might also have coincided with significant innovations in watercraft and in the navigational lore that enabled sailors to make passages out of sight of land for days on end.

Only rarely do these remarkable seafarers come into historical focus. In about 1150 B.C.E., some Lapita canoes landed at Teouma, a wide and shallow bay on the southwestern shore of Efate Island, in the Vanuatu archipelago of the New Hebrides.[6] Here, freshwater came from a nearby stream, so the newcomers founded a village nearby. They also established a cemetery on the coral-rubble beach and in cavities in a nearby uplifted and volcanic-ash-covered reef. Three archaeological field seasons in 2004–2006 recovered almost fifty burials from the cemetery, which bring us face-to-face with a Lapita society that clearly placed great emphasis on relationships with their forebears. Remarkably, the skeletons are all headless, the skulls having been detached by the mourners. Apparently, the living manipulated the corpses of the deceased for some time after burial as part of their transition to revered-ancestor status. Burial customs varied considerably. For example, in one large grave, an adult male lay in a grave with four others, three skulls and the jaw of a fourth person lying on his chest. Isotopic readings from the bones and teeth of the dead in the cemetery generally tell us that most of them subsisted on a predominantly maritime diet, heavy on shellfish. But the four adult males in the large grave produced distinctive readings associated with diets more terrestrial than marine. Very likely these four individuals migrated to the island from elsewhere, a place where their drinking water came from coastal rainfall near sea level, which is isotopically distinct from Efate's spring-derived supply. Where these people came from is still a mystery and may be difficult to pin down, because shoreline environments are similar over a huge area of the western Pacific. Three of the four lay with their heads facing south, as if this direction had some significance to the deceased. Perhaps they were the first settlers, from a land with a more terrestrial diet. Alternatively, they may represent people voyaging between communities to arrange marriages, or for economic or political purposes.

One possible clue may be obsidian flakes found in the cemetery. We know that obsidian from the Bismarck Archipelago traveled to Lapita communities in the southwestern Solomons, to Vanuatu, New Caledonia, and even Fiji. Perhaps the social networks created by these exchanges linked islands out in the Pacific, over the open sea, up to as far as 125 miles (200 kilometers) away. Relatively few people were seafarers. If the Teouma cemetery is any indication, then Lapita passage making was as much a social phenomenon as a matter of colonization and trade. The powerful social and ritual underpinnings of later interisland voyaging might have originated with them.

NONE OF THE Lapita voyages would have been possible without a legacy of seafaring experience from the distant past and without major advances in canoe technology, the means to navigate out of sight of land, and an ability to stay at sea for days on end. For anything more than a day passage, the canoes had to be capable of handling heavy weather and strong winds with no convenient refuges nearby. They had to sail well, often in the face of prevailing headwinds, and also be capable of carrying not only a relatively large crew but also enough food and water. As we saw in Chapter 2, a canoe sailing in waves is far more stable if it becomes a platform rather than a single hull. Two ready solutions must have come into play soon after people plied the waters off Sunda: outriggers and double hulls. Of the two, the double-hulled canoe is the most practical craft for offshore sailing, on account of both its load capacity and its sailing qualities. Unfortunately, the last double-hulled canoes disappeared at least a century ago, leaving us with nothing but drawings by eighteenth- and nineteenth-century artists, notably of elaborate Tahitian war canoes, so we know little about these craft. We know from modern experiments that double-hulled canoes were capable of sailing at a reasonably close angle to the wind, perhaps as close as sixty degrees. This would have made passages against prevailing trade winds entirely practicable, if relatively slow. Thus, one always had the guarantee of being able to return by turning in front of the wind.

The ancient canoe rigs are nearly impossible to reconstruct except from historical analogies, and then only on the assumption that sails and rigs remained little changed over long periods. If this is correct, most Lapita canoes shipped out with a form of spritsail supported by two spars, which came in various forms, including a "clawlike" design with a high sprit, widely used in historical times.[7] These are what sailors call "fore-and-aft" sails, which flap when turned head to wind but fill when the breeze blows to one or the other side. Unlike the traditional square sail used by the Norse, Christopher Columbus, early dhow sailors, and many others, the sprit enables a canoe to sail at a closer angle to the wind—very important for a Pacific canoe voyager.

Like all Pacific canoes, Lapita watercraft were probably based on hollowed-out logs, to which the builders lashed one or more side planks,

Points of sail

Sailors refer to points of sail, a way of describing a sailing vessel's course in relation to the wind direction. No sailing boat, however scientifically designed, can sail directly into the wind, so there is what one might call a "no-go zone" between about thirty and fifty degrees off either side of the wind direction in which a vessel under sail cannot sail.

Close-hauled
A sailing vessel, whatever its size, has to sail at as close an angle to the wind as it can, then change direction to the opposite "tack" by passing through the eye of the wind, aka the no-go zone. So any course against the wind is a zigzag one, which means that it takes much longer to reach your destination than on other points of sail.

For thousands of years, canoes and other sailing craft sailed with the wind, but they never mastered the art of sailing at less than ninety degrees to the wind. Their clumsy square sails could not be sheeted in tight to push the boat at a close angle to the breeze. People waited for favorable winds, or for calm conditions in which they could paddle or row. No one knows when sailors first developed rigs that could sail more efficiently to windward, but the lateen sail, with its long spar, described in Chapter 7, was probably one of the first so-called fore-and-aft rigs to do so, at least 2,000 years ago.

You sail close-hauled, often called beating or sailing to windward, with your sails trimmed in tightly. The helmsperson sails as close to the wind as he or she can without entering the no-go zone, when the sails begin to flap slightly. A modern racing dinghy or light-displacement ocean-racing yacht can approach an angle of thirty degrees to the wind, but the kinds of vessels described in these pages did little sailing to windward. When they did, their angle to the wind was sixty degrees or more, progress was slow, and the boat sagged away from the wind, known as sagging to leeward.

Reaching

A reach is when a boat is sailing at approximately ninety degrees to the wind. A beam reach is a course at right angles to the wind, a close reach one with the wind more forward of the beam. A broad reach is when the wind is at a wider angle, approaching the stern. Reaching is usually the fastest point of sailing for modern yachts and also many traditional sailing craft, including Polynesian canoes.

Running

Running downwind is sailing with the wind behind you, the most efficient course for a square-rigged vessel like a caravel or Norse warship.

Tacking and Jibing

Sailing against the wind, to windward, requires changing tacks by tacking through the eye of the wind. The helmsperson steers through the no-go zone, using the boat's momentum to bring the sails to the other side. If the boat stalls in the no-go zone, it is said to be in irons.

Jibing is the opposite of tacking, the boat turning in front of the wind, a maneuver that can bring the sails and spars across with considerable violence in strong winds. An accidental jibe in strong winds can result in a dismasting.

or patchworks of shorter planks, to increase the freeboard—the distance between the waterline and the deck—in rough water. The canoes were long and narrow, with sides that could be higher than 2 feet 6 inches (0.75 meters), sufficient to make them safe in most seas. If swamped, they still floated. The hulls were long and narrow enough to achieve respectable speeds, a critical factor in making fast passages, or for reaching a safe haven before a storm burst overhead. No accurate speed figures exist for traditional canoes, but they were certainly faster than Captain Cook's lumbering ships and could sail circles around them. Above all, when caught in a sudden squall, a multihulled canoe had its second hull, which prevented excess heeling over and provided additional stability, something that must have saved thousands of lives in the past.

WHAT WAS IT like to sail on a Lapita canoe in Near Oceania? The large canoes of historical times have virtually disappeared, so firsthand accounts of interisland voyaging are hard to come by. Fortunately, the Polish anthropologist Bronislaw Malinowski, who lived among the Trobriand Islanders nearly a century ago, was entranced by their sailing abilities. He traveled with the canoes on major expeditions toward mountainous islands, whose distant peaks hung faintly on the horizon, wreathed in cumulus clouds. Malinowski wrote, "It is a precarious but delightful sensation to sit on the slender body, while the canoe darts on with the float raised, the platform steeply slanting, and water constantly breaking over . . . and be carried over the waves in a manner almost uncanny." He observed canoe builders at work, the intricate carving they lavished on the hulls, the complex rituals that surrounded construction and also protected the crew against the dangers of seafaring. "When the water rushes away below with a hiss, and the yellow [matting] sail glows against the intense blue of sea and sky—then indeed the romance of sailing seems to open through a new vista." When a fleet of trading canoes under sail appeared, "their triangular sails like butterfly wings scattered over the water, with the harmonious sounds of conch shells blown in unison, the effect [was] unforgettable."[8] Malinowski had entered a maritime world steeped in myth and legendary tales passed down the generations that peopled the ocean with vivid personality and realism.

THESE ORAL TRADITIONS and the rituals to appease evil deities masked the real dangers of sailing in these waters, where local knowledge came only from long experience. Razor-sharp coral reefs lurked close to the surface, revealed only by rapidly changing colors in the water, which is why many canoes always had a crewman in the bow when sailing in shallow water. There were other difficulties in sailing in confined waters, especially against the wind. Trobriand canoes could only sail at a wide angle

Figure 3.3 *A Dobuan canoe heading out on a Kula expedition. Photograph by Bronislaw Malinowski. The Library of the London School of Economics.*

to the wind, which meant that they often retraced their steps in the face of a breeze on the nose. Strong winds brought other hazards, too, for even large craft were easily swamped in rough water. They then lost their buoyancy and sagged rapidly to leeward, which put them at risk when close to rocky shores. Calms were especially dangerous, especially in narrow inlets and bays where currents and tides ran strong, sometimes as swiftly as 5 knots (9.3 kilometers per hour).

Nearly all voyages followed well-trodden courses, using familiar landmarks and the same points of arrival, both for navigational considerations and because the crew might be uncertain of their reception at the other end in a world fraught with factionalism and rivalry between neighboring islands. Vivid legends surrounded some islands on or over the horizon. One island, Kaytalugi, was said to be peopled by big, naked women, who ravished men to death on sight.

Surrounded as they were on every side by real and imaginary dangers, the canoes rarely deviated from line-of-sight courses. If rain squalls obscured the landmarks, the skippers noted their position carefully so that they could make for the nearest sandbank or island, normally only a few miles away. Just as when coasting in earlier times, they made use of the prevailing winds, which blew for months on end without changing. They preferred to make voyages during the periods when the winds were shifting, in November–December and March–April, not during the summer monsoon, with its violent northwesterly storms. The people would chant spells into the face of powerful monsoon winds. Malinowski wrote, "I was deeply impressed by this persistent effort of frail, human voice, fraught with deep belief, pitting itself so feebly against the monotonous, overbearing force of the wind."[9]

Sudden squalls, torn sails, a need to run before strong winds—all such incidents, combined with the roar of surf and the rustling of pandanus trees in the breeze, provoked apprehensions and fears felt by generations of canoe voyagers. The Trobrianders told tales of the *kwita*, an enormous octopus with a body so vast that it could envelop an entire village. Its home was in the east, a realm of ocean and islands. Pity the canoe that was caught by the *kwita*. Its tentacles would grip the frail craft for days, until the crew, dying of hunger and thirst, sacrificed one of the boys aboard by throwing him to the octopus. The ocean was the realm of invisible *mulukwausi*, flying witches, malevolent harbingers of shipwreck. "The canoe sails fast; the wind rises; big waves come; the wind booms, du-du-du-du . . . I speak magic to calm the wind . . . The wind abates not, not a little bit. It gains strength . . . The *mulukwausi* scream, u-ú, u-ú, u-ú, u; their voices heard on the wind. With the wind they scream and come flying."[10]

All these myths colored the seascape and gave it meaning. It became something alive and familiar. Individual rocks acquired distinctive personalities. Legendary tales brought alive the shorelines fast approaching on the horizon. Mythic names, vivid stories, passed from the old to the young. A legendary hero cast a rock after an escaping canoe; it became a landmark. Two rocks represented a couple turned into stone. The seascape formed a continual story that linked past and present, the hazards and features of ocean waters near and far. To the Trobrianders and to other Pacific voyagers, the past was a vast storehouse of events, a place where people fished and voyaged, lived and died, in the same ways as their living descendants did. The difference lay in the magical qualities possessed by these remote, mythic ancestors who traveled across the sea. Those who sailed Lapita canoes must have had similar stories, for they must have believed, like the Trobrianders, that one couldn't navigate safely without ritual pathways across open water.

THE LAPITA ANCESTRAL voyages were far more than journeys of exploration. They were deliberate voyages of colonization. We know this because the earliest sites on previously uninhabited islands are clearly permanent settlements, founded as colonies rather than transitory encampments. The newcomers stayed for a generation or more, then some of them went to sea again to find another new island. A rapid-fire sequence of Lapita colonization continued for generations.

Why did Lapita canoes keep on exploring ever outward into the unknown Pacific? Theories abound. The founding populations must have been small, simply because of the limited load-carrying capacity of their canoes. But the constant expansion speaks to rapidly growing populations resulting from high birth rates, low infant mortality, or increased life expectancy, perhaps as a result of less malaria infestation. We do not know. But why would people, having safely colonized a remote island with no close neighbors, feel compelled to keep sailing southward and eastward? Many have argued that population pressure was the cause, but many of the newly colonized islands such as Efate had been large and uninhabited. Centuries would have passed before population densities rose to crisis levels. Thanks to widespread finds of obsidian flakes, we know that the ancestral Lapita were inveterate traders. Their explorations of the Bismarcks and other closer islands might have been searches for new trading opportunities, especially for obsidian outcrops and other valued commodities. However, the farther out into the Pacific the canoes sailed, the fewer opportunities there were for trade.

We are left with intangible motivators, like social organization. According to linguists, Proto-Oceanic words for such terms as *kinship*, *social status*, and so on reveal a strong emphasis on birth and inheritance in Lapita society. Older siblings ranked above younger ones. The firstborn inherited house sites, gardens, and property—this apart from cherished ritual privileges and all kinds of privileged knowledge. The University of California at Berkeley archaeologist Patrick Kirch points out that rivalries between older and younger brothers are a persistent theme in Polynesian myths, which may perpetuate much earlier folklore. He writes, "In such societies, junior siblings frequently adopt a strategy of seeking new lands where they can found their own 'house' and lineage, assuring their offspring access to quality resources."[11] Founders—the original colonists and discoverers—may have assumed great prestige and importance in Lapita society, thereby providing a powerful incentive for bold voyaging into the unknown.

How, then, did Lapita canoes navigate when out of sight of land? Even more puzzling, how did the Lapita detect unknown islands beyond the horizon? The art of navigating the open Pacific developed out of many centuries of coasting and line-of-sight pilotage in Near Oceania. Once seafarers had the watercraft and the motives, it was an easy matter to head offshore, with the confidence both that they could return if need be and that they could maintain a course by sun, moon, and stars until distant signs of land such as irregular wave patterns came into play. Small wonder canoe pilots were highly respected members of society.

COLONISTS REVERED THEIR ancestors, whose names, like navigational lore, passed down the generations: their deeds, fictional or otherwise, were a social glue of oral traditions that linked isolated communities near and far. When oceanic peoples moved from one island to another, they carried with them a rich lode of knowledge about deities and culture heroes, about human existence.

History and ritual beliefs passed by word of mouth were one social bond, but just as important in practical, day-to-day terms were the relationships between individuals and wider kin groups living on other islands. No village was ever completely self-sufficient. Quite apart from subsistence needs, the islanders married outside their communities, which often meant moving to another island. In time, durable kin ties maintained not only social links but also complex trading networks that endured for centuries. Fine-grained obsidian for tool making traveled in canoes from island to island. So did rocks used to fashion stone axes and adzes used for cultivation; seashells, including large ones used to make shell adzes; red feathers; and all manner of objects, many of them having important prestige value—to mention only a few items of exchange. All of this activity, conducted between what were basically egalitarian groups, meant that even sporadic contacts with other islands produced important social and economic networks among individuals and groups that endured from one generation to the next. Over time, their connections developed into direct and indirect relationships that extended over hundreds of miles, far over the horizon.

Material objects tell us nothing of the complex relationships and social dynamics behind the voyages that carried them far from their source. If historical Near Oceanian societies are any guide, factionalism, ever-shifting alliances, and sudden raids were part of island life, as were cherished relationships between individuals living at considerable distance from one another, who might meet face-to-face only once or twice in their lifetimes. Such contacts, often endowed with profound spiritual meaning and frequently reinforced by the exchange of valued objects, formed the umbrella for much wider trading. That such contacts and relationships existed in Lapita society seems unquestionable, for survival on remote islands depended on relationships far beyond the confines of one's own village, as it did right into modern times. The roots of today's elaborate connections go back deep into the past, perhaps even to Lapita times, albeit in different, probably simpler, forms. Most famous and enduring of them all is the celebrated Kula ring of the Trobriand Islands. Such networks, with their constant passages over open water, also contributed significantly to the long process of decoding the ocean between the islands.

THE KULA RING, first studied by Malinowski in 1914, is a form of exchange that links communities and individuals occupying a wide ring of islands north and east of New Guinea.[12] The label "ring" is appropriate, for the exchanges of the Kula form a circuit that passes two kinds of ceremonial objects—*vaygu'a*—clockwise and counterclockwise in a circuit of perpetual motion. Long necklaces of red (spondylus) shells known as *soulava* pass clockwise; bracelets of a white (conus) shell called *mwali* travel in the opposite direction. Malinowski describes how he was shown Kula artifacts, "long, thin red strings, and big, white worn-out objects, clumsy to sight and greasy to touch." The owner would name them with reverence, "tell their history, and by whom and when they were worn, and how they changed hands." For such objects to visit a village is a matter of pride and prestige.[13] An elaborate set of traditional rules and conventions and sometimes rituals surround the Kula exchanges, as the two categories of objects meet each other while they travel in opposite directions. Every island, every village, has a small number of men who participate in the exchanges. They receive arm-shells or necklaces, hold them for a short time, and then pass them on to one of their partners, receiving the opposite commodity in exchange. No one retains a Kula object for any length of time. Kula partnerships between two men, however distant from one another, are permanent and last a lifetime. And the movement of the artifacts never ceases.

The Kula is not, in and of itself, a decoding of the surrounding ocean, but, in what must have been earlier forms of the same institution, it was enormously important in cementing relationships between distant communities separated by often challenging waters. Carefully planned voyages lay at the center of the Kula, voyages that traveled over familiar and less familiar waters imbued with all manner of spiritual meaning. In a sense it was, and still is, a reenactment of the process of understanding the ocean, making open water as familiar a landscape as that of island and village. The Kula created and maintained social bonds that ensured a deep continuity between generations and lasting ties between individuals near and far.

This well-ordered institution of ceremonial exchange is an umbrella for all kinds of secondary activities, especially ordinary trade involving the barter of essential commodities, like ax and adze stone. There is little that is spontaneous about the ring, for it unfolds periodically on carefully arranged dates. The participants are recruited with care at periodic gatherings. Sometimes membership passes through family generations. Kula partnerships involve mutual duties and privileges that bind

Figure 3.4 *A Kula gathering in the Trobriands, with more than eighty canoes drawn up along a half mile (0.8 kilometers) of beach. More than two thousand people assembled here. Photograph by Bronislaw Malinowski. The Library of the London School of Economics.*

members of different groups together on a very large scale and over long distances, a highly adaptive way of maintaining contact between isolated landmasses. Participants help each other in many ways, with a partner at greater distance, outside the immediate circle of close relatives, acting as a host and ally in places of danger and insecurity, where sorcery may prevail. He provides safety, food, and a place to gather when visiting. The Kula provides every participant with friends near and far, with friendly allies in more dangerous lands farther afield.

The Kula is an interwoven fabric of relationships that encompasses men living hundreds of miles from one another, bound together by direct and indirect ties. Over the generations, a vast intertribal network of ideas, cultural influences, art motifs, songs, and alliances travels down the Kula routes. Thousands of men scattered over hundreds of square miles enjoy Kula relationships.

Rich mythology surrounds the Kula, telling of ancient times when mythic ancestors sailed on distant voyages. Their magical knowledge enabled them to surmount obstacles, to defeat their enemies, and to escape danger. The magic of these remote personages, along with maritime lore and navigational information, has passed down countless generations to the present Kula participants. Such voyaging goes back far into the past, involving periodic expeditions to other islands. No question, such knowledge played an important role in carrying canoes safely over unfamiliar waters.

LAPITA CANOES COLONIZED a mosaic of islands deep into Remote Oceania with remarkable speed. At Samoa, the seafarers paused, for reasons that are little understood. East of Samoa, landmasses are smaller, more isolated. But sometime in the late first millennium C.E., voyaging resumed. By 1000 C.E., drawing on the ancient voyaging expertise of their Lapita ancestors, people were sailing to the Cook and Society islands, in the

Figure 3.5 Tonga Canoes *(oil on canvas), attributed to John Webber (1750–93). © Peabody Essex Museum, Salem, Massachusetts/The Bridgeman Art Library.*

heart of Remote Oceania. In western Polynesia, the traditions of inter-island contact expanded into a form of maritime empire centered on the large island of Tongatapu.[14] A sacred paramount chief, the Tu'i Tonga, presided over a carefully controlled system of chiefly governance based on deliberately nurtured connections across open water far beyond the Tonga archipelago, into Fiji to the west and Samoa to the east. Long-distance voyaging along familiar routes lay at the core of this "empire," combined with strategic marriages that cemented ties over hundreds of miles. Prestigious goods such as mats, feathers, sandalwood, bark cloth, canoes, and pottery flowed into Tongatapu, the pinnacle of what became a highly stratified, quite stable society. Tongan royal power depended on a seamless knowledge of surrounding waters that blurred the distinctions between land and sea. Such blurring, inherited from Lapita ancestors, was, here as everywhere, one of the keys to decoding the ocean.

CHAPTER 4

A Pattern of Islands

POLYNESIA: APPROACHING HUAHINE, in the Society Islands. I woke before dawn the day before landfall, blinking from the torpor of deep sleep following a midnight watch. The boat rolled gently like a slow rocking horse, as it had for days. All was just as it had been when I came off watch hours earlier. On deck, the utterly predictable northeast trade wind, soft and sensuous, caressed my bare chest in the gray light before sunrise. I went forward to the bow; two porpoises plunged and swam with the bow wave. Endless soft trade-wind clouds processed across the sky, tinted light gold as the sun burst abruptly above the horizon. Two hundred miles (321 kilometers) of sailing still lay ahead.

The day and following night passed without trimming a sail or adjusting a line. We sailed effortlessly on a deep-blue ocean, the horizon a hard line on every side. I fingered the sextant anxiously, for this was long before the days of satellite navigation. My last sun sight had placed us about 30 miles (48 kilometers) away from landfall, but I'd convinced myself that we'd miss the target. Anxiously, I watched mounting clouds, black with rain, on the horizon ahead, remembering how ancient canoes used such clues to find land that interrupted the trade winds' flow. The storm clouds rose, soon evaporated, and then came together again, this time in one place. Soon dark island peaks loomed through the distant rain showers as we drew near to land.

For days, we had sailed across deserted ocean, our small vessel seemingly motionless in a featureless seascape of whitecaps and cerulean blue. The daily routine never changed—sunrise, the sun high in the heavens and the noon sight, occasional rain squalls, glorious, colorful sunsets, and the brilliant stars of the small hours. Day after day, we traversed the open Pacific just like the ancient Polynesians, who colonized some of the remotest islands on earth more than a thousand years ago. I never felt threatened by the isolation, the feeling of being a tiny dot on open water. There was an intimacy, a closeness to the ocean, a familiarity with its moods that I had never experienced before. For a few days, I shared some of the feelings that must have passed through the minds of the first navigators who ventured into Remote Oceania.

THINK OF A random pattern of islands scattered over thousands of square miles of open water, most of them lying upwind against the prevailing trades, and you can visualize the challenge facing those who first deciphered the vast waters of eastern Polynesia beyond Samoa. These seagoing journeys were the last great expansion of *Homo sapiens*, a complex diaspora that had begun south of the Sahara some 100,000 years ago. (The date when our first modern ancestors left Africa is a matter of debate.) Fully modern humans had settled in Southeast Asia by 60,000 years before present, or perhaps earlier; had replaced Neanderthals in Europe and Central Asia by 45,000 years ago; and had crossed into North America by 15,000 years ago. As we've seen, by that time small numbers of fisherfolk and seafarers had long since settled in New Guinea and the southwestern Pacific—on the Solomon Islands and in the Bismarck Archipelago. After 1500 B.C.E., their successors, the Lapita people, farmers and expert seafarers, navigated from island to island by line of sight until they ventured offshore to the Santa Cruz Islands, then ultimately to Tonga and Samoa, where they had arrived by 800 B.C.E. There the seafarers paused for many centuries.

The last pulse of the great diaspora reached more than five hundred islands in eastern Polynesia, an area of the Pacific larger than North America—from Hawaii to Rapa Nui and as far south and west as New Zealand and the Chatham Islands. Some canoes may even have reached South America.

Tracing these voyages has engaged a small regiment of scholars since

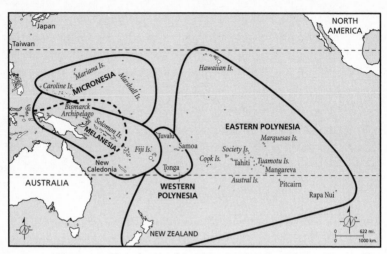

Figure 4.1 *Map showing locations mentioned in Chapter 4.*

Captain Cook's day.[1] All manner of ingenious approaches have been attempted to decipher the colonization of Remote Oceania, including elaborate computer simulations and experimental voyaging. The former are, of course, theoretical exercises that are only as good as the data behind them, but they argue strongly against one-way voyages. The simulations also highlight the increasing difficulty of voyaging and navigation as one sailed east. When sailing into unknown waters, the pilots probably went by indirect routes if they could, as well as by some form of latitude-like sailing using the stars. As in Lapita explorations, each canoe traveled into the teeth of the prevailing easterly winds, taking advantage of periods when the trades were down. This ancient, conservative strategy allowed them to discover new lands over the horizon while always knowing that they could return safely home.[2]

We'll never know much about these voyages. Many of the probes must never have sighted land. One imagines two canoes sailing close to one another, food and water running low, the pilots talking quietly across the water. They look at the sky, see telltale trade-wind clouds, a sign the winds are changing. After careful deliberation, they reverse course, using familiar constellations to return home safely. On many occasions, too, the canoes would never return, victims of severe squalls or prolonged

The Pacific's waltz of atmosphere and ocean

Early human settlement of the offshore Pacific revolved, in part, around enduring, large-scale meteorological phenomena that are still little understood. Ultimately, most of them depend on what one might call an elaborate, usually slow-moving waltz involving two partners—the atmosphere and the ocean.

The North Pacific High and the Aleutian Low. A complex interplay between the North Pacific High and the Aleutian Low dominates the climate of the North Pacific. The former is a massive, semipermanent subtropical anticyclone centered northeast of Hawaii, one of several such high-pressure systems around the world. The latter lies near the Aleutian Islands. During the summer, the North Pacific High lies farther north and is stronger, intensifying the easterly trade winds. The Aleutian Low, now far to the north, weakens and is much smaller. The winter months see the reverse, with a much more intense low bringing persistent westerly winds and rain to Alaska and the West Coast of North America.

The Hadley cell. The North Pacific High is associated with the large-scale circulation of air in the so-called Hadley cell. Within the Hadley cell, rising air heated near the equator climbs toward the atmosphere and spreads outward. At about thirty degrees north, the heated air cools and descends, a process associated with the North Pacific High. The cooler air then moves across the surface back to the equator.

Surface winds flowing out from the North Pacific High region deflect to the right, owing to the Coriolis effect, which deflects circulating air in that direction in the Northern Hemisphere. The northeast-to-southwest-flowing surface winds to the south of the high are the trade winds. During the summer, the trade winds intensify as the high moves north and is stronger. In winter, the prevailing westerlies move to the south as the high weakens.

The Intertropical Convergence Zone. Often called the Doldrums by sailors, the ITCZ circles the earth in an area of the equator where winds originating in the Northern and Southern hemispheres come together. Here, the rising limb of the Hadley cell brings warm, moist air and often heavy rainfall. The ITCZ is marked by a band of clouds and thunderstorms that circle the globe and move north and south depending on the seasons and El Niño conditions.

El Niño/La Niña. Everyone has heard of El Niño, an unpredictable climatic seesaw that is said to be the single most influential factor, after the passage of the seasons, in determining global climate. Under normal conditions, the trade winds blow toward the west across the tropical Pacific. This tends to pile up warm water in the western Pacific. Cold water upwells off the Pacific coast of South America, creating rich coastal fisheries. During El Niños, the trade winds weaken and the warm water piled up in the western Pacific migrates eastward, reducing upwelling, warming sea-surface temperatures, and causing heavy rainfall in the east, while there are droughts in the west. During the opposite, La Niña condition, trade winds strengthen and warm water again piles up in the western Pacific. Quite what causes this El Niño–Southern Oscillation (ENSO) is unknown, but it is connected to complex interactions between the atmosphere and ocean temperatures that act as an irregular seesaw, the gyrations of which are hard to predict far in advance. El Niños appear to occur every two to seven years. The frequency of ENSO events appears to be linked to the so-called Pacific Decadal Oscillation, a still little-understood cycle of coupled atmospheric and oceanic conditions that seem to alternate to create long periods of dominant El Niños with periods of predominating La Niñas. For instance, we are currently in a phase of more frequent La Niñas and fewer strong El Niños that began in 1998.

calms, of starvation. If they did sight land and found it suitable for settlement, the canoes would have to return home first. They knew well that repeated visits would be needed to establish a viable island community.

The initial explorations might have involved just men, but deliberate colonization would have brought women, children, crops, and animals to the newly discovered land. Perhaps later voyages would have carried skilled artisans, as well as single women to maintain a viable sex ratio if too many people died. Such voyages were long and dangerous to undertake, so it's hardly surprising that the tempo of passage making slowed once the new community flourished. Oral traditions suggest that later voyages were matters of piety or social connection. For instance, canoes from all over Polynesia made pilgrimages to the Taputapuâtea temple, on Raiatea in the Societies, the religious center of eastern Polynesia. Here priests and navigators gathered to make sacrifices to the gods and to exchange genealogical and navigational lore. Adventurous Tahitian chiefs occasionally sailed to Hawaii to marry into noble lineages or to visit long-departed kin. But eventually the voyages ceased as new priorities at home revolved around war and the shifting sands of competing alliances.

When did the voyages take place, and how long did colonization take? Dating them was largely a matter of guesswork until the University of Chicago chemist Willard Libby and his research team developed radiocarbon dating in the late 1940s. For the first time, there was a way of dating the settlement of Polynesian islands—or so it seemed. By 1993, 147 dates had produced a mosaic timescale for first settlement, with the colonization of the Society Islands and surrounding archipelagos in the 900–950 C.E. range. This chronology appeared just before accelerator mass spectrometry (AMS) refined carbon dating dramatically.[3] Now excavators could obtain dates from samples as small as individual seeds adhering to a pot.

The rules of the dating game have changed completely since AMS arrived. The newer dates, a tenfold increase over 1993, are much more accurate, their contexts more carefully researched. Instead of looking at individual dates, one can treat them as statistical groups. A recent study of first settlement uses no fewer than 1,434 samples from at least forty-five eastern Polynesian islands, carefully appraised for accuracy and for their associations with human activity or with what are called commensals, animals like the Pacific rat that lived only with humans. We now have an even shorter chronology of remarkable precision that spans thousands of square miles of the Pacific. The 1,434 dates reveal a dramatic burst of ocean voyaging.[4]

For about 1,800 years after arriving there, in about 800 B.C.E., the Lapita ancestors of the Polynesians stayed around Samoa and the Tonga archipelago. Then, suddenly, between about 1000 and 1300 C.E., Polynesian seafarers discovered, and usually colonized, nearly every other island in the eastern Pacific in a relatively narrow time span.

The colonization dates speak for themselves. A wave of canoes arrived in the Society Islands between 1025 and 1121 C.E., in the Marquesas between 1200 and 1400. Other voyagers reached New Zealand between 1230 and 1280, Rapa Nui between 1200 and 1263, and Hawaii between 1219 and 1269. Some Polynesian pilots might even have sailed to South America and back. The rapid pace of colonization might account for the remarkable similarities in artifacts such as adzes and fishhooks in places as widely separated as the Societies, the Marquesas, and New Zealand. A mere three centuries of ocean voyaging wrote the last chapter in the 100,000-year journey of *Homo sapiens* across the world. By the time European voyagers arrived a few centuries later, farming, imported animals, and promiscuous hunting had changed the environments of Polynesia's islands beyond recognition.

THE PILOT WATCHES the fading stars, feet apart, balancing easily against the pitch and roll of the fast-moving canoe. Except for the steersman, he's the only one awake. After days at sea, the crew are weary and hoping for land. He sniffs the wind, watches birds wheeling overhead, and looks closely at the swell. As the darkness lightens and the stars vanish, the weathered navigator leans over, eyes shut, feeling the movement of the waves through his swinging testicles. After several minutes, he straightens up, looks again at the water, and then points to a course slightly more downwind. Hours later, the cross-waves are stronger, washing far offshore after colliding with island cliffs. As the sun sets, the pilot climbs high in the rigging and points slightly to leeward. A low cliff stands clear above the horizon. Without a word being said, the steersman alters course close to the wind, knowing that they will wait until dawn to approach the unknown island.

How did the Polynesians find their way over trackless ocean? The answer lies in the heavens, as visible at sea as on land. A Polynesian navigator acquired his knowledge by apprenticeship to experienced pilots when he was still a child. The late Mau Piailug, a master navigator from the Caroline Islands, in Micronesia, started his apprenticeship at age five, listening to his grandfather talking about passages he had made. As Piailug grew older, he accompanied his grandfather on interisland voyages, learning about stars, swell patterns, and birds. When he was a teenager, Piailug studied with an uncle who taught him not only practical knowledge but also complex magical and spiritual lore. At age fifteen, he was initiated as a *palu*, a navigator, and subjected to intense oral drilling day and night for a month as he memorized star tracks across the heavens. Only then was he allowed to sail offshore as a pilot.

Mau Piailug might have lived out his life in quiet isolation, had it not been for the English physician David Henry Lewis, an expert small-boat sailor who abandoned medicine for the sea. He sailed through the Carolines in the 1960s, learned something of traditional navigational practices long assumed to be forgotten, then piloted his catamaran from Tahiti to New Zealand with the help of a Micronesian pilot, steering by the stars just as the ancients had done. Subsequently, Lewis apprenticed himself to Melanesian and Micronesian navigators from the Caroline Islands and Tonga.[5] Meanwhile, in the late 1960s, the American anthropologist Ben Finney began long-term experiments with replicas of ancient Polynesian canoes.[6] *Hokule'a*, designed by Hawaiian Herb Kawainui Kane, was 62 feet (19 meters) long, with double hulls and two crab-claw-shaped sails. Finney, Mau Piailug, and a mainly Hawaiian crew sailed *Hokule'a* from Hawaii to Tahiti and back in 1976. They followed this journey with a two-year voyage around the Pacific using only indigenous pilotage. Thanks to the successful *Hokule'a* experiments and other replica voyages, ancient Polynesian navigational skills have been preserved for posterity.

Nowhere are the challenges to a navigator greater than in Micronesia,

Figure 4.2 *Hokule'a in Hawaiian waters.* © *Douglas Peebles Photography/Alamy.*

which is effectively a vast desert of ocean dotted with low-lying atolls and shallow reefs. Yet Micronesian navigators like Piailug found tiny islands again and again with effortless panache. They had to, for less than two tenths of the Caroline archipelago is land, the rest a huge expanse of water. Open-water passages of 150 miles (240 kilometers) were routine, carried out with no instruments whatsoever. When at sea, the navigator had to judge both the direction in which he was sailing and the distance he had traveled. Lewis found that Carolinian canoes would make a point of arriving at the latitude of an island that lay to windward but arrive slightly upwind of it, the island being to the east. The strategy is somewhat like the latitude-sailing method used by the Norse and others (see Chapter 11), which involved sailing to the latitude of the zenith star of one's destination island, then running with the wind along the latitude to make landfall. Carolinian pilots knew which zenith stars pass directly over different islands, so when exploring unknown waters they would sail upwind, always knowing that they could reverse course and use zenith stars to return home. They also used a form of star compass, based on the North Star, five positions of the Southern

Cross, and thirteen constellations. Star bearings defined thirty-two compass points. Each navigator regularly visited a range of islands, each with its own star points. The changing stars were a familiar tapestry to the navigators, who used the rising and setting points of different constellations to maintain direction.

This explains direction, but how did they judge distance traveled? Again, they used a conservative strategy based on long experience. Each passage unfolds along a course with the changing star bearing of a third island lying to one side or the other. The island is usually invisible, but the star bearing allows the seafarer to judge the distance traveled as the island moves from ahead to astern during the voyage. Note that it is the island that moves, not the canoe—a fundamental thought process in Micronesian passage making. As the anthropologist Thomas Gladwin puts it: "The canoe is a familiar little world . . . On either side of the canoe, the water streams past, a line of turbulence and bubbles merging into a wake and disappearing into the darkness. Overhead there are stars, immovable, immutable. They swing in their paths across and out of the sky but invariably come up again in the same places. You may travel for days on the canoe, but the stars will not go away or change their positions aside from their nightly trajectories from horizon to horizon."[7]

This is *etak*, a system of expressing distance used by pilots who well know that the notion of a stationary canoe is a fiction. They work with mental images, with a bearing of a reference island to the side of their course. Thus, the imagery of the star bearing set on the horizon that shows the position of a moving island is entirely logical as a navigational device. In this way the navigator minimizes the number of moving systems around him. He mentally allows the canoe and stars to remain stationary while the islands move around in a perception of the ocean that enables him to know he has reached his destination when the reference island has the same bearing from the canoe as it does from his destination island.

Etak is a timeless exercise, for the duration of longer passages across open ocean is not an important consideration for navigators whose primary concern is to reach their "target," not how long it takes to get there.

THE GREAT VOYAGES were long over when Bougainville, Cook, and other European explorers arrived in Polynesia in the mid-eighteenth century. However, the deeds of the great pilots linger in Polynesian oral traditions as part of the common beliefs and values transmitted from one generation to the next. Great culture heroes like Maui, the fisher of lands, and Rata, an expert canoe builder, figure in historical narratives throughout much of Polynesia and may date back to Lapita times.[8] Maui snared the sun, fished up islands, and obtained fire, a symbol of the human struggle to harness the forces of nature. Rata, the canoe builder, perhaps himself a voyager, figures in traditions that may be at least 3,000 years old. The oral traditions preserve the names of great navigators like Hiro. He was born in the Societies and, as an adult, acquired a passion for sailing, stealing, and womanizing. He is said to have sailed to the Marquesas, Hawaii, the Australs, and Rapa Nui in large canoes with sewn planks. Whoever the navigators were, they carried far more than sailing lore with them. Generic place names meaning "passage" and "reef" traveled around with them throughout Polynesia. They designated small islands at the entrances to natural harbors as places of sanctuary for visiting canoes waiting to see if it was safe to go ashore. The mosaic of oral memories provides some names, some shared cultural traditions, but does not answer the question of questions: Why did small numbers of people suddenly decide to sail over the horizon in search of new lands?

What prompted such deliberate voyages? Were they quests for religious enlightenment, for the realm of the ancestors, or simply a reflection of those most human of all qualities, curiosity and restlessness? We don't know. Whatever the motivation, to sail eastward toward sunrise into unknown waters was a hazardous enterprise, given the prevailing northeasterly trades. To cover any distance would require setting sail when the trades were down, something that happened for only a few weeks a year between January and March, except when El Niños dampened the trades. It might be no coincidence that the eastern voyages occurred during a documented spike of El Niño activity during the early second millennium. Even with unexpected breaks from the wind, the social reasons for taking off into the unknown must have been compelling. We can only speculate about them.

Like their Lapita forebears, early Polynesian societies placed great emphasis on birth order, inheritance, and kin ties. As was the case farther west, older siblings outranked their younger brothers and sisters. Oral traditions are full of rivalries between older and younger brothers. Some siblings sailed away to seek new homelands, where they could found their own privileged lineage and pass land to their offspring. Such ventures were expensive but prestigious, requiring superlative navigational skills acquired over many years. Thus, successful voyages over the horizon acquired a mystique that was passed down the generations, not necessarily because their leaders were exceptional pilots but because they became founders of descent lines firmly anchored in new lands.

Long-distance voyaging was a privileged activity. Most Polynesians stayed at home, fishing in lagoons and cultivating their gardens. Cultivable acreage was the basis of social life, even on the larger islands. The social structure associated with agriculture revolved around inheritance and access to the land. Birth order was all-important. So the driving force behind colonization of Remote Oceania may have been a quest for land and the privileges of inheritance. Prestige and power also came from maritime expertise, from knowledge of a deciphered ocean. To those who traveled across them, Polynesian waters became not a barrier but a network of watery highways that connected one's island to many others.

With these pathways came economic, social, and other ties, some of which endured for generations, while others were but transitory. Soon after initial settlement, a complex network of interconnections linked island to island, settlement to settlement, individual to individual—economic, ritual, and social ties maintained by navigators and seafarers over many generations. Just as with the Kula, contacts with other islands resulted in trade and exchange, and also sometimes in marriage partners. Much of the contact was with near neighbors, with whom people shared a common history as well as close cultural and other ties. This meant, for example, that the Tongans sailed regularly to Samoa and Fiji.

Etak still flourishes in a world of tiny, isolated Micronesian atolls. Elsewhere, navigational traditions virtually disappeared until the

The prestige of a canoe

Canoes were far more than mere utilitarian objects. Of course, there were humble dugouts and small fishing canoes, but watercraft used for longer voyages and for ceremonial passages were imbued with ritual meaning and acquired a history of their own, accumulated from dangerous journeys. In many societies, songs and stories surrounded larger canoes, many of them adorned with carvings, shell ornaments, or painted designs with deep symbolic meaning. Kula canoes were seagoing vessels, often with names, each with a complex history. They were owned communally, but each was under the direction of a chief or some other prominent person, who served as the master. There were respected specialists, too—carvers, canoe builders, and ritual experts. Every stage of construction, from selecting the trees for the dugout hulls to the final caulking and painting, involved appropriate rituals. There were spells and other magic incantations that ensured the canoe was fast and seaworthy. Since the average life of a canoe was about fifteen years, new vessels were constantly being built, giving those who constructed and sailed them a powerful leadership role in society.

Canoe captains were often men of unusual status. Canoe builders in the Pacific Northwest of North America enjoyed such prominence. So did the Chumash Indians who built and owned planked canoes in Southern California. An influential guild, the Brotherhood of the Canoe, enjoyed unique power and prestige, so much so that canoe captains wore bearskin capes. Their power came from their ability to control trade between the islands and the mainland in shell beads and acorns, a Chumash staple.

Nearly every ancient society where deep-sea watercraft were in use treated those who built, skippered, and piloted them with great respect. They truly were men apart, often with considerable ritual power and wealth gained by their mastery of the ocean. There is every reason to believe that such prestige extended to canoe skippers in waters as diverse as those of Northern Europe, the Mediterranean, and the Erythraean Sea.

twentieth-century revival. They were alive and well in 1769, when James Cook arrived at Matavai Bay, on Tahiti, to observe the passage of Venus across the sun. There he met a navigator-priest named Tupaia and other pilots, who astounded him with their knowledge of neighboring islands. He wrote: "Of these they know a very large part by their Names and the clever ones among them will tell you in what part of the heavens they are to be seen in any month when they are above their horizon."[9] Cook, himself a consummate navigator, learned that Tupaia knew the names and locations of more than a hundred islands around Tahiti. He compiled a chart of seventy-four islands from Tupaia's verbal accounts of their bearings on the horizon. They ranged from Fiji, Samoa, and Tonga in the west to some of the Marquesas, Australs, and Tuamotus in the east, a huge swath of the Pacific. Tupaia might not have visited them all, but he had the knowledge (using the word in the same sense as London cabdrivers do). Much of his information was probably in the form of oral traditions, some of which must have dated back to the much earlier days of regular long-distance voyaging. Subsequently, Tupaia guided Cook's ship some 500 miles (800 kilometers) from Tahiti through the Society Islands and from Raiatea to the Australs. With each destination, he always "pointed to the part of the heavens where each isle was situated, mentioning at the same time that it was either larger or smaller than Taheitee, and likewise whether it was high or low, whether it was peopled or not."[10] According to Tupaia, the longest a canoe could stay at sea without reprovisioning was about twenty days.

Another explorer, Spaniard Domingo de Bonechea, carried Puhoro, a Tuamotan navigator, on a voyage to Lima in 1775.[11] During the voyage, Puhoro dictated a list of fifteen islands east of Tahiti, including most of the Tuamotus, and twenty-seven to the west, both in the Societies

Figure 4.3 *A sailing canoe of Otaheite, from* Views in the South Seas *(1792), by John Webber (1750–93), an artist who sailed with Captain Cook. Private Collection/The Bridgeman Art Library.*

and the Cooks. He also enumerated the topography and reefs of each island, the main products, the hostility or friendliness of the inhabitants, and the number of days needed to sail to each one, and he described the sixteen points of the wind compass used in conjunction with star paths.

ONCE THE TEMPLATES of surrounding waters lay in navigators' minds, the routines of passage making were well established in seeming perpetuity, despite a virtual cessation of very long trips. Dangerous voyages lasting weeks gave way to shorter journeys that were part of the tapestry of everyday existence. People sought wives on neighboring islands, visited shrines, and traded foodstuffs. As island populations grew, different communities acquired reputations for such items as red feathers used in important rituals, shells for adze blades, and ax stone. We know from sourcing studies of basalt adze and ax blades (akin to those from obsidian) that there were repeated contacts between many island groups.

Basalt found in a rock shelter on Mangaia Island came from American Samoa, nearly 1,000 miles (1,600 kilometers) away. Adze stone from the Marquesas traveled by canoe to Moorea, in the Society Islands, to mention only two examples of such contacts documented from finds in archaeological sites. Trade networks ebbed and flowed, prospered, then ceased to operate. For generations, the inhabitants of the southern Cooks relied on exotic pearl shell and other materials for both ornaments and such prosaic artifacts as shell fishhooks. After regular contacts with other islands ceased, the villagers turned to inferior local materials instead.

The arrival of humans on Pacific islands led to immediate, often fundamental environmental changes—deforestation from agriculture, widespread erosion, and the rapid extinction of many intensively hunted sea and land birds as well as indigenous animals such as the giant turtles of Efate Island, in the Vanuatu archipelago, some of them up to 8 feet (2.4 meters) long. Many islands in Remote Oceania abounded in birds, fish, and shellfish and enjoyed salubrious, malaria-free climates but lacked vegetable foods until farmers arrived. When people started clearing land and planting, the islands rapidly became largely cultural environments, whose productivity varied widely with soil and rainfall. Ingenious and highly productive farming systems, combined with fishing, produced large food surpluses in many places, despite rising population densities. The wetter landscapes of the Society Islands supported dense farming populations, while the ancient taro pond fields of Hawaii fed thousands of people and are in use to this day.

Inevitably, political and ritual power passed to those who owned the best land. By 1600 C.E., some Polynesian societies had developed into elaborate chiefdoms headed by small elites of chiefs, navigators, and priests, especially in areas where wet, swamp-based agriculture was possible. Inevitably, the escalating demands of chiefs and priests questing for ever more prestige threatened the fine line between subsistence and surplus. Rivalries led to war. In the Society Islands, chiefdoms turned in on themselves as they juggled slippery alliances and warfare in vicious competition for good farming land and for political and ritual power.[12] The inhabitants were aware of islands over the horizon, of a much wider world, but their cultural horizons were confined more to landscape than to seascape, as if the broad expanses of the ocean were no longer relevant.

The Society Islanders maintained at least tenuous contacts with outlying archipelagos, but the Hawaiians flourished in isolation after some centuries of sporadic voyaging.[13] Judging from esoterica like the designs of shell fishhooks and adzes and also linguistic similarities, it seems likely that the first settlers in Hawaii came from the Marquesas. Hawaiian oral traditions speak of a subsequent "voyaging period" in which great navigators like Moʻikeha and Paʻao sailed to a mythic homeland, "Kahiki"—perhaps Tahiti—and back. The great passages ceased after 1300. Complete isolation ensued, except for the symbolic return of an anthropomorphic god, Lono, who was said to journey from Kahiki each year to renew the land. When James Cook anchored off Kauai in 1778, the local people thought his ship was a floating island. The islanders learned that he had come from Tahiti, so they assumed he was Lono, who had traveled there many generations earlier and promised to return. Cook promptly became a great ancestor. By this time, at least 250,000 people lived on the Hawaiian Islands, under the rule of powerful chiefs.

Isolation was no barrier to Polynesian navigators, who sailed enormous distances—not only more than 2,500 miles (4,000 kilometers) to Hawaii but to New Zealand and Rapa Nui, and perhaps even farther afield. Thirteenth-century Polynesian navigators from the Cooks, the Societies, or the Australs are said to have followed cuckoos to New Zealand (Aotearoa), the last, and largest, Pacific landmass they colonized. A pleasing legend, for the long-tailed cuckoo indeed flies south from Polynesia to New Zealand in September. There must have been more than a few voyages to achieve lasting settlement in what was a heavily forested, unfamiliar environment. Then the voyages ceased, as they did elsewhere. A now isolated Maori society developed into a mosaic of competitive, warlike kingdoms, but their oral traditions list the achievements of twenty or more generations, recounted with the aid of notched sticks. What is actual history ultimately merges into the mythological, but, like other Polynesians, they have a profound sense of their maritime ancestry and a strong bond with the great ocean, which their ancestors traversed centuries ago.[14]

Aotearoa, some 600 miles (1,000 kilometers) southwest of Fiji and Tonga, was an enormous target by Polynesian standards, very different from the tiny islands of the east, such as Rapa Nui.[15] Some canoes were sailing there by about 1200–1269 C.E. The human population grew steadily in isolation, achieving sustainability by using ingenious agricultural methods in the face of the deforestation caused by the depredations of rats that arrived in the canoes, as well as humans. The carving of great ancestral stone statues (*moai*) and the building of temple platforms using communal labor were important ways of maintaining social cohesion, which fell apart after Europeans arrived.

Were Aotearoa and Rapa Nui the last frontiers of Polynesian exploration? Or did canoes venture 2,200 miles (3,500 kilometers) farther east, to the Americas, a distance roughly equivalent to that from the Society Islands to Hawaii? In theory, canoe navigators who had located tiny specks on the ocean were perfectly capable of sailing to the massive continents to the east. According to the archaeologist Geoffrey Irwin, the most likely routes to South America would have been from southeast Polynesia, passing south of the high-pressure area that endures in the eastern South Pacific before sailing to the coast ahead of southerly winds, using a northbound current.[16] Similar conditions would have pertained for canoes sailing northward from Hawaii until clear of the

Figure 4.4 *Rapa Nui* moai. *iStockphoto.*

North Pacific High, at which point they could turn eastward, as many sailing yachts do today. In both cases, returning canoes could ride the prevailing trades. But did they actually do it? No one has yet found Polynesian artifacts anywhere on American coasts, despite claims to the contrary. We know that the American sweet potato and the bottle gourd reached Polynesia, the latter as much as a thousand years ago. Coconuts, which originated in Southeast Asia and Melanesia, were established on the west coast of Panama before Europeans arrived. The chances of any of these plants having drifted east or west for months, then germinating, are infinitesimal, so canoes may well have carried them to new home-lands. A potential smoking gun comes from an unlikely source: chicken bones. The mitochondrial DNA from chicken bones found on Tonga and Samoa is identical to that from chicken fragments found at a coastal settlement named El Arenal-1, in south-central Chile, dating to 1321–1407 C.E., nearly a century before Columbus landed in the Bahamas and before the time of the great voyages.[17] Perhaps, then, Polynesian canoes reached South America soon after the colonization of Remote Oceania, bringing chickens with them. Perhaps they picked up plants like sweet potatoes and bottle gourds and brought them back to Polynesia.

If such voyages took place—and the genetic science seems impeccable—what was the nature of the contacts between Polynesians and Americans? Were they fleeting or more lasting? Did any of the visitors from beyond the horizon stay in Chile or elsewhere and marry into the local population? We may never know, but there is nothing in the story of the human decipherment of the Pacific that suggests that such voyages were impossible. We should never forget that as long as the land and the ocean are seen as one, people will venture offshore and decode the most demanding of seascapes.

POSEIDON'S WATERS

Suddenly wind hit full and the canvas bellied out
and a dark blue wave, foaming up at the bow,
sang out loud and strong as the ship made way,
skimming the whitecaps, cutting toward her goal.

—Homer, *The Odyssey*[1]

The Mediterranean was another cradle of seafaring, many millennia after humans had paddled or sailed into the southwestern Pacific. A case can be made that much earlier humans crossed to Crete perhaps before 100,000 years ago, but such—presumably accidental—voyages are a very different matter from deliberate journeys from the mainland to the Aegean islands, which began at least 10,000 years ago. We're concerned here not with triremes and classical Greek warships, or with Phoenicians or Romans, whose maritime exploits are well known—although, obviously, they deserve brief mention in these pages. Here we delve into the remotest chapters of Mediterranean seamanship, into the many centuries when dugout canoes and other humble craft paddled from island to island deep into the Cyclades Islands of the central Aegean. There were few obvious incentives to undertake such passages, for fertile island soils were in short supply, and fish were far from abundant. At first, the canoes came to collect obsidian, the fine-grained volcanic rock that makes razor-sharp stone tools, as well as exotic rock for axes, adzes, and grindstones. By 3000 B.C.E., the Aegean had changed from a secret world known to toolmaking specialists into a place where small island communities eked out livings from the soil and depended on one another for survival. Soon, intervillage trade networks became part of a much wider maritime world in the hands of Minoan traders from Crete, who sailed as far as the eastern Mediterranean coast and the Nile. The famed Uluburun shipwreck in southern Turkey bears witness to a coastal trade that flourished for thousands of years far from the spotlight of ambitious monarchs and vying civilizations. We briefly trace the fortunes of the Phoenicians as the pace of Mediterranean sea history quickens after 500 B.C.E., for these remarkable mariners and traders were the first from the south to explore Northern European waters in search of tin. But, many centuries earlier, Egyptian ships were plying the Red Sea and trading as far south as the mysterious Land of Punt, on the margins of the vast monsoon world of the Indian Ocean.

CHAPTER 5

A World of Ceaseless Movement

Crewmen sat to the oarlocks, each in line.
They slipped the cable free of the drilled stone
    post . . .
The ship like a four-horse team careering down the
    plain,
all breaking as one with the whiplash cracking smartly,
leaping with hoofs high to run the course in no time—
so the stern hove high and plunged with the seething
    rollers
crashing dark in her wake as on she surged unwavering,
never flagging, no, not even a darting hawk,
the quickest thing on wings, could keep her pace,
as on she ran, cutting the swells at top speed.[1]

HOMER'S IMMORTAL WORDS DESCRIBE a Phaeacian ship surging across the "wine-dark sea" at full speed. His epics tell of a fearsome, turbulent realm—unpredictable, often vicious, under the god Poseidon's arbitrary rule. Poseidon is long departed, but the Aegean remains the same nearly 3,000 years later—a deep-blue, island-studded ocean racked with powerful summer winds that can blow for days.

I remembered Homer's Phaeacian ship when a powerful summer *meltemi*, the Etesian wind out of the north, thrummed in our rigging.

We pitched violently in the following sea, mainsail well out to starboard, tightly secured fore and aft to stabilize the boom. The rough water sparkled in the effervescent sunlight, the horizon and the Greek mainland sharp against the cerulean sky. Kea's dark peak loomed on the horizon, a precipitous island some 12 miles (19 kilometers) off Cape Sounion, the southeastern tip of Attica, on the Greek mainland. We drew close to land at sunset. With startling abruptness, the *meltemi* switched off, leaving us becalmed. Short, wicked Aegean seas beset our stationary boat—from bow and stern, from either side. Mainsail and jib slatted violently. Fortunately, we had a reliable diesel engine to take us into port. But I thought of Homeric sailors equipped with only oars being beset by the same seas, moving more up and down than forward, waiting patiently and uncomfortably for the calm water of nightfall.

The Aegean is an island-crowded sea, compact and challenging to traverse because of the strong winds and short, steep waves. In a sense, it's an inland ocean within the much larger Mediterranean world. Mainland coasts surround it on three sides; Crete forms the fourth. There are only four large islands—Euboea, off mainland Greece; Crete; Rhodes; and Lesbos, close to Turkey. Demanding, often hazardous waters by any standards, but it was here that some of the earliest seafaring occurred.

My passage to Kea was the first leg along a string of islands explored by simple canoes as early as the late Ice Age, long before farmers settled on the islands some 8,000 years ago. Kea lies at the edge of the Cyclades (in Greek, Kukloi, meaning "rings"), so called because they surround Delos, the ancient shrine and important trade center at the heart of the Aegean. The poet Callimachus wrote, "Asteria [Delos], island of incense, around and about thee the isles have made a circle and set themselves about thee as a choir."[2] The Cyclades are some distance from the mainland coasts of Greece and Turkey. Other Aegean islands lie closer or form lines out to sea, like the Sporades, north and east of Euboea. As Aegean archaeologist Cyprian Broodbank aptly remarks, the Cyclades were, historically speaking, "both on the edge of everywhere *and* at the center of the whole, a deeply ambivalent position."[3]

For thousands of years, the isolated Cyclades were a realm unto themselves, insulated from wider historical forces by often fierce winds

Figure 5.1 *The Aegean Sea.*

and rough seas. Nevertheless, Aegean sailors, like their counterparts in other parts of the Mediterranean world, traveled from mainland to island and from island to island in an intricate jigsaw of routes that are almost impossible to trace. We can only turn to archaeology for insights. By studying artifacts, raw materials, and their sources, scientists can obtain chronological information about changing trade patterns and other human activities.

Eventually, the Cyclades became part of a much more complex eastern Mediterranean world. Aegean islands became potential stepping-stones, as Broodbank puts it, "from everywhere to everywhere else."[4]

The Cyclades are very different from the tropical environments of islands in Southeast Asia and the southwestern Pacific. Vast expanses of
the open Pacific, a marine desert, if you will, bound those waters, where
seafarers passed from island to island along generally linear routes. Long
corridors of interisland movement developed, whereas in the Aegean
there were many lines of approach from the landmasses that surrounded
the islands.

As I FOUND at my own cost, the Aegean's winds can blow strongly for
days. We lingered at anchor or in port as the *meltemi* howled in the
rigging with malicious intensity. The best season for Aegean seafaring in small boats was, and still is, during the calmer periods between
May and September—especially for longer passages involving a few
days at sea. But the *meltemi* can blow throughout the sailing season
and can close down any form of seafaring for days on end, especially in
July and August, when winds are strongest. Even downwind passages,
while fast, can be hazardous, especially in boats with low sides that can
easily fill among steep waves. There are short periods of calm conditions during most Januaries, but they are useful only for short passages. Close inshore, away from open waters, local conditions can be
very different. An expert sailor makes use of local conditions—downwind
breezes flowing through coastal valleys, gentle land and sea breezes
that allow a vessel to waft its way along the coast, often at night, when
a soft offshore breeze triggered by cooling temperatures fills in. I vividly remember coasting effortlessly from headland to headland southward along the eastern Peloponnesian shore in the small hours. A full
moon, a smooth sea, and a warm land breeze just sufficient to fill the
sails allowed us to sail under Monemvasia's towering cliffs and the
ramparts of its imposing medieval fortress as the wind dropped at
dawn.[5]

With care, short journeys in any direction would have been possible
for the ancient voyager, provided that the traveler knew, and was prepared to accept, that sometimes lengthy delays were inevitable. Here, as
elsewhere in the ancient world, there would have been a high premium set

on seafaring and climate expertise that passed from one generation to the next. But just as much depended on seaworthy boats.

THE SIGHT OF a replica Athenian trireme being rowed at full speed is something you never forget. Power, speed, endurance: the surging warship makes you realize that the Aegean has always been a sea where human power ruled. Triremes are mesmerizing, so much so that one tends to forget that they had their origins in much more humble watercraft. Unfortunately, the harsh realities of preservation leave our knowledge of early Aegean watercraft as incomplete as that from other waters. All we have to work with are two- and three-dimensional representations that range from humble inland dugouts to images of multi-oared or paddled craft pecked on rocks.[6] At this stage in the research, we can be reasonably confident that there were two basic forms of early watercraft in the Aegean cradle. Both were canoelike vessels, depicted in rock engravings or on clay pottery. The smallest, and presumably the earliest, was a dugout-like craft, apparently paddled by a small number of people. Then there were larger boats—slender, longboat-like designs with angled hulls for speed and a post-like stern capped with a carving of a fish. Alas, none survive, but they are known from depictions on pots. These may have been between 50 and 65 feet (15 and 20 meters) long, sizable enough to cover open water fast when paddled by large crews. Clearly, these faster vessels required considerable boatbuilding expertise. Quite when they first came into being is still a mystery, but it appears to have been before 3000 B.C.E.

Unpredictable Aegean waters, with their prolonged calms, were, above all, a paddler's and oarsman's world, and it was human power that propelled warships and large merchant vessels for much of the time in later millennia. We can be almost certain that the first crossings from mainland to island were in small dugouts, vessels commonly used in sheltered water, paddled offshore on calm days and moonlit nights when safe passages for 15 to 20 miles (24 to 32 kilometers) were feasible, provided one could reach shelter before the wind came up.

Exactly when sailing began is a mystery, but any form of rig, even a square sail and a short mast, requires a more stable, wider hull than a dugout, and there are no depictions of these before the third millennium B.C.E. Outriggers were unknown in the ancient Mediterranean, so any sailing would come after major changes in boatbuilding, especially the development of planked hulls built on rigid frames. Such designs would have increased both the beam of the boat and the height of the sides, as well as permitted at least partial decking. Initially, at any rate, the most a small sail would have done would have been to increase speed for a dugout running before smooth seas and a light wind.

Small vessels like dugouts had advantages in these waters. They never required artificial ports, for any shallow creek or beach would suffice. They also had disadvantages, notably a lack of freeboard and no decks, a serious problem in the short, steep seas for which the Aegean is famous. Dugouts with a couple of planks sewn or mortised on either side would be problematic in steep seas, as opposed to long ocean swells, for they could easily arch and buckle in the kinds of waves that we experienced off Kea in a modern yacht. Contrary winds and head seas would have been like a stone wall. Even a zigzag course would present difficulties and make any passage a slow, laborious enterprise. Nor could dugouts carry heavy cargoes, for there would be little room, let alone weight-carrying capacity, with even a small crew, in a long 20-foot (6-meter) boat. Such loads as they did carry must have been confined to containers filled with small luxury items such as beads or compact bundles of toolmaking stone. They certainly could not transport large animals or enough food and freshwater for a journey of more than a couple of days.

Early Aegean watercraft cannot have covered long distances, even under optimal conditions with a fresh, energetic crew. Maximum speeds in the range of four to six knots (seven to eleven kilometers per hour) might have been possible in calm water, but actual speeds must have been much slower. An experiment with a replica of a twenty-foot reed boat that traveled from Attica to the island of Milos with a crew of five to six paddlers produced an average distance of 9 to 12 miles (15 to 20 kilometers) a day—when the *meltemi* abated.[7] (Whether early Aegean seafarers used reed boats is, of course, a matter of pure speculation.) The much faster longboat, apparently of later times, would have had a maximum speed of about six miles (ten kilometers) an hour and might have covered 25 to 30 miles (40 to 50 kilometers) a day. These are all hypothetical figures, based on data from a variety of sources, but it's worth noting that the distance covered by a canoe in a day was about the same as that recorded for portage on land.

Fortunately for early seafarers, the Cyclades form a series of small island chains within the range of a crossing of six miles (ten kilometers) made in a day. You can reach much larger groups when you undertake a one-way journey of 12 miles (19 kilometers). Some islands, such as Thera (Santorini), of later eruption fame, remain cut off by longer distances. The navigational contrasts are also striking. In some places, such as Naxos, local navigation was practically in landlocked waters. Many other island settings involved more sea than land, which created additional navigational problems. As a gross generalization, you can paddle from one end of the Cyclades to the other in a week. However, the time required doubles or becomes even longer when you allow for delays because of strong winds. In the Cyclades, travel time was a more important factor than the distances between islands, just as it was in the southwestern Pacific (see Chapter 4). By the standards of later times, these interisland distances were vast for people navigating in small, paddled canoes. Compare this with French historian Fernand Braudel's estimate of sixty to eighty days for a vessel in Renaissance times to traverse the entire Mediterranean.

Broodbank and others have suggested that a day's travel, some 12 miles (20 kilometers), was a common maximum for uninterrupted passages. Animals can be difficult to handle after a couple of days, too. Quite apart from these limitations, weather conditions in the Aegean are so unpredictable that voyages longer than about 30 miles (50 kilometers), spread over two days and a night, involved higher, and perhaps unacceptable, risk. Interestingly, however, this distance effectively brings all Aegean islands within passage-making range from other land.

How did the ancients decode Aegean waters? Again, we are hampered by a lack of archaeological evidence to track what was an extremely complex process of exploration, exploitation, and colonization. Why would anyone want to settle permanently on the islands in any case? Sustaining farming communities on the Cyclades was never possible without continuous interactions with communities on other islands. The islands were, at best, marginal for farming, for they possessed little flat arable land. Island farmers had to resort to hillside terracing, which seems to have developed relatively late. Larger islands like Naxos, with its coastal plains and inland valleys, possessed more cultivable acreage than precipitous ones like Kea. Milos, on the other hand, of much the same size as Kea and Naxos, had shallower contours and more farmland. Freshwater was another issue, for the Cyclades are among the driest Aegean islands, especially as one sails south. Groundwater is scarce; occasionally small springs nourished local oases, especially on Naxos. Every island lived under the threat of drought in a world where annual rainfall fluctuated dramatically from year to year. We do not know what climatic conditions were like during the late Ice Age or immediately afterward, but chances are, they were always relatively dry. On Milos, for example, today's farmers expect a drought at least once a decade, often more frequently.

For all their drawbacks as farmland, the Cyclades had other assets.[8] They possessed one priceless commodity for Stone Age hunters: obsidian, the finest of all toolmaking stones, a rarity on the mainland. Thanks to high-technology sourcing of trace elements in artifacts and natural outcrops, we know that obsidian in mainland settlements came from two locations on Milos, which also provided another valuable commodity for people living off wild plant foods or cereal crops: volcanic rocks for grinding stones. (In later times, other valuable commodities came from the Cyclades. Marble passed to the mainland from Naxos and Paros. Copper, lead, and silver came from several islands, as did small amounts of gold.) Almost certainly, the first exploration of the Cyclades was purely exploitative and revolved around toolmaking stone.

The story of exploitation begins during the late Ice Age, when the Cyclades were very different from today. With sea levels up to 300 feet (91 meters) lower than today, the Cyclades then formed a large island covering slightly more than 2,300 square miles (6,000 square kilometers), known, inevitably, to geologists as Cycladia. Kea was part of the mainland; Milos and other islands formed another large landmass off Cycladia. Much of Cycladia itself was low-lying, so it flooded rapidly directly after the Ice Age, leaving slightly expanded versions of the islands of today.

Cycladia was a large place—two thirds the size of Cyprus.[9] We know that dwarf mammals lived there, including diminutive elephants and possibly deer. But there are no signs of human occupation or of short-term hunting visits. Most likely, people didn't get there before rising sea levels isolated animal populations on ever-smaller territories until they died out. Mainland hunting groups were aware of what island landscapes offshore could provide them, notably toolmaking stone. When Ice Age sea levels were much lower, even small canoes or rafts could have paddled readily along a line of islands to the west of Cycladia to obsidian-rich Milos, with only short distances across open water involved. A less likely alternative to somewhat indirect island hopping would have been to travel between what were then larger islands off the mainland coast, from the Argolid, in modern-day Peloponnese, to Milos, with passages of between 12 and 22 miles (20 and 35 kilometers).

As the climate warmed after the Ice Age, a sparse population of hunting bands lived on the Greek mainland, apparently land-based, but there are reasons to believe that they had a strong maritime orientation. Such groups might not have been viable without wide networks of people living both close by and at a distance. Some experts believe that these people traveled from island to island for much of the year, spending long periods either close to the water or moving from one nearby island to the next. For example, we know that hunting groups visited Franchthi Cave, in the southeastern Argolid, from about 18,000 years ago right up to 6000 B.C.E., when farming began in the area. After about 7000 B.C.E., large but fluctuating numbers of tunny-fish (northern blue-fin tuna) bones appear in the cave, as well as fragments of Milos obsidian. Whether the Franchthi people were fishing in deep water or venturing to Milos is something we will never know, but it's clear that by this time obsidian from the Cyclades was in wide circulation.[10]

There's other evidence of hunters at sea, too. Far to the north, people with much the same habits as Franchthi's people visited Cyclops Cave, on the small island of Gioura, at the eastern end of the northern Sporades

Islands, as early as the ninth millennium B.C.E. Large numbers of fish bones and a few obsidian fragments come from these cave levels. It may be no coincidence that Gioura, with its 581-foot (177-meter) peak, is a conspicuous landmark visible from a considerable distance, as I can personally attest. The distances when island hopping from the mainland to Gioura, like those to Milos, would not have been insuperable for simple watercraft, provided the paddlers chose their weather carefully. We should remember that these tenuous networks of people, of shared intelligence about obsidian resources, fishing, and so on, were constantly on the move as part of a way of life that encompassed mainland, island, and ocean. Such knowledge enabled people to travel from one island to the next over considerable distances long before farming took hold in about 6000 B.C.E.

VISITING ARID, ROCKY islands for their toolmaking stone is one thing. Settling there permanently with crops and domestic animals is a far more ambitious enterprise. Permanent settlement changed the dynamics of seafaring in the Aegean. Contacts between different islands now assumed extraordinary importance in a seagirt world where no individual community could survive on its own.[11] A patchwork of radiocarbon dates from excavations throughout the islands tells us that farmers had settled on Naxos as early as the fifth millennium B.C.E. Between 4000 and 3000 B.C.E., farming communities flourished on Andros, relatively close to the mainland, as far out as Paros, and possibly on Mykonos, in the heart of the Cyclades. As far as one can tell, the early settlers avoided smaller islands, with their tiny patches of arable soil and often sparse water supplies. As for obsidian-rich Milos, it was certainly visited for fishing and fine-grained stone, but the first date for permanent occupation remains an open question. Throughout the Cyclades, the founding settlers seem to have preferred larger and medium-size islands, even if they were far from the mainland. This speaks volumes about the seaworthiness of what by now must have been larger boats. Quite apart from anything else, such vessels would have had to transport sheep and goats across open water for as long as two days.

Why, then, did people colonize islands far out in the Aegean? One theory argues that regular visits in search of obsidian, or for tuna fishing in otherwise inaccessible waters, might have led in due time to permanent settlement. Archaeological finds on the mainland do not support the obsidian hypothesis, for early obsidian finds are merely fragments, apparently carried back haphazardly. It was only much later, some centuries before 3000 B.C.E., that much greater quantities of obsidian arrived on the mainland, deliberately prepared in a variety of ways, arriving as cargoes that included carefully hewn blocks of the volcanic glass. Whether greater loads resulted from colonization or simply from an increase in the tempo of exploitation and visitation is a matter for discussion. Nor is fishing a particularly compelling reason for colonization. Fish were never more than a dietary supplement in these waters, where marine life was far from abundant. Tuna migrations move rapidly and unpredictably, usually heading south in the fall. Laborious voyages in search of such an unreliable food source were not worth the trouble or the risk, given the difficulty of predicting them.

Living permanently on the Cyclades was never easy, for survival depended on diversifying one's crops among carefully selected microenvironments. Barley, wheat, and pulses were staples, while goats and sheep thrived on rugged island slopes. Olives and vines became important crops later, when they were widely traded commodities, but almost certainly not in earlier millennia. The uncertainty of the Aegean agricultural year meant that storage of foods of all kinds, including animals on the hoof, was of great importance, a process that must have involved sharing among neighboring communities and perhaps even between one island and another. Unlike mainland farmers, islanders could not fall back on a cushion of reliable wild plant foods or game like fallow deer. The realities of daily life meant that most island communities were small and widely dispersed over generally rugged island terrain. Populations were tiny, to the point that people in the Cyclades were a scarce resource. Few islands attained self-sufficient populations and marriage networks of about three hundred to five hundred people. There were many more people living in a single early Mesopotamian city such as Uruk, one of the earliest urban settlements in the world in the fourth millennium B.C.E., than in the entire Cyclades.[12] Inevitably, then, there was a high degree of interdependence among the islands, for exchange of food and other commodities and mobility were the only long-term survival strategies.

The constant movement touched every facet of island existence— marriage and kin ties, planting and harvest, food storage, the need for toolmaking stone and other commodities as prosaic as grinding stones, movements triggered by drought, excessive rainfall, and other short- and long-term climatic events, chance migrations of tuna shoals, and all the complex demands of ceremonial life and ritual observance. Seafaring here operated within ever-changing lattices of interaction that linked people over considerable distances and across often turbulent seas. This restlessness and constant movement began long before farming, perhaps as early as the late Ice Age. It began because no one could stand on their own, and it moved offshore because islands could be clearly seen on the horizon, within easy reach of familiar surroundings on the mainland. Deciphering the ocean here came about not because of any great mysteries lurking in the seascape but because people accustomed to constant movement thought of the ocean and its islands as a natural part of their daily landscape.

THE CYCLADES ARE an irregular scatter of islands large and small, so much so that to map any ancient routes between them is futile. In practice, the entire area was a cradle of seafaring. The general configuration of the islands and the mainland, as well as predictable wind directions and good intervisibility, were conducive to experimentation and seafaring. Further, this is an area where powerful draws such as farmland, fish migrations, and toolmaking stone may have pushed seafarers ever farther offshore, from one accessible island to the next, until there were only more challenging ones to explore. Under these circumstances, one could argue that the perceptions of open water and distance became ever more stretched as such traveling extended farther out and became as commonplace as shorter crossings.

Broodbank identifies two viable short-range entrances into the Cyclades.[13] One of the routes starts in Attica (or on the long island of Euboea, which is effectively part of the mainland), then makes one-day crossings out to the islands. Euboea, Attica, Andros, and Kea half-enclose a square of the ocean, an area that would have been a starting point for journeys to obsidian-rich Milos. As sea levels rose, people living on the shores of these isles would have acquired detailed knowledge of the winds and currents, with Kea in particular serving as a stopping point for canoes trapped by strong westbound currents. Paddling from Attica to the Cyclades would mean straightforward crossings to Makronisos or Kea, with the prevailing northerly winds astern. A canoe heading offshore from Euboea would cross to Andros. Next, a wide and turbulent open-water channel through the center of the northern Cyclades would send seafarers on one of two interisland routes. One ran down the western Cyclades out to Milos; the northern route passed down the coasts of Andros and Tinos, then out to Mykonos, Delos, and Syros.

The other entry direction to the Cyclades requires longer crossings, from the eastern Aegean islands of Ikaria and Astypalaia, with open-water passages that were as long as 31 miles (50 kilometers), a very long day's paddle in calm water. The southeastern Aegean region, off Turkey, with its slender peninsulas and convoluted coastline with plentiful bays, was an even more spectacular starting point than the more sheltered Euboean route. A screen of islands protect the mainland. Beyond, short open-water passages lead to large islands like Samos, Kos, and even Rhodes. Scatterings of smaller islands extend even farther into the Aegean toward the Cyclades, with ever more challenging journeys as one paddles farther offshore. The western Turkish coast displays the same kind of continuity between island and mainland as Attica and its offlying islands. Chains of large, well-watered islands that can be seen from one another lie farther offshore, to say nothing of smaller, more arid islands within paddling distance.

Crossings from the southeastern Aegean involved longer passages of more than one day and often required crossing the notoriously turbulent Ikarian Sea, albeit with favorable winds and currents. Ikaria lies just west of Samos, the latter a spectacular island with rugged mountains and gullies that even the phlegmatic *Admiralty Pilot* describes as "fantastic." This is no place for cautious sailors. I was blown on my beam ends in a large boat by violent *meltemi* gusts off Samos. We hastily returned to port to wait for quieter conditions. Farther offshore, the more visible islands are Naxos, with the conspicuous peak of 3,290-foot (1,003-meter) Mount Zas, the highest peak in the Cyclades, visible from far offshore, and the rugged profile of Amorgos. From there settlers could travel easily to Mykonos and more low-lying islands. These were high-risk passages for small canoes, but the presence of farming sites on the islands proves beyond all doubt that such crossings took place.

As Broodbank points out, there may have been prestige in undertaking such voyages, with a higher cultural value being placed on the opportunities of a rough passage than on the risks involved. Whatever the canoes used at sea, these were impressive passages by any standard. Broodbank compares the distances covered by sailing canoes in the southwestern Pacific in a scaling ratio with the much shorter distances covered by Aegean seafarers. He estimates that these longer Aegean passages were the equivalent in difficulty of Pacific voyages of 60 to 120 miles (100 to 200 kilometers).

The process of colonization was both prolonged and complex, especially once Naxos and other larger islands came under cultivation. Some of the more marginal islands were only settled 2,000 to 2,500 years after the earliest farming communities crossed into the Cyclades. As far as we can tell from the very limited data, the earliest farming villages often lay on bluffs overlooking major bays with good water supplies close at hand. This may have maximized opportunities for fishing, an important supplemental food source for people short of good arable land. The pattern changed dramatically after 3500 B.C.E., when islanders began to settle in small one- or two-family farmsteads close to patches of arable land and colonized smaller, rugged islands such as Erimonisi. Why this change took place is unknown, but it may be connected with drier climatic conditions across the Aegean. At the same time, there was an increase in maritime activity throughout the Aegean, an acceleration of trade in obsidian, pottery, and ritual objects such as figurines. For the first time, as Broodbank eloquently puts it, "the Cyclades shifted from a silent, secret world penetrated by specialist mainlanders to a space full of voices."[14] The Aegean world—and its decoded sea—had become a human landscape.

LONG BEFORE RECORDED history and Homer's time, the Greeks coined a word for their verbal sailing directions: *periplus*, a journey around coasts and islands. *Peripli* began as oral recitations, almost mnemonics, passed from father to son and amplified by firsthand experience. Thousands of years later, some were set down in writing, the most famous being *The Periplus of the Erythraean Sea*, a guide to Indian Ocean coasts set down in the first century C.E. (see Chapters 7 and 8). By then, the genre was a familiar one, but only occasionally do we glimpse much earlier directions. A few passages in Homer, notably in the *Odyssey*, are clearly drawn from mariners' navigational lore. Witness the sailing directions used by the Phaeacians to land Odysseus on Ithaca:

> There on the coast a haven lies, named for Phorcys,
> the old god of the deep—with two jutting headlands,
> sheared off at the seaward side but shelving toward the bay,
> that break the great waves whipped by the gales outside
> so within the harbor ships can ride unmoored
> whenever they come in mooring range of shore.[15]

Aegean navigation involved a great deal of line-of-sight passage making as canoes voyaged from one scattered island to another. The seafarers would have acquired firsthand experience of conspicuous headlands, mountain peaks visible from afar, cliffs of unusual color, even caves and large "branching olive trees." Prominent human-constructed landmarks such as burial mounds of legendary heroes sometimes served as navigational marks. The great mound erected over the bones of Achilles and Patroclus lay on a headland above the Dardanelles, a landmark from far offshore. No traces of it remain today.

The effectiveness of distant landmarks depended on visibility. Sometimes high peaks projected above summer haze or spume stirred up by strong winds near land. Dust in long, dry summers could restrict visibility, as could heat haze. Refraction, on the other hand, could cause normally invisible islands to appear on the horizon, but such conditions are rare and usually vividly remembered. Aegean navigators generally had it easy, for they could, at least in theory, travel without ever being out of sight of land. However, one could not always glimpse Crete's high mountains from the Cyclades or the coast of Euboea from Skyros. At night, and sometimes even in times of poor visibility by day, the seafarer turned to the sun and the stars, using the polestar to establish direction. When Odysseus sailed away from Calypso's sacred island, he

> steered his craft,
> sleep never closing his eyes, forever scanning
> the stars, the Pleiades and the Plowman late to set
> and the Great Bear that mankind also calls the Wagon.[16]

For seventeen days, he kept the stars hard to port until he made landfall.

Every expert Aegean seafarer had a mental picture of the ocean and islands around him in his head, even if the destinations were still over the horizon. This knowledge allowed him to set out with confidence, using other clues to make landfall, just like the Polynesians—unusually bumpy swells that had bounced backward off invisible cliffs, birds flying toward land, and so on. There were also currents and drift to leeward to be accounted for, which could be calculated at least provisionally by taking a backsight on a prominent landmark as one left land. It was no coincidence that later seafarers erected an imposing temple to Poseidon on Cape Sounion, at the extremity of Attica. Once, heading toward Athens on a hazy day with the lightest of northerly breezes, I estimated we were close to land but could see nothing for the haze. Then, suddenly, the salt-encrusted columns of Poseidon's shrine stood out in the afternoon sun. We steered for the temple until the cliffs came in sight; I imagined countless ancient steersmen sighting the bright flash of the white columns from far offshore in the sunlight of early morning or by moonlight, happy to be closing in on their destination.

Deciphering the Aegean was an easy task in terms of establishing basic geography and overcoming the fear of crossing open water. What

Figure 5.2 *The Temple of Poseidon, at Cape Sounion, Greece, a landmark for seafarers since classical times.* © *Sunpix People/Alamy.*

required prolonged experience and intense decipherment was the acquisition of a mental chart of the ocean around one, of different islands and their anchorages and beaches, of places where you could haul ashore while the *meltemi* churned the ocean into a froth of whitecaps. As it was everywhere, early seafarers learned to think of the Aegean and off-lying islands on the horizon as part of their landscape of daily existence. It was only a matter of time before they incorporated the seascape into their daily lives. Once they did, they could live on the islands at their doorstep only by interacting constantly with other local communities across the sea. At first, the decipherment and the interaction were local. However, after 3500 B.C.E., new, larger watercraft may have allowed people to travel longer distances at higher speeds and, perhaps, also under sail. At the same time, too, maritime powers outside the local confines of the islands impinged on the islanders and their neighbors, who were now sucked inexorably into the wider maritime world described in the next chapter.

CHAPTER 6

Timber and Mekku-Stones

Hoisting the pinewood mast, they stepped it firm
in its block amidships, lashed it fast with stays
and with braided rawhide halyards hauled the white
    sail high. . . .
A dark blue wave, foaming up at the bow,
sang out loud and strong as the ship made way.[1]

ANOTHER IDYLLIC HOMERIC VOYAGE: Homer's sailors either had fair winds or terrible storms, and not much in between. That's voyaging in the Mediterranean for you, whether you are close to shore or out of sight of land. Like Homeric sailors, I've spent days just waiting in a sheltered bay for a headwind to drop or a favorable breeze to arrive, even for a calm day when I could make progress under engine. There are dozens of such bays, like one nameless indentation in southern Spain where I whiled away three days waiting for a gale to subside. We had the place to ourselves, a narrow cove with precipitous, nearly bare cliffs where landing was impossible. High above us, a ruined stone watchtower looked out over the ocean. Solitary residents we may have been, but we were certainly not the first people to anchor there. The measured tones of the British Admiralty's *Mediterranean Pilot*, compiled in the days of sail, informed me that "anchorage may be obtained in 4 fathoms [7.3 meters] with the watchtower bearing ENE."[2] And it was so. Sailing in Mediterranean waters requires infinite patience and a tolerance for unpleasant, vertical-faced waves.

Unlike the Atlantic coast of Europe or the Pacific, the Mediterranean is to all intents and purposes a huge lake, or, as Fernand Braudel once remarked, a "sea of seas," a world unto its own where a variety of distinctive marine environments fostered seafaring, colonization, and trade. He called it a series of small seas, each with known coasts.[3] But we are still left with the fundamental question: Why did people venture into deep water here when they were well aware of the dangerous winds and high seas that battered them ashore? Almost invariably, they did so not out of curiosity, but to follow trading opportunities. It all may have begun with humble intervillage exchange in a Middle Eastern world where no community was completely self-sufficient. By 8000 B.C.E., dozens of villages received volcanic obsidian for toolmaking via hand-to-hand exchanges that linked farmer to farmer over hundreds of miles. Much of the obsidian came from Lake Van, in Turkey, the quantities diminishing the farther it traveled down the line from source. Obsidian is a visible commodity, as are exotic seashells, but much of the trade would have been in foodstuffs and other, more prosaic items. As populations rose, the ocean was no barrier to exchange and quests for more agricultural land. For example, we know that farmers had crossed to Cyprus by the late tenth to mid-ninth century B.C.E., a 50- to 75-mile (80- to 120-kilometer) passage across the open sea, but a straightforward one in calm weather and good visibility, from either the Latakia area of Syria or southern Turkey. The mountains at their destination would have been clearly visible on the horizon far offshore. We have no idea what vessels carried people to the island, but they were probably large dugouts, perhaps somewhat similar to those used in the Aegean, described in Chapter 5. The same craft must have navigated close to often rugged mainland shores, carrying heavy loads such as grain, hides, and timber.

BYBLOS, LEBANON, SUMMER OF 2600 B.C.E. Piles of sweet-smelling cedar logs lie on the stone quays of the small harbor. Flat-bottomed cargo ships from the Nile lie alongside, their decks almost level with the tops of the stones. Sweating crew members and timber laborers roll trunk after trunk to quayside, then lever them carefully down ramps into the hold with fiber-and-hide ropes. The skipper directs the loading from above, carefully placing each log so that the weight is evenly distributed. A high-ranking Egyptian official in a clean white kilt watches the loading from a distance as his scribe carefully records the length of each log. The skipper calls out. His ship is fully loaded. His crew dismantle the ramps and stow them, then pole the laden vessel out of the harbor; a few oarsmen create steerageway as the skipper anchors close offshore to wait for others in the convoy. Meanwhile, another empty vessel comes alongside the quay and loading resumes.

"Bringing of forty ships filled with cedar logs," wrote a scribe when praising the accomplishments of the pharaoh Snefru, who ruled Egypt in about 2600 B.C.E.[4] The Nile Valley is short on good-quality timber, so the pharaohs had to look beyond their homeland to build boats, adorn temples, and assemble coffins. We know from exotic artifacts, perhaps carried by land, that Snefru's predecessors had been in touch with the Levant for centuries, but it is only with the testimony of an anonymous scribe that we learn that the Egyptians had now ventured out of the Nile and into the open sea. Asses can carry only relatively light loads, and the logistics of supplying them with forage and water, to say nothing of the hazards of marauding robbers, conspired against intensive trade on land. So the pharaohs turned to the ocean, especially for bulk cargoes like timber.

Whether Snefru's fleet was the first venture, we don't know, but the cedar trade turned Byblos (near modern-day Beirut) into a major hub of international trade at a time of intensifying economic and political competition between the states that bordered the eastern Mediterranean's shores. The Egyptians went so far as to call seagoing merchantmen "Byblos ships," regardless of their destination. Copper from rich outcrops on Cyprus soon joined the mix of valuable commodities transshipped to Byblos. The trade in Lebanon cedar flourished for centuries until the royal monopoly on the traffic ended in around 2200 B.C.E. Lamented a wise man of the day: "No one really sails north to Byblos. What shall we do for cedar for our mummies, those trees with whose produce our priests were buried and with whose oil nobles were embalmed?"[5]

The Nile was a natural highway that traversed the length of the Egyptian kingdom. Virtually all cargoes traveled by water, including massive loads of building stone for constructing temples and pyramids. Larger Nile vessels had gently rising bows and sterns and spoon-shaped hills without keels. The early voyages to Byblos probably involved riverboats, their hulls braced with a trussing rope that ran fore and aft, tightened amidships by a spar that twisted the strands. In this way, the two ends of the ship received support when paddling or sailing through waves, an important consideration for inland vessels venturing offshore.

The Lebanon voyages involved coasting passages, carried out during the summer sailing season. The ships would have passed from landmark to landmark, always looking for shelter, often waiting for days on end for favorable winds or calm conditions. The Egyptian river pilots who first sailed into the ocean were excellent seamen—they had to be, for they navigated among shallows and in muddy waters, where sounding poles and lead-and-line were in daily use. Deciphering more open water would have involved simple, well-honed skills. Everyone would have shipped out with a sounding rod or a knotted and weighted cord similar to those used by land surveyors, carefully unrolled from a neat coil, as depicted on a wall painting of the second millennium B.C.E. Thus, the pilots would gauge their distance from the land and their location from soundings, knowing from experience where shallows extended some distance offshore. They were expert at taking and interpreting depths, familiar with the vagaries of local currents, and well aware of the feel of winds as they blew from different quarters. Much of their knowledge of landmarks must have come from inshore fisherfolk, and also from voyage after voyage along the same, often featureless coastline, where subtle landmarks and distinctive coastal profiles would guide them to their destinations.

As the mariners gained experience and met seamen from other cultures, they modified their ships. By the second millennium, Egyptian

Figure 6.1 *Locations and sites mentioned in Chapter 6.*

merchant vessels in the Red Sea had high bows and sterns, twin steering oars, and ten to twenty oarsmen on each side. A square sail set on a yard supported by stays and shrouds allowed the ship to make use of favorable winds. How far Egyptian ships ventured before 2000 B.C.E. is a matter of conjecture, but it is likely that they reached Crete, for Cretan vessels resemble them quite closely, and Egyptian artifacts have been found in island palaces.

A FAVORABLE WIND was all-important to a Mediterranean sailor in a heavy, square-rigged merchantman, especially when the sail was loose and billowing. In storms from astern, you lowered the sail and relied on oarsmen; in calms and adverse winds, you either waited or rowed. Every Mediterranean voyager, whether coasting or sailing offshore, knew the prevailing wind patterns, which marked the passage of the seasons on land and at sea. The northerly Etesian winds blew across the eastern Mediterranean during the summer sailing season, as did the strong northwesterly *meltemi* in the Aegean. With such a wind blowing from astern, even a lumbering craft could sail readily from

Crete or Rhodes to the Nile, a distance of about 400 miles (644 kilometers).

THE GREAT RIVER made the passage easier by announcing its presence far offshore. The peripatetic Greek traveler Herodotus, who experienced the approach firsthand, wrote, "The physical geography of Egypt is such that as you approach the country by sea, if you let down a sounding line when you are still a day's journey away from land, you will bring up mud in eleven fathoms of water. This shows that there is silt this far out."[6] Quite how long a "day's journey" would have been in Herodotus's day is unknown, but with a good following wind, the distance could have been as much as 60 miles (97 kilometers). Modern charts tell us that the depth that far offshore is about 100 fathoms (183 meters), so maybe some anonymous scribe copied the depth wrong. However, it's interesting that Herodotus's captain not only used a lead-and-line to find soundings, but also some substance like wax to bring up a sample of yellow Nile mud from the bottom. By sounding, he could receive advance warning of approaching land.

With the prevailing summer northerlies, a coasting vessel could time its journey to move westward along the Turkish coast, perhaps calling at Cyprus for copper, then sailing to Crete or the Aegean islands. Later in the summer, the skipper would complete what became a classic mercantile circuit by riding before the Etesian wind to North Africa and the Nile. From Egypt, one coasted northward along the Levant coast, and the entire rotation began once again the next season. This, presumably, is how the Egyptians visited Crete and how the Minoans of that country regularly visited the Nile.

There is a land called Crete . . .
ringed by the wine-dark sea with rolling whitecaps—
handsome country, fertile, thronged with people
well past counting—boasting ninety cities,
language mixing with language side-by-side.[7]

The greatest of all Crete's "cities" (actually palaces) was Knossos, on the north side of the island. King Minos, the legendary ruler of the Cretans, was said to be "master of the seas," the man who swept pirates from Aegean waters. According to the Greek writer Thucydides, Minos established the first maritime empire, whose dark-hulled ships traveled throughout the Aegean—to ports on mainland Greece and Turkey, to the Levant coast, and across the Mediterranean to the Nile during the second millennium B.C.E. Pictures of Minoan ships abound on seals and frescoes, impressive vessels that were probably about 50 feet (15.25 meters) long, powered by a square sail and fifteen oars on each side. But for all these large merchantmen and warships, there were thousands of much humbler craft, which plied from port to port and fished year in, year out.

Only one Minoan wreck is known, from the waters of a Bronze Age settlement at Pseira, at the northeast corner of Crete. Apparently the ship capsized, for the cargo landed on the bottom upside down.[8] All

Figure 6.2 *A Minoan frieze from Akrotiri, Santorini Island, Greece, showing traders in longships.* © World History Archive/Alamy.

that remains of the vessel and cargo are tumbled amphorae that once held olive oil and wine. According to pottery experts, the clay containers date to between about 1800 and 1675 B.C.E., a time when Minoan rulers were expanding their maritime ties and building palaces. The excavator, the Greek archaeologist Elpida Hadjidaki, believes that the ship was between 32 and 50 feet (10 and 15 meters) long. If it was anything like the one depicted on a seal excavated at the town of Pseira itself in 1991, it had a high prow and stern and was powered by a square sail set on a single mast. The Pseira ship was probably a local coaster that plied its way along Cretan coasts, working from town to town, where the skipper had personal contacts.

Minoans built on the maritime experience of early millennia but expanded the range of the coasting trade to encompass lengthy voyages. Their homeland was a stepping-stone at the southern edge of the Aegean Sea, a short distance from the Greek mainland, little more than a day's sail into the heart of the Cyclades Islands, and a series of easy hops via Rhodes and other islands to the Turkish coast. These coasting routes were familiar waters long before Minoan times, but it was probably Cretan or Egyptian skippers who first sailed directly to the North African coast, then coasted eastward to the mouth of the Nile. We know of extensive, if irregular, contacts between Crete and Egypt, where written records speak of a distant land across the sea known as Keftiu. Depictions of Minoan traders bringing gifts to the pharaoh appear on Theban temple walls.

The Egyptian city of Avaris lay in the northwestern region of the Nile delta. Between about 1783 and 1550 B.C.E., this busy port is said to have catered to more than three hundred ships during a summer trading season. The Hyksos rulers of Lower Egypt at the time were invaders from the east, who seized the delta by force in about 1640 B.C.E. and ruled much of Egypt for a century until they were expelled by the pharaoh Ahmose I in about 1530 B.C.E. They were cosmopolitan rulers who fostered international trade, so much so that a strong Minoan presence developed in their city. A temple erected during the Hyksos period boasts rooms with Minoan friezes identical to those on the walls of the Palace of Minos, at Knossos.[9]

By Minoan times, hundreds of itinerant skippers knew the eastern Mediterranean like the backs of their hands. The volume of traffic, mostly in relatively small vessels, was enormous, the value of some of the cargoes staggering by ancient standards. By now, no state monopolized the coasting trade, even the commerce in Lebanon cedar that once was the perquisite of the pharaohs. This was a cosmopolitan subculture of seamen from many lands. Many of them spent their lifetimes afloat, nuzzling into bays large and small, fighting off pirates and repairing their ships on quiet beaches. I never encountered pirates, but I've done the same kind of coasting in a small sailing yacht off mainland Greece, sailing close to steep cliffs and remote beaches. Day after day, we slipped quietly along, heeling to occasional mountain gusts, ticking off landmarks on the chart, using the *Mediterranean Pilot* as our guide. All we encountered were occasional small fishing boats catching octopus near the rocks. As the sun dipped to the west, we would cast our anchor in a remote bay, the only sound that of sheep bells on the hillsides.

IN ABOUT 1316 B.C.E., a heavily laden cargo ship staggers in a strong northwesterly wind, square sail flogging violently in the squalls. The steersman wrestles with the heavy steering oar as the skipper watches the looming cliffs of nearby Uluburun, in what is now southern Turkey. Savage gusts and steep waves cast the heavily laden vessel onto Uluburun with brutal force. The crew leap into the swirling breakers, only to be dashed by the waves against sharp rocks. The ship breaks apart and plunges to the bottom. Only a few timbers float on the surface.

Thirty-three centuries later, a Turkish sponge diver would spot a pile of flat copper ingots on the seabed off Uluburun, each with distinctive handles at the corners, designed to be easily stacked for transportation on donkeys' backs. The archaeologist Cemal Pulak spent eleven seasons excavating the undisturbed wreck, which lay at a depth of 140 to 200 feet (43 to 61 meters) below the surface. The meticulous investigations provided a mine of information on the trade routes plied by this and many other ships of the day.[10]

The heavily built merchantman was between 49 and 59 feet (15 and

18 meters) long, with planks at least two inches (five centimeters) thick. Dense wattle fencing ran along the gunwales to protect the crew and deck cargo from waves and spray. This slow, lumbering vessel must have been difficult to sail, even with a large square sail. A strong wind from aft of the beam would have been needed to move it along at four to five knots (seven to nine kilometers an hour). Even a moderate, steep-sided sea, such as is commonplace in these waters, would have stopped the boat dead in its tracks. Hardly surprising, the Uluburun ship carried twenty-four stone anchors, the heaviest at the bow, weighing a total of 3.36 tons (3,048 kilograms). The crew's safety depended on being able to cast such weights overboard in strong winds. Hundreds of ships like this plied eastern Mediterranean waters for many centuries, sailing from port to port, bay to bay, to places where water could be obtained, or to remote villages where cargoes were sold.

The Uluburun ship sailed at a time when powerful states were competing for the lucrative eastern Mediterranean trade. To the north ruled the Hittites, expert traders and warriors, whose kings eyed the prosperous entrepôts of the Levant. To the south was Egypt, a brilliant civilization at the height of its power, headed by pharaohs with territorial ambitions in what is now Syria and Israel. To the west lay the palaces of Crete, rich in olive oil, timber, and wine. Even farther west were the lords of Mycenae, on the Greek mainland, whose ships sailed as far as copper-rich Cyprus. The Lebanese coast was the nexus of the trade. Port cities such as Byblos, Tyre, and Ugarit were places where donkey caravans from deserts and cities far to the east converged.

Hemmed in on every side by powerful neighbors, the Lebanese farmers, herders, and merchants presided over bustling, cosmopolitan harbors, their markets polyglots of donkey drivers, skippers, and merchants from many lands. Battered merchant ships vied for lucrative cargoes to be carried along age-old coastal shipping routes, in an endless circulation of slow-moving sailing vessels that took advantage of prevailing currents and winds.

The Uluburun ship would not have stood out alongside the crowded wharves of a Canaanite port, its short mast and square-sail yard lashed to the rail. But its payload was unusual and far from prosaic, a windfall for archaeologists studying the complex trading relationships of the day. The hold carried more than 350 copper ingots, set in rows of eight to eleven rectangular plates. More than a dozen tin ingots also came from the cargo, one of the rarest metals in the ancient world, but vital for forging strong-edged bronze weapons. Enough copper and tin shipped out in the Uluburun vessel to fabricate well over three hundred bronze helmets and corsets. The metal for more than six thousand weapons lay aboard, enough for a sizable military force. Sourcing minerals is now a highly sophisticated technology; we know from lead-isotope analysis that the Uluburun copper came from outcrops on nearby Cyprus. The tin probably came from central Turkey or Afghanistan, carried to the Levant by caravan then offloaded onto ships. The Taurus Mountains of Turkey and Attica's Mount Laurium region, in Greece, provided lead for the fishing weights on board.

Most of the Uluburun metal came from sources east of the wreck. So did nine storage jars, one of which had tipped over, cascading a stack of brand-new Cypriot pottery across the seabed. Laden Canaanite amphorae came from the eastern Mediterranean coast. Some of the cargo lay in late Minoan or Mycenaean jars from Crete or mainland Greece, as if some of the load had been destined for a distant palace to the west. Scarabs and a stone plaque inscribed with Egyptian hieroglyphs hint at connections with the Nile trade. A number of short ebony (African blackwood) logs were in the cargo, the same timber used to fashion a bed, a chair, and a stool in the teenage pharaoh Tutankhamun's tomb. Complete and partial elephant tusks and hippopotamus teeth, one carved into a fine ram's-horn trumpet, lay aboard. There were glass ingots, commonly used, so cuneiform records tell us, as tribute, called "mekku-stones." Thousands of these glass beads came from the wreck, as did gold objects including a chalice and a golden scarab bearing the name of the celebrated Egyptian queen Nefertiti. There were even some amber beads from the Baltic aboard. A group of faience (glass) cylinder seals are of a type that were widely used from northern Mesopotamia and Iran to Lebanon, perhaps made in a workshop near Ugarit. Two species of Mediterranean mollusk aboard would have yielded a much-prized purple dye used to color prestigious raiment until as late as

Roman times. As for the crew, they might have come from the east, for their smoke-discolored oil lamps are invariably of Syrian design.

This was an international ship with cargo from at least nine lands. Judging from the cargo, their voyage was probably from east to west, passing through familiar waters that took advantage of the prevailing winds. The ill-fated ship left a Canaanite port, sailed across to Cyprus, where she loaded copper ingots, then approached the Turkish shore and hugged it toward the Aegean and the Greek mainland. Apparently, the skipper misjudged the weather and sailed too close inshore, for perhaps unseasonal winds pinned him on a lee shore as he was rounding Uluburun, a fatal mistake for a heavily laden vessel. Had the vessel reached Greek ports, she might have sailed to points beyond, such as southern Italy or Sardinia. The final segments of the voyage would have taken them across open water to the North African coast before heading eastward to the Nile. On a previous circuit, perhaps, the skipper had picked up the exotic Egyptian commodities in the cargo.

The Uluburun ship, with its remarkable load, was a tiny part of an inconspicuous trade, often dangerous, for pirates lurked in deep bays and behind headlands. For all the hazards, the trade continued unabated, driven by the insatiable demands of growing states for all manner of commodities, not just such luxuries as gold ornaments and semiprecious stones. Egyptians craved Cretan and Lebanese timber. Olive oil, wine, and metals were important cargoes; so were such prosaic items as almonds and olives. Sometimes, a ship carried a king's ransom in cargo—diplomatic gifts or dowries for political marriages. For obvious reasons, such loads traveled inconspicuously. The Amarna tablets from Upper Egypt, a priceless archive of diplomatic activity from around 1300 B.C.E., speak of one such cargo. "I herewith send you 500 [units] of copper. As my brother's greeting gift, I send it to you," writes the king of Alashiya (Cyprus) to the pharaoh of Egypt.[11] Many such cargoes must have traveled by sea—they were too heavy to dispatch by land. The value of the coastal trade was enormous, but always dispersed, in the hands of individual ship owners and small-time merchants backed by interests ashore. Risks were enormous, for there was no insurance. But the profits could be immense, which is why so many ships went to sea.

One can liken this ancient coasting trade to a leisurely perpetual motion machine, a slow-moving ballet of laden ships that passed along circular routes, with few long stops ashore. The ships themselves were unspectacular workhorses, kept hard in service for as long as possible. For instance, another wreck of a later date, the Kyrenia ship, which sank off northern Cyprus in the fourth century B.C.E., had been repaired several times.[12] The excavators painstakingly reconstructed the ship's lines and its convoluted history from traces of repairs found on the surviving planks. They discovered that the owner hauled her ashore at least twice, replaced rotted planks, added a second layer of bow planking, and patched the keel where it had cracked. Eventually he sheathed the hull with lead to keep out worms and prevent further leaks. On her last voyage she carried about 25 tons (23 metric tons) of cargo, including ten thousand well-preserved almonds, perhaps from Cyprus; nearly four hundred amphorae filled with olive oil or wine; and millstones fashioned of volcanic rock from the island of Nisyros, south of Bodrum on the Turkish coast, popular merchandise in many places. Iron arrowheads found under the hull testify to a sudden attack, perhaps by pirates, that sank her in 100 feet (30 meters) of water.

All running gear secure in the swift black craft,
  they set up bowls and brimmed them high with wine
  and poured libations out to the everlasting gods . . .
  and the ship went plunging all night long and through the dawn.[13]

Libations to the gods, offerings to Poseidon: the immortals were never far from sailors' minds even long after the Minoans and Homer's day. Every seaman placated the deities that brought calm, storm, and a safe landfall. Then, around 1200 B.C.E., this relationship seems to have changed profoundly from one of awe to pragmatic familiarity. The entire Mediterranean now became the stage for vastly expanded long-distance trade, for colonization, and for a new phenomenon: deep-sea naval warfare.

Around 1200 B.C.E., widespread economic and political instability descended on the eastern Mediterranean. Minoan and Mycenaean civi-

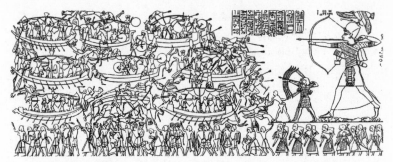

Figure 6.3 *Ramses III battles the Sea Peoples.* © *Interfoto/Alamy.*

lization finally evaporated; lawlessness prevailed on the ocean as pirates flourished. The enigmatic Sea Peoples now appear on the historical stage, a polyglot confederacy of seafaring raiders whose cultural origins remain a mystery. They spread havoc, wanderers on society's margins—professional seamen, merchants, and warriors who had always lived from hand to mouth and were particularly vulnerable to drought and famine. When crop failures caused widespread hunger, the desperate Sea Peoples turned against the Hittite Empire and overthrew it. Large numbers of homeless people prowled coastal waters. They then descended on the Nile by land and sea. In about 1187 B.C.E., the Egyptians fought off hundreds of ships accompanying land-based invaders trying to settle along the river. Pharaoh Ramses III and his archers led his troops to victory. More than two thousand attackers perished. A fascinating relief on the north wall of the king's mortuary temple at Medinet Habu, on the west bank of the Nile, near modern-day Luxor, recounts how military scribes brought a tally of the enemy dead to the pharaoh. They pile 175 severed right hands in front of him. Ramses questions the numbers, until the scribes dutifully assemble the enemy's penises and the numbers coincide.

POLITICAL STABILITY DID not improve until about 1000 B.C.E., when coastal trade picked up once more. The enterprising Phoenician merchants of Byblos, Tyre, and Sidon, on the Levant coast, seized the opportunity. They were astute businessmen whose fortunes had come in

part from the lucrative purple dye trade. Geography helped, for the Phoenicians operated at the hub of long-distance trade routes that passed
overland to Mesopotamia and the Persian Gulf, and to Egypt and down
the Red Sea, where frankincense and myrrh were to be obtained. Now
they invested heavily in seaborne commerce. Between 1000 and 800 B.C.E.,
the Phoenicians had the ancient eastern Mediterranean trade routes
virtually to themselves all the way to their western limits in Sicily and
Sardinia. But their quest for new profits also carried them far south and
west—to North Africa, where they established outposts at Carthage
and Utica before exploring the broad waters of the western Mediterranean world. By 700 B.C.E., Carthage was a major trading center.

The western expanses of the Mediterranean are not my favorite sailing ground. I've traversed them in midwinter, from Gibraltar to Malta,
in a World War II tank landing ship whose welded deck rippled in the
fierce seas on our bow. Our progress was glacially slow; the motion was
hideous; it was bone-chillingly cold. Years later, I sailed my own boat
from the Balearic Islands to Corsica in summer. We eased along with a
northwesterly on our beam with smooth seas for a day, then the breeze
shifted ahead and strengthened. Steep-sided waves slowed us to a crawl
and we got drenched. Headwind gave way to baffling calm—futile drifting, sails flapping, and endless chasing after puffs of air. Finally the northwesterly came back until we made landfall. A pleasant sailing ground of
gentle breezes for the most part, and thus easy to master, one is tempted
to believe, until the ghosts of the past remind you that this can be a savage world for heavily laden ships.

During our voyage, we anchored among the sheltering boulders of
Lavezzi, at the southern end of Corsica, on a beautiful, calm summer's
day. The anchorage overlooks the Strait of Bonifacio, with the mountains of Sardinia as a backdrop. We sunbathed and drank wine, but the
strait is not always so welcoming. In 1855, the French sixty-gun frigate
Sémillante left Toulon with a crew of 301 plus 392 soldiers bound for the
Crimean War. On February 15, she entered the Strait of Bonifacio in a
fierce gale. A thick fog enveloped the ship. A sudden midnight gust drove
her onto the rocks at Îles Lavezzi, with the loss of all hands. Six hundred
corpses floated ashore, all but one of them battered beyond recognition.

They lie in two Lavezzi cemeteries. The *Sémillante* tragedy has faded into history, but the crying birds in a nearby wildlife refuge shrieked all night like tortured souls. None of us slept well that haunted night.

Like all ancient sailors, the Phoenicians went to sea during the summer sailing season, which meant that they missed the dreaded mistrals of the winter months. They faced northwesterly winds, which made hugging the North African coast a dangerous proposition. So they sailed north far offshore, then tacked in an anticlockwise direction to the southwest for eastern Spain and the Strait of Gibraltar. Homeward-bound, they coasted safely along North Africa. Once past Gibraltar, they turned north to Gadir (modern-day Cadiz), where they acquired that most precious of metals, tin. The ore came not from Spain but from mysterious islands far to the north, probably Cornwall in southwestern England, where tin abounds. Having mastered western waters, they kept their mouths shut to protect their carefully acquired monopolies.

The Phoenicians soon had competition from inveterate wanderers from Greek city-states. After 600 B.C.E., shiploads of Greeks fanned out across the Mediterranean and into the Black Sea, founding about 250 colonies, some of which are still important cities today. Some colonists were seamen and merchants, but many were land-poor farmers, driven from home by famine and land shortages. The city of Rhegium, on the Italian side of the Strait of Messina, between Italy and Sicily, is a case in point, founded by citizens of the city of Chalcis, who were told to leave when hunger struck. But Greek colonists never arrived at an unknown destination. Both seamen and merchants had been there before them, for the Mediterranean was now a deciphered ocean.

Perhaps the most spectacular act of colonization was that of the Phocaeans, citizens of a small city on the west coast of Turkey. Unlike other Greeks and the Phoenicians, they traveled not in merchant vessels but in packs of warships, swift galleys known as penteconters—fifty-oar ships. Phoenicians and Carthaginians in the western Mediterranean had been able to protect their monopolies against occasional merchantmen, but fleets of well-organized warships were another matter. The Phocaeans sailed westward to the Strait of Gibraltar, then beyond, up the Spanish coast and southward along Morocco. In about 600 B.C.E., they

founded a colony known as Massalia (Marseille today), at the mouth of
the Rhone River, which gave them access to a lucrative trade in wine
and other luxuries with Celtic tribes to the north. Fortunately for the
Phocaeans, the Phoenicians were preoccupied with wars in the east.
But, inevitably, furious naval battles ensued. The Carthaginians were
the victors and had reestablished their sphere of influence over all of
the western Mediterranean by 480 B.C.E., except in northeastern Spain,
southern France, and western Sicily, where Greek colonies maintained
a hold.

Decipherment of sea routes, trade, colonization, warfare: the sequence
of events unrolled like a historical carpet. By 500 B.C.E., the open pirate
vessels of earlier times had given way to carefully designed warships. A
Greek city, Corinth, a major maritime power, led the way with specialized warships with rams that projected from their prows. Fighting platforms came into use from which soldiers fought, the oarsmen protected
by the deck as they rowed from low in the ship. Warships became faster,
lower, and sleeker. They now boasted two banks of oars, which eventually developed into the celebrated trireme, the warship par excellence of
the classical world.

The Mediterranean was now a world of mercantile towns and cities.
Trade routes now crisscrossed deep water. Coasting voyages transported
cargoes along now familiar shores from the outer reaches of the Black
Sea and the Levant to the Nile, south from the Po, in the Adriatic, and
through the Strait of Gibraltar to Cadiz. Piraeus, the port of Athens, lay
at the center of a vast web of trade routes that carried grain and a host
of other commodities in and out of the city. Grain, olive oil, and wine
were the basic commodities of the ancient world, where prices rose and
fell on news of poor harvests or military campaigns that might endan-
ger supplies.

Fourth-century Piraeus was a commodious harbor with a narrow
entrance. Every ship that arrived paid a toll and port dues. On the southern side lay the trireme sheds for warships. The eastern shore was the
commercial port, with stone quays and five colonnades, the longest of
them for the grain market, the most important commodity of all. Ath-

ens imported about eight hundred boatloads of grain a year to feed its 300,000 people. At this greatest of ancient markets, one can imagine the diversity of the ancient world's trade networks. To quote the historian Lionel Casson: "From here rose a babel in every language of the Mediterranean seaboard as traders laid out miscellaneous wares from all quarters and bickered with officials or bargained with dealers. Here one could buy carpets or pillows from Carthage, seasonings and hides and ivory from Libya, flax for cordage and papyrus paper from Egypt, fine wine and incense and dates from Syria, furniture from Miletus, figs and nuts from Asia Minor (slaves, too from the same area), pigs and beef and cheese from Sicily and Italy."[14]

For all the volume of business, this was still mostly a world of individual skippers, who chartered ships, and small-scale merchants, who borrowed money from high-risk investors at interest rates that could rise as high as 30 percent for the five-month sailing season in waters where pirates lurked.

MANY GENERATIONS LATER, when foul weather drove a huge Roman grain carrier into Piraeus during the second century C.E., all Athens walked down to see it. The writer Lucian joined the crowd. "What a size the ship was! One hundred and eighty feet [55 meters] in length, the ship's carpenter told me, the beam more than a quarter of that."[15] She carried enough grain to feed everyone in Athens for a year—all of this steered by one "little old man, woolly-haired, half bald." The Romans were farmers and soldiers, never willing seamen. They rarely maintained large war fleets, but did succeed in banishing much piracy from the seas. However, economic and political realities, especially the feeding of armies and teeming cities, took them into the bulk trade business, into shipping grain and luxuries on a grand scale. Their bulk carriers traversed fixed routes, from large port to large port, just as the Atlantic liners of today cross the ocean from Southampton to New York on rigid, predetermined schedules. Yet in their shadow and far from hustling ports, the ancient routines of itinerant trading persisted, as they do to this day, except that the diesel engine has replaced oar and sail. I once moored in Mykonos harbor, in the Aegean, close to a small, weathered coaster laden with wine barrels and bottles of olive oil. The crew carried the olive oil ashore, but they pumped the wine from barrel to taverna with a small diesel pump. One can be sure that their remote forebears would have used such a device had one been available. Ingenuity and improvisation are the marks of sailors everywhere.

THE MONSOON WORLD

It is . . . desirable that you should know all the coasts
and their landfalls and their various guides such as mud,
or grass, animals or fish, sea-snakes and winds. You
should also consider the tide, and the sea currents and
the islands on every route . . . [The captain] should not
load [the ship] more than is the custom, nor set out unless he is properly in command nor with an unprepared
ship nor in a closed season.

—Ahmad b. Majid al-Najdi,
Kitab al-Fawa'id, c. 1460 C.E.[1]

Mesopotamia, the "land between the rivers," and the Nile were two
cradles of civilization. So, somewhat later, was the Indus Valley in what
is now Pakistan. All lay close to or within the world of the monsoon
winds. The next three chapters describe this enormous realm where the
predictable reversals of the monsoon allowed sailing vessels to sail from
the Red Sea to India and back within twelve months. The decoding of
the Indian Ocean began thousands of years in the past with the beginnings of unchanging rhythms of coastal trading, often called cabotage
or tramping, dictated by the seasonal directions of the monsoon winds.
Just as it did in the Mediterranean, such coasting flourished far from
the historical spotlight, in the shadows of warring rulers and international diplomacy. Cabotage fostered interconnections between peoples
and states living hundreds, if not thousands, of miles apart, linked only

by the rhythms of predictable winds. Thus came into being the closely interconnected monsoon world, which extended from the East African coast and the Red Sea to India, Sri Lanka, and as far as Southeast Asia and China. Sometime before the time of Christ, more ambitious skippers, some of them Greeks from Alexandria, started sailing nonstop to India's Malabar Coast from Arabia and the Red Sea, then, later, from East Africa, too. An astounding range of commodities and luxuries traveled along the monsoon trade networks—soft, easily carved African elephant ivory, frankincense from Socotra, hut poles from mangrove swamps in what is now Tanzania to Arabia and Mesopotamia, glass beads and cotton cloth from India, tropical exotics from Africa to Chinese ports. Many of the ships used in the trade had teak hulls constructed in India. Inevitably, Chinese emperors cast eyes on the trade of the "Western Ocean," easily accessible with the monsoon winds. The eunuch Zheng He's seven voyages around the Indian Ocean between 1403 and 1433 provided strange exotics for the imperial court and at least nominal tribute in one of the first global diplomatic initiatives, made possible by much older decodings of the cycles of the monsoon winds.

CHAPTER 7

The Erythraean Sea

"BEYOND THE RIVER SINTHUS there is another gulf . . . the water is shallow, with shifting sandbanks occurring continually and a great way from shore; so that very often when the shore is not even in sight, ships run aground, and if they attempt to hold their course they are wrecked." In the first century C.E., an anonymous seafarer, probably an Egyptian Greek, compiled *The Periplus of the Erythraean Sea*, a sixty-eight-chapter-long description of the coastlines around the Indian Ocean. ("Erythraean Sea" means "Red Sea," but the Greeks used the term to refer to both the Indian Ocean and the Persian Gulf.) The *Periplus* is the work of an experienced traveler who has seen the anchorages, ports, and dangers of the great ocean firsthand, from the southernmost reaches of East Africa to the Indian coast, where there were numerous sea serpents and "very many rivers and a very great ebb and flow of tides."[1]

By the time of the *Periplus*, the coasts and wide expanses of the Indian Ocean were the front door of societies from Sri Lanka and India to the Persian Gulf, the Red Sea, and the East African coast. The great ocean and its predictable monsoon winds linked the Mediterranean world with Mesopotamia and India. Geography favored sailors in these waters. From Arabia, one could cross to the East African coast to obtain tropical products like elephant ivory and mangrove poles, and a sailor from Arabia could also coast along the shores of Iran to India. Most important of all, the Red Sea and the Persian Gulf steered commodities and valuables of all kinds from the Nile, Euphrates, and Tigris into the trade routes of the Indian Ocean.

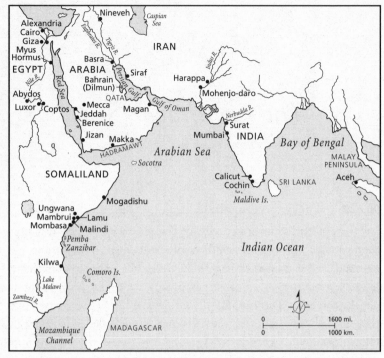

Figure 7.1 *The Indian Ocean.*

The historian Felipe Fernández-Armesto argues convincingly that what really drives decoding the oceans is understanding wind systems, especially such phenomena as monsoon winds and the trades, whose predictability is apparent to anyone fishing or living along their shores.[2] The secrets of the monsoon were common knowledge around the northern Indian Ocean, sometimes called the Arabian Sea, long before recorded civilization. In these usually benign waters, the monsoon winds blow from the northeast from November to March and somewhat less predictably from the southwest between May and September. Summer heat warms the continental landmasses north of the ocean. The hot air rises and creates a low-pressure zone at the earth's surface, causing moisture-laden air from the sea to move into the low-pressure area. As this air climbs on rising air currents, rain-bearing clouds bring monsoon rains. In winter, the pattern reverses, for the ocean cools more slowly than the land. The winds now blow toward the ocean.[3]

The seasonal reverses of the monsoon winds are most prominent in the Arabian Sea, between East Africa, Arabia, and western India. The monsoon made this stretch of generally well-behaved ocean a wonderful area for long-distance voyaging, for the reversing monsoon winds could guarantee a return journey. For instance, a sailor leaving the East African coast on the wings of the southwest monsoon could more or less be certain that he would return within a year, simply by being intelligent about the winds.

The northeast monsoon wind is the major player, a lovely breeze that blows virtually continually, never at gale force, almost never dropping to a flat calm, never changing direction dramatically. This is a sailor's delight. For thousands of years, it wafted sailing ships from the Red Sea and the Persian Gulf to India and East Africa, and from the incense shore of southern Arabia as far as the Maldive Islands. Back in the 1930s, the Australian sailing writer Alan Villiers coasted eastward along the Arabian coast in a lateen-sailed dhow, making progress against a northeasterly on the nose. The ship sailed as close as forty-five degrees to the wind (a modern racing yacht can achieve thirty degrees), navigating close to the beach, the skipper spinning the ship around by turning it in front of the wind to head offshore when the breakers were too close, a few ship lengths away. Once the ship turned west and altered course down the African coast some weeks later, with the monsoon astern, the crew winged out the sails and sailed fast and upright, with Africa to the right, the ocean to the left. "The only sounds were the soft sighing of the monsoon wind and the swish of the sea as the dhow passed gently, shadowing the rippling, deep-blue sea as she ran."[4] One can imagine similar voyages along the desolate shores of what are now Iran and Pakistan—laden sailing ships coasting close inshore, trimming their sails to the twists and turns of the northeast wind, maximizing soft land breezes, conning their way from one headland to the next without charts or compasses, just the stars overhead, familiar to every mariner and desert traveler. Such voyages unfolded year after year along ancient coast routes that flourished inconspicuously far off the historical radar screen, their existence known only from scatterings of exotic archaeological finds dropped far from their homelands.

Storms came with the more powerful southwesterly monsoon of summer, which sometimes delivered gale-force winds and heavy rainstorms. This was not a good sailing breeze by northeast monsoon standards, but a well-equipped ship could make a fast passage from East Africa to Arabia or India within a relatively short time. However, most coasting dhows stayed ashore, for their high rigs were potentially lethal in the face of hard-blowing squalls.

The Red Sea and the Persian Gulf were more challenging. A ninth-century Arab traveler wrote of ships from the Gulf port of Siraf that dreaded the Red Sea. "This Sea is full of Rocks at the Water's Edge; because also upon the whole Coast there are no Kings, or scarce any inhabited place, and, in fine, because Ships are every Night obliged to put into some Place of Safety, for Fear of striking upon the Rocks."[5] Everyone anchored at night and sailed during the day. The Persian Gulf was

Figure 7.2 *An Indian Ocean* boom, The Triumph of Righteousness, *under sail. Photograph by Alan Villiers.* © *National Maritime Museum, Greenwich, London.*

the gateway to Mesopotamia, whose cities lay upstream in the flat, torrid landscape of the Euphrates and Tigris delta. It was notorious for its unpredictably strong northwesterly winds and sandstorms.

The world's earliest cities, such as Eridu and Uruk, now in arid desertic landscapes, were once close to the Euphrates and connected to it by river meanders and canals. Oceangoing ships moored at Ur's wharves, some of them bound for remote anchorages along the Persian Gulf and even farther afield. The Gulf was less hazardous, but the mariner had trouble obtaining freshwater along the uninhabited and pirate-infested shoreline. As a result, contacts between the cities of Mesopotamia and places like Dilmun (Bahrain) and Magan (Oman), at the mouth of the Gulf, were irregular. But they did occur, for transport by land was even more arduous and expensive, especially for bulk commodities such as grain, dates, and timber.

THE BEGINNINGS OF Indian Ocean seafaring lie deep in the remote past, among humble fisherfolk who worked the marshes and channels of great rivers such as the Euphrates, Indus, Nile, and Tigris. As sea levels rose after the Ice Age, so major rivers backed up and became slower-flowing. Floodplains and marshes teemed with fish and waterfowl. When villages became towns, and towns the first cities, the rivers became natural highways for emerging Egyptian and Mesopotamian civilizations. Both the Nile and the Euphrates came alive with watercraft of all kinds—dugouts and reed canoes, rafts, and larger craft that carried substantial loads. The Egyptians used reed boats fabricated from papyrus bundles for hunting or short journeys. Small pieces of cedar formed wooden boat hulls, securely lashed together much like papyrus vessels. Prevailing northerly winds carried heavily laden sailing boats upstream against the current. (Square sails may first have come into use on the Nile for this purpose.) If there was no wind, the crew towed the vessel from the bank. The current helped them drift downstream despite the constant headwinds.

The earliest recorded Egyptian sailing boat appears on a pot dating to about 3200 B.C.E.[6] Funerary boats excavated at Abydos, in Upper Egypt, were long and narrow, about 82 feet (25 meters) overall, rowed by about

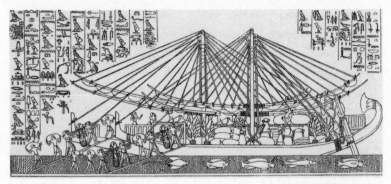

Figure 7.3 *Two of Queen Hatshepsut's ships in Punt, from reliefs in her temple at Deir el-Bahri, Thebes. James Hornell. Courtesy Antiquity Publications Ltd.*

thirty men. Another imposing example of an early craft lies alongside the Pyramids of Giza, near Cairo. Such was the demand for timber that the Egyptians carried loads of cedar trunks from the Lebanon coast to the Nile (see Chapter 6). Such maritime coasting probably began before 3000 B.C.E., as river sailing expanded to coastal and ocean pilotage. In later times, Egyptian skippers also sailed through the coastal islands of the Red Sea as far south as the Land of Punt, probably in the Horn of Africa, part of present-day northern Somalia. Queen Hatshepsut (1508–1458 B.C.E.) mounted an imposing expedition to Punt. Her temple friezes show ships being loaded with sacks of precious myrrh resin and myrrh trees, their root balls protected by baskets. Men carry ebony, gold, ivory, incense woods, and leopard skins. Glass beads, bangles, and weapons paid for the rich cargo.

Hatshepsut's venture provides a glimpse of what was obviously a long-established coastal trade along the inhospitable shores of the Red Sea. Once skippers had deciphered the patterns of winds and currents, they knew that northerly winds prevailed during the summer months, generating southerly currents. In winter, the winds in the southern Red Sea blow from the south, with the current now flowing in the same direction. In the north, however, strong northerly winds often prevailed year-round. Steep seas and constant gale-force winds blowing desert sand made paddling northward virtually impossible for much of the year. It was no coincidence that much Nile commerce ended at Berenice and other ports far from the head of the Red Sea, at the closest points on the western shore to the Upper Nile.

No one knows for certain when seafaring began in the Persian Gulf, whose waters lap southern Mesopotamia, where life also revolved around rivers and waterways. When the Englishman Wilfred Thesiger lived among the Marsh Arabs of the south during the 1930s and '40s, he found himself in an isolated world governed entirely by water.[7] Anyone wanting to go anywhere had to step from their hut into a reed boat, even when just visiting a neighbor, let alone a nearby village. Reed boats thrived in the marshes and swamps of the south from the very earliest days of human occupation, perhaps as early as nine thousand years ago, when farmers moved onto the southern plains of Mesopotamia. Many communities made use of natural outcrops of asphalt to waterproof their boats, for the glutinous tar smeared on reeds makes for a waterproof seal. In the south, the marshes gave way to the Persian Gulf, a dynamic stretch of water whose shores changed constantly as sea levels rose after the Ice Age, when it had been little more than a narrow gulch. Anyone who lived along its shores would have been familiar with inshore waters, given that boats were about the only way of staying in contact with others with such harsh desert on land. Certainly, reed vessels with pitch-coated hulls could have paddled along the desolate Gulf shorelines and inside islands lying close offshore.

The remains of one such asphalt-coated craft have come to light at As-Sabiyah, in Kuwait, dating to between 5300 and 4900 B.C.E.[8] The tar-encrusted reeds even bear traces of the barnacles that once clung to the hull. Supplies of the asphalt traveled considerable distances. Just how effective reed craft would have been for longer journeys, given their penchant to become waterlogged even when coated with tar, is an open question. In anything but calm water, they would have been difficult to handle. Almost certainly, anyone coasting seriously in the Gulf would have needed a wooden-hulled ship.

Mesopotamians had virtually no wood stocks except for palm trees, whose trunks have soft, pithy interiors, so they had to obtain planking from elsewhere. The nearest plentiful sources were on the Indian coast, beyond the Gulf of Oman, on the other side of the Arabian Sea. For this reason, we can reasonably assume that both wooden boatbuilding and coasting along the shores of the Arabian Sea began in a place where boat-building timber of all kinds abounded—along western Indian shores. Ancient boatbuilding traditions along this coastline produced a great variety of watercraft, among them light, flat-bottomed river- and surf-boats of thin planks sewn together with fibers, which were flexible enough to buckle to the contours of the bottom when landing in turbulent swell. In 1810, a British official's wife, a Mrs. Maria Graham, wrote of such craft that they "give to the water like leather, other wise they would be dashed to pieces."[9]

The sea does not loom large in Indian creation legends. The ocean was *kala pani*, "the black water," a place where fishing and coastal trading lay in the hands of lower members of the social hierarchy. In the larger spiritual arena, the god Vishnu plays a leading role in the struggle between the gods and demons. He appears on temple walls reclining on the coils of the serpent Shesha, asleep on the cosmic ocean during intervals between the periodic annihilation and renewal of the world. When the weakened gods gather atop Mount Meru, the world's navel, Vishnu persuades them to churn the waters of the sea to tease out the *amrita*, the elixir of immortality. The sun and moon emerge, then Vishnu's wife Lakshmi, and finally Dhanvantari, the physician of the gods, bearing in his hands the *amrita*. The strength of the gods is restored. In the Puranas, religious texts telling of ancient times, the journey of life is likened to a voyage across the oceans, an experience fraught with trials and tribulations. Interestingly, as the Australian historian Michael Pearson points out, India may have been the focus of Indian Ocean trade and seafaring for thousands of years, but the sea was peripheral to a continent that was very largely self-sufficient.[10] To trade on the ocean was something that Pearson calls "discretionary." At best, the initial contacts were sporadic. Over the centuries, however, a few merchants and seafarers developed connections with people in places like Oman at the head of the Persian Gulf, which, in turn, maintained ties with Mesopotamian cities to the north.

The anonymous rulers of Harappa, Mohenjo-daro, and other Indus cities had no interest in the sea. But their merchants traveled along desolate coasts to the Gulf to find new markets and also to obtain exotica for sale at home. In Indian Ocean waters, the secrets of the ocean were deciphered not because of overwhelming curiosity about what lay over the horizon—that was generally known—but because river-based civilizations in Mesopotamia and, to a lesser extent, in Egypt needed a broad spectrum of basic commodities, something quite apart from the exotica prized by kings and queens.

THE PERIPLUS OF THE ERYTHRAEAN SEA paints a gloomy picture of the western Indian coast, with its fast-running tides and extensive sandbanks. This was not a coastline to approach with a wind blowing from astern, especially during the strong southwest monsoon of summer. Nevertheless, by 2000 B.C.E. the Indus Valley, cradle of the Harappan civilization, with its great cities, was a hive of long-distance commerce, much of it carried great distances by water, apparently in vessels constructed from teak planks. We have no idea what these vessels looked like, but some of them may have had sewn hulls.

The catalyst for this trade lay not in India but in Mesopotamia, among rulers who presided over cities on a sandy delta, without rocks or minerals or even enough timber for beams and boatbuilding. Sumerian kings of 5,000 years ago craved gold and copper, exotic semiprecious stones and pearls, ornaments, ivory, carnelian, and even unusual animals such as monkeys. Rulers and their henchmen sought such rarities, but there was much more extensive commerce in commodities such as foodstuffs, cloth, and timber.

Thus it was that Mesopotamian seafaring began, linking, albeit indirectly, the Indus Valley and western India with Oman and Bahrain. We know of the trade from convoluted references on cuneiform tablets from Ur and other cities between the Tigris and Euphrates, as well as from a scatter of Harappan artifacts found in Mesopotamia and in Persian Gulf sites.[11] Such artifacts inevitably reflect the traffic in prestigious luxuries and valuable cargoes, but most trade flourished in the hands of small traders coasting from anchorage to anchorage and port to port in small ships. Their vessels were like mobile bazaars, laden with foodstuffs and rolls of cloth, with cheap baubles and such prosaic items as axes and sickles. They traveled in short hops, following the same routes year after year, staying ashore when the southwesterlies blew strong, coasting east and west close inshore when the gentle northeasterlies returned. Cabotage under sail continued into the twentieth century and in some places endures to this day, the rhythm basically unchanged from the earliest times, whatever the advances in technology or raw materials.

We know little about this coasting except for occasional passing references, so the flavor, and sometimes the drama, is lost to history. However, far to the west, in 1938, Alan Villiers took passage from Aden to Jizan, on the eastern Red Sea coast, in a "tough, hungry, and exceedingly primitive" *zarook*, a coastal dhow less than 50 feet (15.25 meters) long, with two short masts.[12] Ahmed the Yemenite's *zarook* was an open boat with a lateen sail, pieced together from odds and ends of timber and old iron. She lay low in the water, the only protection from waves a belt of palm-leaf matting lashed above the bulwarks. Villiers traveled in this battered craft, with its cheap Japanese cotton sail, for 600 miles (965 kilometers), sailing by day and anchoring at night, for these are dangerous waters with numerous reefs and submerged rocks. The skipper had no charts or modern compass. He knew every rock and headland, every beach and sheltered anchorage. Food was inadequate; everyone was hungry, but the boat sailed well. The skipper and his crew lived a hand-to-mouth existence, where delays meant nothing and one day passed timelessly into the next. Villiers remarked that he lost all sense of time, for life revolved not around the clock, the day, or arrival times but on the wind and current.

These were the unspectacular voyages that decoded the arid coast between the Gulf and the Indus, passages that could take months to complete as one waited for calm conditions or a favorable breeze. This decipherment was born of the dependency of a river civilization on the products and commodities of other lands. In time, the ships that used these waters carried kings and high officials, military detachments and diplomatic missions, but their voyages began out of economic necessity.

We can imagine a weathered merchant ship with short mast and matting sail lying alongside wooden quays in the heart of Ur and Eridu, the crew hefting sacks of dates up the narrow gangplank, herding bleating goats aboard. The next morning, the laden vessel slips away with the light northern wind of dawn, bound for the Gulf. The first part of the journey takes the ship through narrow canals and marshlands, shimmering in the intense heat. She emerges into the wide Euphrates, moving steadily downstream into the reeds of the maze-like estuary, pausing at the head of the Gulf for water and more cargo before sailing out. The skipper knows that the southward passage must be made in the cooler winter months after October, when the winds are mostly northerly. Once in his southernmost port, he waits for the south-westerly monsoon, which will carry him north. He has learned to be patient, for the winds are often light, with prolonged calms, especially close inshore, which is the route he takes, coasting from landmark to landmark using knowledge passed on to him by his father. The ship stays inshore because dust haze is a serious problem, especially during the summer months. But the crew can never relax, as pirates lurk among the islands, knowing that some of the ships carry valuable cargoes.

Clay tablets from Ur's archives record that the city was a port of entry for copper into Mesopotamia, which came from Bahrain, in the Gulf.[13] A group of enterprising merchants exchanged woolen garments for copper in the island's markets, but Bahrain itself had no ore. The kingdom served as a neutral entrepôt for all kinds of transactions—in gold, ivory, and exotic animals, to mention only a few items—from northeastern Arabia and two fabled areas: Magan, now Oman, and Meluhha, the Indus Valley. On returning to Ur, the merchants would make an offering of gold, copper, or silver to the goddess of reeds, Ningal, consort of the Moon God. The merchants in this trade formed a small group, for their ventures required exceptional skill. The trade seems to have expanded. In about 2300 B.C.E., King Sargon of Akkad proudly recorded that ships from or destined for Meluhha, Magan, and other ports berthed in the harbor outside his city.

THREE THOUSAND YEARS ago, voyaging down the Red Sea and from India to the Persian Gulf was commonplace. By this time, the center of long-distance seafaring between India and points west lay to the south in the Indian Ocean, not in Mesopotamia, where conquerors along the two rivers imported their seafarers. When the Assyrian monarch Sennacherib (705–681 B.C.E.) sought to capture a rebel king in northeast Arabia, he brought Phoenicians and timber to his capital at Nineveh, had them build seagoing ships there, manned them with Mediterranean sailors, and paddled or portaged the vessels about 550 miles (885 kilometers) down the Euphrates to the Gulf.[14] There an army embarked and defeated the rebels in a brief land campaign. Three and a half centuries later, Alexander the Great hired Phoenicians to navigate the Persian Gulf, even importing prefabricated ships to carry his regiments. Some of these vessels reached Bahrain, where they observed the pearl fisheries, but no one ventured farther. Meanwhile, Arab and Chaldean seamen frequented coastal waters along Arabia and from the Gulf to India. They sailed habitually close inshore to India and back, using the gentle northeastern monsoon to waft them on their way.

Long before the advent of Islam, Arabs handled much Indian Ocean cabotage, sailing, as far as we know, in boats fashioned from sewn planks, a technology borrowed from Indian boatbuilders of centuries earlier. Coastal voyages along what are now the Yemeni and Saudi Arabian coasts carried spices such as myrrh. The Greek writer Agatharchides memorably remarked, "A heavenly and indescribable fragrance seems to strike and stir the senses of everyone. Even far out from the land it happens that the fragrant odours blowing from the myrrh bushes and others of the kind reach the neighboring parts of the sea."[15] Much of the spice trade revolved around the island of Socotra, at the mouth of the Red Sea, where trade routes from Egypt and India met.

As far as we can tell, this was a coastal trade, carried out by seafarers in ways that had changed little for thousands of years. Then, between 120 and 110 B.C.E., a skipper named Eudoxus of Cyzicus sailed from Egypt down the Red Sea, then he shaped a bold offshore course straight for India. Perhaps on this expedition or on one soon afterward, a Greek navigator, Hippalus, learned how to sail directly from Arabia to India using the summer southwesterly monsoon wind. *The Periplus of the Erythraean Sea* tells us that Hippalus "observed the locations of the ports and the conditions of the sea" as he sailed nonstop.[16] Almost invariably, the passage was a rough one. I remember getting horribly seasick in a small coastal sailing vessel off the Kenya coast in the summer monsoon. The boat pitched and rolled like a dervish possessed. I was very thankful when we found shelter behind a coral reef. Originally, skippers used the shortest possible distances over open water to cut across from the northernmost coasts of the Arabian Sea to the Indus delta. But they became progressively bolder with enhanced experience until they were sailing direct from the Red Sea across to India's Malabar Coast.

Hippalus did not, of course, discover the monsoon winds, which were common knowledge long before his time. All he worked out was how to use the southwestern monsoon for the outward voyage—a boisterous enterprise, as anyone who has experienced the summer winds will testify. The traditional voyage to India under Arab command had dhows leaving Aden and coasting along the Hadramawt coast of Arabia until they were sufficiently north and east that they could fall off and use the gentle northeasterly monsoon as a beam wind. This was a straightforward passage compared with the much more hazardous open-water voyage of summer.

The offshore route was competitive, because it was weeks faster than coasting, provided a ship left Egypt in July, using the prevailing northerlies, then bore off before the southwesterly when clear of the Red Sea. The monsoon would bring a ship to the Malabar Coast in September, when weather conditions had eased somewhat and one could approach port safely. These direct voyages were, apparently, a Greek innovation, for there is no evidence that Arab sailors with their sewn-hulled ships made such voyages. The hulls of their vessels were too flexible and fragile for tumultuous summer seas. The Greeks used framed, rigid hulls fastened with iron nails that were well suited to rough seas.

Once the direct passage became widely known, open-water voyaging took off. By the geographer Strabo's time, in the first century C.E., at least 120 ships sailed annually from Myus Hormus, on the Red Sea, to India. Roman coins were now commonplace in India; cargoes of silks, cotton, and other fine cloth, as well as spices, filled Greek holds. The Red Sea trade began in Alexandria, the exports traveling up the Nile to

Coptos, then overland to Myus Hormus or Berenice. Here large ships made sail for India, taking one of two routes. If bound for the Indus region in the northwest, they would coast as far as Cape Syagrus (Ras Musandam) before sailing offshore. Vessels bound for the Malabar Coast of southwestern India would sail straight from the Red Sea, a passage that took about forty days with the monsoon astern. Some ships would pass down the African side, then steer for Socotra before sailing nonstop across the ocean. Indian Ocean merchants of the time had used the monsoon to sail as far afield as the mouth of the Ganges River, in the Bay of Bengal. Sri Lanka was known but was not a regular stopping place.

The *Periplus* makes it clear that Arab seafarers were active in places like Muza, on the Yemen coast (near the modern town of Mukha), by this time, sailing across to "the far side" (Eritrea and Somaliland), to Socotra, where "Arab, Indian, and Greek traders" lived, for its frankincense, and to northwest Indian ports. They must also have been sailing farther south to the Malabar Coast for centuries, as this was where the timber for their ships came from and where many were built. The East African coast was closer to the Arabian Peninsula and a reliable source of all kinds of raw materials—gold, iron ore, mangrove poles for house beams, skins, and also slaves. Much of the traffic was in elephant tusks, much prized for making bracelets and other ornaments. By 150 C.E., Greeks were coasting as far south as Rhapta, in the Rufiji River delta, in present-day Tanzania, were sailing to Sri Lanka, and were familiar with the ports of the Bay of Bengal. Some skippers had even visited the Malay Peninsula, perhaps also traveling to the borders of China. Between the fourth and sixth centuries C.E., Chinese ships traded with India, where they may have received African products such as ivory and tortoise shells. Sixth-century Sri Lanka was a meeting point for Chinese and Persian ships, the main commodity being silk. We know little of these mercantile enterprises, which, from the Chinese perspective, were conducted "far out on the western ocean." Han Dynasty merchants experienced "special difficulties" on these western routes, "the force of the winds driving them far away across the waves of the sea."[17]

WITH THE RISE of Islam, a great expansion of commerce enveloped the Indian Ocean. Arab seafarers inherited earlier commercial traffic. By the time of the Umayyad and early Abbasid caliphs (660–870 C.E.), their ships sailed from the Persian Gulf to Canton (Guangzhou), in China.[18] Strong empires flourished at both ends of the route, so safe voyaging was assured. Commercial interests—insatiable demands for raw materials and such luxuries as silk—drove the trade in its entirety, and it required tough vessels capable of sailing well in open water under boisterous conditions. Unfortunately, we have virtually no record of Arab ships before the arrival of the Portuguese in the late fifteenth century, but there is no reason to believe that ship design changed radically over the centuries.

Arab boats were double-ended, which is to say the bow and stern were both pointed.[19] There were many forms, everything from small coastal carriers and fishing boats to large oceangoing merchant ships. Teak or coconut wood formed the planks, the former being very durable and easy to work and growing widely in southern India and imported from India to the Persian Gulf as early as Babylonian times. Coconut wood abounded on the Maldive and Laccadive islands, where a flourishing boatbuilding industry fashioned ships entirely of these trees, right down to masts, fiber ropes, and sails. Construction methods were very simple: the builder shaped the keel on the beach, then sewed horizontal planks to it with stout coir fibers passed through holes laboriously bored with simple hand drills near the edges of the flush-set planks. In 1185, the Arab writer Ibn Jubayr, visiting Basra, at the head of the Gulf, noted that boatbuilders thrashed the coir until it "becomes stringy, then they twist from it cords with which they stitch the ships."[20] They also strengthened the hull with strong ribs before adding the remaining planks, making for a flexible yet strong craft. For all this strengthening, sewn hulls were weaker than iron-fastened ones and leaked continually. Iron nails were known but were probably too expensive and required elaborate fabrication. A mixture of pitch or resin and whale oil caulked the coir-filled seams. Finally, fish oil sealed the planks. Villiers tells us this treatment made dhows extremely odoriferous, especially when partially decked, which trapped the smell belowdecks.

The lateen rig

The lateen rig, from the French word *latine*, meaning Latin, is a large triangular sail set on a generally short mast, with the forward end of the sail secured at the bow. The leading edge of the sail stretches out along a long spar, the rig being controlled by a sheet at the aft end. Lateen rigs appear to have originated in the Mediterranean at least as early as the first century B.C.E. By the mid-first millennium C.E., the lateen had replaced the square sail throughout the Mediterranean and become the standard rig of Byzantine galleys. Generations of historians assumed that the lateen used by Arab dhows had arrived in the Indian Ocean with Islam, but this does not seem to have been the case. In fact, lateens seem to have arrived with the Portuguese, who used them on their caravels. Arab skippers soon realized the advantages of lateens. By 1500 they were in widespread use in the monsoon world.

Lateens, with their long leading edges, allow ships to sail much closer to the wind than square-sailed vessels. This was an obvious advantage for coastal merchant vessels working the light winds of the northeast monsoons close inshore. Lateens are not so efficient when running before the wind, which is why Portuguese caravels often replaced lateens with square sails in the Atlantic, with its trade winds. But the maneuverability of lateen-rigged vessels made them ideal for Indian Ocean traders, who often worked close inshore and in shallow water.

The lateen has disadvantages, however. It is a large sail, which requires careful handling when tacking through the wind. The flapping yard and sail can overwhelm the crew as they wrestle with it, a potentially fatal misjudgment when altering course close to shore. Almost invariably, a dhow changes direction by turning in front of the wind rather than tacking through it, which requires laboriously bundling the sail and setting the yard on the other side of the mast. It is also difficult to reduce sail on such a craft. Many dhows used to carry two yards with different sails, the smaller one serving for rougher conditions.

Figure 7.4 *Aloft on the lateen yard. Photograph by Alan Villiers.* ©
Villiers Collection, National Maritime Museum, Greenwich, London.

All early dhows had square sails of leaf matting or cotton. In later
times, they adopted the lateen, a tall, triangular fore-and-aft sail that
had a high peak—so much so that Arab writers said they looked like
whale fins from a distance. Above all, the lateen is highly effective at sailing close to the wind, especially in lighter breezes such as the northeasterly monsoon. This may indeed be the reason why lateen use spread—as
an effective way of ghosting along desolate coasts. For most of the time,
a large lateen allowed Arab and earlier seafarers to coast along inshore
routes, where local transactions were as important as those conducted
by larger ships carrying more precious goods.

FEW RECORDS OF what is was like to sail on an Arab merchant ship have
come down to us, and the diesel engine long ago replaced the more leisurely world of trade under sail. Generations of desert travelers such as
the English archaeologist Gertrude Bell and the famed scholar and soldier
T. E. Lawrence waxed lyrical over the challenges of traveling in trading
caravans or with desert nomads. They never turned their eyes to the

Indian Ocean, where boat travel was as old as civilization itself. Fortunately, Alan Villiers spent a year just before World War II on an Indian Ocean *boom*, a large variant of the dhow, which he boarded at Aden. Villiers lived among the crew, sleeping on the captain's bench on the quarterdeck, observing a trading voyage whose rhythm was unchanged for many centuries.[21]

The *boom* was a large seagoing vessel with a mast that towered 90 feet (27 meters) above the sea. The ultimate destination seemed of no concern. Stays at anchor could last for days, depending on cargo and passenger. Perhaps it was just as well, for the labor of getting under way was enormous. Just hoisting the lateen yard with the sail secured lightly with fine cord took at least an hour. But once the anchor was aboard, a tug at the cords unleashed the great sail and the dhow crept out of the anchorage under perfect control. When possible, the *boom* sailed in company with others, steering close enough on occasion for a conversation. The shipboard muezzins would call for prayers every day, breaking the silence of dawn with their chants. After prayers, breakfast, and ablutions, the crew bailed the hold before tackling whatever work was needed. Much of the time, they sailed within a stone's throw of the beach, sometimes tacking a short distance offshore when there was a stronger breeze or anchoring for a while when becalmed.

Mogadishu, Lamu, Mombasa, Zanzibar: the *boom* coasted slowly from port to port along an ancient East African cabotage route, offloading passengers, selling its cargo, and engaging in some judicious smuggling. South of Zanzibar, Nejdi, the skipper, entered the mangrovechoked Rufiji River, on the southern Tanzanian coast, to load straight, standard-size timber poles for sale in Bahrain or Kuwait, a dhow cargo for many centuries. Then came the return journey in front of the southwestern monsoon—but a longer way round, coasting the entire way home, within sight of land. Villiers never discovered why Nejdi preferred this strategy, but a vicious squall off the Somaliland coast had the ship laboring heavily under its enormous lateen sail. The sail tore to shreds as the crew struggled to lower it, giving a hint as to why many dhow skippers preferred coasting, where the winds were gentler, the seas smaller, and the tides and currents weaker.

Figure 7.5 *A heavily laden Kuwaiti* boom. *Photograph by Alan Villiers. © Villiers Collection, National Maritime Museum, Greenwich, London.*

It was here, close inshore, that the unique skills of the Arab sailor came into play. On the last leg of the voyage, the ship raced in a fresh wind from Bahrain to Kuwait. Nejdi elected to sail close inshore so he could beat his rivals to port. He sprinted homeward along the Persian Gulf's western shore through a maze of coral reefs and sandbanks that had never been charted. A man stood at the bow holding a lead-and-line with a lump of camel fat wedged in the base. As the boat twisted and turned between reef and sandbank, Nejdi examined the grit, sand, and shell brought up with the lead, as if following a map. The shore was so low-lying that it was practically invisible, but the skipper knew every foot of the bottom, every minute variation in depth, from ten years of pearling in these waters. He looked at the ocean and the sky, for even minor nuances in the colors of either could signal small changes in depth. The skipper knew almost by instinct the set of the tides, the directions they ran in, and how to predict them, all without a chart or tide table anywhere aboard.

Safe in port, Nejdi remarked that the moon was enough—just the moon, the stars, and the behavior of the sea itself. All the way from Aden to Zanzibar and beyond, then back to the Gulf, he sailed without a chart, for, as he said, "he knew the way." He sailed only on established routes for commercial purposes, going where the cargoes and passengers took him, drawing on the sailing experience of thousands of years' worth of earlier traders, to whom the waters of the *Periplus* were as familiar as the heavens that guided them from landmark to landmark. Centuries earlier, Ibn Jubayr had watched his dhow skipper ease his ship through narrow channels that led to Jeddah, on the Red Sea: "It is extraordinary how they bring [the ship] through the narrow channels and lead it among them like a rider on a horse which is sensitive to the rein and easy under the bridle; and in this they show marvelous skill, difficult to describe."[22] There was an artistry in dhow seamanship honed by generations of seafarers, stretching back to the earliest days of civilization and enduring into modern times.

CHAPTER 8

"A Place of Great Traffic"

I TEASED THE LAST OF THE GRAY ASH away from the shell beads at the man's neck. Eleven hundred years ago, his anonymous mourners had buried him knees to chin in a shallow grave dug into the gray soil by the side of his thatched hut. The tightly packed beads still lay in place, just like those from other burials. But this time there was a difference. A single red glass bead stood out among the thin shell disks. I picked it up with tweezers, placed it carefully in a plastic bag, then turned it from side to side. Dull red and well worn, this tiny bead was from the far side of the Indian Ocean—and we were digging in southern Zambia, more than 700 miles (1,127 kilometers) from the East African coast.

What a story this solitary bead would have to tell! Mentally, I traced its journey from the distant coast, at first part of a large string of multicolored Indian beads carried inland by a trader, perhaps to a village in the hinterland. From there, the string would have traveled along narrow paths through the bush, perhaps by canoe, pausing in settlement after settlement, growing ever smaller as bead after bead changed hands—perhaps for food, perhaps for fragments of copper or iron, even an ivory bracelet. Eventually, months, or even years, later, a few glass beads traveled up narrow escarpment trails from the low-lying Zambezi Valley to the plateau of the far interior, where perhaps just one or two arrived at a small community at the very end of an exchange network that stretched back to India. This far inland, they were exotic items, much treasured, perhaps heirlooms, sometimes buried with the dead. The fruits of commerce carried by the monsoon winds traveled deep into Africa for many centuries.

Studying Indian Ocean glass beads

Glass beads were a staple of the Indian Ocean monsoon trade. Brightly colored, easily carried in large strings, they became one of the standard items carried by nineteenth-century European explorers as they traveled through East Africa. By that time, glass beads had become so commonplace that fashions changed arbitrarily from one place to another and from one year to the next. One early student of glass beads in southern Africa talked of a "bead saturation point," when they were so little valued that people dropped them and barely noticed. In earlier times, it was another matter, for such exotics must have had considerable prestige attached to them. We have, of course, no idea of their value in terms of commodities they "bought" a thousand years ago and during the height of the Islamic dhow trade. The Ingombe Ilede burials in the Zambezi Valley wore thousands of red beads, and also blue, turquoise, and some green wound beads, reflecting fashions during the early fifteenth century.

But where were the beads made? Early researchers attempted to classify them by place of origin, but with little success, except for later, highly distinctive Venetian beads and other forms. In recent years, bead specialists have turned to spectrographic analysis, as well as neutron activation, to study the composition of individual beads, on the argument that the chemistry varied from one area to another. Unfortunately, the recipes for glassmaking varied little over long periods, so any detailed studies of provenance are still impracticable. In general, however, the glass beads found in eastern and southern Africa dating to before the tenth century appear to have come from Mesopotamia and Iran. With the decline of the Abbasid caliphate in the tenth century, the focus of the trade shifted to western India, where beads were made with mineral-soda-alumina glass. Millions of these so-called trade-wind beads traveled throughout the monsoon world, a significant number also coming from Sri Lanka. Most likely—though it has not been analyzed—my solitary red bead ultimately came from an Indian source.

By the time the Portuguese explorer Vasco da Gama arrived at the mouth of the Zambezi in 1497, the monsoon trade had reached impressive proportions along the East African coast, driven by insatiable demand for the raw materials that Africa had to offer in such abundance. Iron, timber, and skins were staples for dhow merchants, but the most valuable commodities were gold, copper, elephant ivory, and slaves. The exotica arrived at the coast in canoes or more often on the shoulders of the enslaved, for there were no draft animals to carry heavy loads and the trader could sell his porters as well as their cargo. Just how organized the interior trade was and what volume it attained is unknown, but it was always one-sided in strictly economic terms. Those who provided the raw materials exchanged them for trade goods that were commonplace in the wider world—cheap Indian cotton fabrics, glass beads, and seashells large and small, among them the disk-like base of the cylindrical conus shell and the diminutive cowrie, much used for hair decoration and clothing adornment. Far inland, even a single cowrie was of considerable value.

The middlemen in this trade were often powerful chiefs, like the rulers who presided over cattle kingdoms based at the imposing stone enclosures at Great Zimbabwe, far south of the Zambezi River, and at Mapungubwe, a hilltop village in the Limpopo Valley, on the northern

Figure 8.1 *Great Zimbabwe. © Images of Africa Photobank/Alamy.*

Figure 8.2 *A richly adorned Ingombe Ilede burial, Middle Zambezi Valley, Zambia. The man wears brass bangles, four conus shells— one with a gold backing plate—and numerous strings of glass beads. Lengths of copper wire and wire-making tools lie above his head. Conus shells, or at least the spiral-formed disks that serve as their bases, were symbols of chieftainship and prestige. When the Scottish missionary David Livingstone visited a chief in the far reaches of Central Africa in 1855, he found that a single conus was worth the price of two slaves. Such ornaments were so valuable that porcelain replicas remained in circulation until the early twentieth century. Photograph by James H. Chaplin.*

frontier of modern-day South Africa. This is a long way from the southern limits of dhow routes, which ended just south of the Zambezi estuary. Some measure of the wealth that accrued to trading chiefs comes from nine intact fifteenth-century graves at Ingombe Ilede, a village on a low hilltop in the Middle Zambezi Valley, to the north, occupied just before the Portuguese arrived on the coast. Nine people lay in graves atop the hill, among them a man in his early twenties who wore no fewer than nine conus shells around his neck, one with an eighteen-karat-gold backing plate. He and others wore long lengths of bronze bangles on their arms and legs. Fragments of cotton fabric, perhaps from robes, survived with the bangles. Thousands of glass beads and, in one case, a gold necklace adorned the bodies. Cruciform copper ingots and complete sets of wire-making tools lay with several bodies, as did long-bladed ceremonial iron hoes and gongs, the latter ancient symbols of African chieftainship.[1]

These were powerful, wealthy men, who dwelt at a strategic location, close to extensive salt deposits, a highly prized commodity in African farming societies. Salt may have been one of the commodities they exchanged for copper, which came from south of the Zambezi. Elephants abound near the village to this day, so one major source of wealth was close at hand. How often traders came to Ingombe Ilede, and how the trade functioned, may never be known to us, but it would never have developed had not the predictable cycles of the monsoon winds brought Asia in touch with Africa many centuries ago.

THE EAST AFRICAN coast is a languorous place, caressed for much of the year by the gentle northeasterly monsoon. Life unfolds at a leisurely pace inside the coral reefs, where small coastal boats, *mtepes*, still fish and sail slowly from port to port. Long before the first outsiders sailed to East African shores, a scatter of small settlements of Swahili fisherfolk and hunters lived along the Indian Ocean, from the Mogadishu region to as far south as Zanzibar and beyond—a coastal society linked by inshore sailing craft and inter-community trading.

A seemingly remote shoreline, divorced from the larger world, one might easily assume, but Greek and Roman traders sailed here long before Islam rose to prominence along the Red Sea. We know of these voyages from *The Periplus of the Erythraean Sea*, which describes Opone, a stopping place now known as Ras Hafun, in northern Somalia—famous 2,000 years ago for its cinnamon "and slaves of the better sort, which are brought to Egypt in increasing numbers; and a great quantity of tortoise shell, better than that found elsewhere."[2] This ancient port of call hosted Egyptian and Phoenician ships and also vessels from Arabia and the Persian Gulf. Greek and Roman sailors sailed farther southward along Azania, the African coastline that stretched into the southern distance, so named as early as Roman times. We learn from the *Periplus* of anchorages sheltered by islands and reefs and, far to the south, of the island of Menuthias, perhaps Zanzibar, remarkable for its sewn boats and dugout canoes. Two days' sail beyond lay Rhapta, "the very last market-town of the continent of Azania [East Africa] . . . in which there is ivory in great quantity, and tortoise-shell," a stopping place much frequented by large trading vessels from the Arabian coast. Beyond, the unexplored ocean curved around to the west, ultimately to mingle with the "western sea."[3]

The *Periplus* would have us assume that Azania was a mere coastal strip, bounded on its eastern side by the Indian Ocean, a world of which it was part, but isolated from the vast African interior to its west. In fact, coast and interior were a seamless cultural whole, linked by flourishing exchange networks and social ties. Azania itself, and its off-lying islands, including Madagascar, the fourth-largest island in the world, enjoyed great environmental diversity, with semiarid terrain and irregular rainfall in the north; savanna, huge tracts of mangrove swamps, and rainforest to the south. Fish and shellfish abounded; timber was plentiful; coral could be used for building; iron ore existed in abundance in some locations. The *Periplus* says that the inhabitants of parts of the coast were "very great in stature" and "of piratical habits"—forerunners of today's Somali pirates.

What first attracted monsoon sailors to this long coast is a mystery, but the prevailing winds must have stimulated voyaging southward. The incentives may have been iron ore and timber, the latter a valuable raw material in virtually treeless desert lands. These items remained the staples of the East African trade until modern times and would have been sufficient to link Azania to the wider Indian Ocean universe. More exotic and highly prized raw materials, such as copper, gold, elephant ivory, and hides, came into play later, driven by demand from distant lands. The tenth-century Arab geographer al-Masudi went so far as to claim that East Africans valued iron and copper as much as gold and silver for ornaments.[4] Elephant tusks soon became a staple of the trade, for the tusks of the African elephant are larger, softer, and more readily carved than those of the Indian species. An insatiable demand for wedding bracelets and other ornaments across the Indian Ocean created a monsoon trade in tusks carried to the coast on the backs of slaves. The humans went to Arabia and the Persian Gulf, the ivory to India.

No one knows when coasting ships from the Red Sea first explored Azania, but it could have been as early as Phoenician times. The earliest known archaeological finds are four Roman glass beads dating to between 200 and 400 C.E. They came from a small settlement in the Rufiji delta, far to the south in Tanzania, farther south even than Rhapta, one of only two major trading centers along the coast mentioned in records as dating to earlier than 800 C.E.[5] Quite where and what Rhapta was is a problem that has engaged generations of scholars. Perhaps it was nothing more than a temporary camp, a transitory place rather than a village or a town.

We can imagine such a sprawling encampment, which mushroomed at a convenient anchorage when the northeast monsoon brought sailing ships down the coast. A cluster of thatched huts and shelters, perhaps with a palisade, appeared in short order, a polyglot encampment where Africans, some from far inland, mingle with merchants and sailors who spend most of their lives afloat. There are small piles of elephant tusks, perhaps some copper ingots, and, more rarely, fine gold dust packed in porcupine quills, for many centuries the container of choice for this precious commodity. Ships load mangrove poles cut in the swamps nearby; slaves squat despairingly in carefully guarded enclosures; merchants and

Africans bargain over strings of beads, bales of cloth, and bags of sea-shells. The camp bustles for a few weeks, then everyone departs, leaving just empty huts and rotting fences behind them.

Only a few archaeological discoveries testify to what must have been at best a sporadic monsoon trade. Some Greco-Egyptian glass fragments have come from a location 12 miles (20 kilometers) north of the Rufiji delta. There was occupation here as early as the first century B.C.E., and Middle Eastern wares of the third century have also been found. Wheel-made potsherds manufactured in the Mediterranean area during the fifth and sixth centuries have come from a site on Zanzibar. Mere hints of activity tantalize us. Judging from archaeological sites near Lamu, in northern Kenya, there were already extended contacts between the coast and the interior when Islam first arrived on the coast in the late eighth century C.E.

Initially, these exchanges with inland peoples revolved around day-to-day commodities such as fish, grain, and iron. As contacts with the north and east increased, the interior trade expanded to encompass other, more precious raw materials. A constellation of diverse African farming and pastoral groups now came in contact with Islamic merchants and dhow skippers from elsewhere. Swahili society remained distinctively African, but its members took pride in many identities, acquired by their partici-pation in long-distance trade across the Indian Ocean monsoon routes and far into the interior. Arab sailors knew the coast itself as Zanj, "the land of black people."

Much of the earliest Islamic trade came from the Persian Gulf, per-haps linked to the rise of the Abbasid Dynasty and the growth of Bagh-dad. Ships from ports like Siraf and Sohar, on the Gulf, sought cargoes of timber, for African mangrove poles roofed many Middle Eastern cit-ies, among them parts of Baghdad. They also carried African slaves to Mesopotamia, where they drained some of the swamps of the lower Euphrates. On return voyages, they brought consignments of porcelain vessels from the Tang Dynasty workshops in China. Why did Chinese porcelain reach East Africa so early? The answer, once again, is the pre-dictable monsoon cycles. Merchant ships from the Persian Gulf carried African ivory and ambergris from the sperm whale hunted by Indonesians, used as a fixative for perfumes, from the Gulf to India and Sri Lanka, then north and east to South China Sea ports.

Inevitably, small Islamic communities, perhaps only a few merchants, settled along the coast. As early as 750 C.E., a handful of foreigners resided at Qanbalu, on the northern Kenya coast. The Shanga village, in the same region, boasted of a small mosque as early as 750–780.[6] Its foundations lay atop a burnt tree stump at the center of the stone enclosure that had been the central feature of the site in earlier times. This may represent symbolic continuity between indigenous religious beliefs and those of Islam, both of which professed belief in a supreme god, even if the African version communicated with believers through intermediaries. Shanga has yielded Chinese, Persian, Arabian, and Indian ceramics, numerous glass fragments, and beads and a seal ring inscribed with an Arabic inscription. Coins minted at Shanga and Kilwa, farther down the coast, hint at connections with other coastal centers. Early Muslim burials dating to the ninth century have been found as far south as Chibuene, in southern Mozambique, perhaps an anchorage for merchants trading with the interior.

By the ninth and tenth centuries, too, the Comoro Islands, some 200 miles (320 kilometers) offshore, were already engaged in long-distance Indian Ocean trade, perhaps acting as a transshipment point between Madagascar, Indian Ocean traders, and the East African coast. A few Comoro settlements of wattle-and-daub houses contain more Persian Gulf ceramics than large centers on the mainland coast. Some of these villages were major iron producers, the iron produced for export to India—a trade reported on by the Arab geographer al-Idrisi. Ancient Indian merchants were said to have liked the malleability of African iron, which was superior to local ores.[7] Zanj's ironworkers, both on the Comoros and on the mainland, produced a commodity that became a major staple of the Indian Ocean trade.

THE PERSIAN GULF trade from Arabia and the Persian Gulf to Azania declined during the late ninth century, in part because of a massive revolt of African slaves in Mesopotamia. China's Tang Dynasty ended in

906; political instability resulted, and China's trade with India faded. By this time, merchants from the Red Sea and the Gulf of Aden had entered the picture—not only Muslims but also Jews based in Cairo, as recorded in a synagogue archive called a genizah.[8]

Aden, on the Yemen coast, was a bustling, prosperous crossroads for the Indian Ocean world, strategically placed, easily defended, and accessible during both the Red Sea and Indian Ocean sailing seasons. This was where ships waited, often for months, to sail east or west, transshipped cargoes, and repaired their hulls. We can imagine the days of waiting at the end of the sailing season for dhows to arrive. Remarked a Muslim traveler, "A man's return from the sea is like his rise from the grave, and the port is like the place of congregation on the Day of Judgement: there is questioning, and settlement of accounts, and weighing, and counting."[9] Anxious traders kept watch, calculating potential profits and losses. Aden was a place where rulers and merchants worked together to create a safe and predictable environment both of fair taxation and necessary mercantile services. They also fostered a shipbuilding industry by developing personal contacts with Indian merchants who provided artisans, timber, and other boatbuilding supplies.

Thanks to the Cairo genizah, we know that Jewish traders played an important role in Aden's commercial life. Some served in important positions in such institutions as the customshouse. The Cairo archive tells of lasting relationships and lawsuits conducted across thousands of miles of open water. We learn how merchants' representatives at Aden created trusting partnerships between foreign traders and reliable businessmen living in Aden. These individuals, with their integrity and dependability, were powerful guarantees to trading partners living as far apart as Cairo and the Malabar Coast, who needed not only efficient services but also information on ever-changing market and voyaging conditions. Personal relationships and trust developed among people who may rarely, if ever, have met one another.

The Cairo genizah reveals a world of competition and of occasional conflict, but also of remarkable collaboration that transcended geographic, ethnic, and religious boundaries. The Jewish Adeni traders who appear in the genizah documents were truly cosmopolitan. Of course, they maintained close ties with individuals who shared their faith in Egypt, India, and beyond, relying heavily on family and religious ties to conduct their business. However, the most important connections they maintained were with their Muslim and Hindu counterparts at home and far away over the horizon. Port cities such as Aden were the anchors of social connections that moved trade between India, Africa, Arabia, and the Mediterranean world.

THE LATE FIRST MILLENNIUM was a time of major economic, political, and social change in the Mediterranean world. The Holy Roman Empire was founded in southern Germany; the Byzantine Empire was at the height of its power; the Fatimid rulers of North Africa had extended their political overlordship to Cairo, one of the great caravan junctions of the Mediterranean world. Arts and crafts and elaborate architecture blossomed, and demand for luxury goods skyrocketed, triggering unprecedented demands for exotic and hard-to-find raw materials. Among them were gold, ivory, and transparent quartz, all of which could be obtained along what the British archaeologist Mark Horton calls "the Swahili Corridor" on the East African coast—Azania.

The demand was extraordinary, especially for ivory, traditionally obtained from North Africa and the Red Sea region. In about 600 C.E., supplies appear to have dried up. Artisans turned to walrus and narwhal, even to fossil mammoth ivory from Siberia. The ivory shortage lasted about three centuries, until about 960, when cascades of African elephant ivory suddenly appeared in Christian and Muslim Europe, especially in Spain. As Horton has pointed out, many of the new ivory pieces were more than 4.3 inches (11 centimeters) across, a diameter achieved only by the tusks of African elephants, hunted in eastern Africa. Almost simultaneously, Fatimid workshops in Egypt produced numerous masterpieces in clear quartz. But gold was the ultimate catalyst, an art medium and also a commodity of great market value. The strictly controlled Fatimid mints produced dinar coins that were 96 percent pure, purity so great that the major gravity of commerce shifted to southern Mediterranean, Muslim-controlled ports. However, to produce the coins, the mints needed a continuous supply of new metal. Much of this came from mines at the southern edge of the Sahara in West Africa, but a significant quantity also arrived from the Indian Ocean.[10]

The coastal trade expanded rapidly as foreign merchants developed lasting relationships with local rulers and prominent trading families. The newcomers brought new architectural and artistic styles with them and brought the artisans to put them into practice. In their train came a new way of life that aped that of Muslim courts in the Middle East. At Shanga, earlier wooden buildings were replaced by a central enclosure with a central stone mosque built of plastered coral blocks and an enclosure wall that followed the old corral fence. By all appearances, the local people adopted new practices and displays of wealth, as well as religious beliefs from outside at least superficially, even if agriculture and herding remained the staples of everyday life. The same changes occurred at other settlements both near Lamu and at good anchorages such as Kilwa, on the Tanzanian coast.

More than four hundred archaeological sites, most of them small villages, document East African coastal settlement before the arrival of the Portuguese. There were, however, a few important towns such as Shanga, Manda, and Ungwana, as well as Kilwa and Sofala in the far south, with hundreds of stone houses and populations that were perhaps as high as ten thousand people in some places. These "stone towns" were the ports of call for oceangoing dhows engaged in the monsoon trade, strategically located close to trade routes to the interior. Here dhows could find safe anchorage, sheltered places where ships could be careened (hauled down on their sides for cleaning and repair). Some of the densest populations thrived around natural harbors like Lamu and Mombasa, and also near Malindi, in the north, and Kilwa, in the south, where fertile hinterlands produced ample food supplies.

Most trade along the Swahili Corridor was in the hands of local people, linked to major merchant families and outsiders by the common bond of Islam. There were shared beliefs and, perhaps more important, common moral values, which enhanced the security of commercial transactions in a world where communication was often glacially slow. The Swahili brought unique maritime skills to the trade. Their pilots had long mastered the challenges of sailing through the reefs and shallows of the corridor. Local *mtepes*, coasting vessels, sailed far south into waters where the monsoons were less reliable and conditions more hazardous. Their skippers knew every reef, every minor channel, anchorages where trade goods could be found and where local headmen and rulers were friendly. They were the seafaring experts in these difficult waters, drivers of the freight trains of the trade. But they knew nothing of the wider world over the horizon. Up north, they transferred their cargoes into deep-sea Arab dhows, which carried merchandise to the Red Sea and the Arabian coast.

To acquire raw materials from the interior required a whole different set of political and social relationships that were infinitely harder to maintain. The Swahili, being Africans with long experience of the interior, carefully preserved links with long-distance exchange networks that extended, spiderweb-like, far inland. These routinely carried grain and skins, ornaments such as seashells, and salt from village to village. It was these networks that ultimately carried my solitary red bead more than 700 miles (1,126 kilometers) into the far interior.

By acquiring trading partners inland, the Swahili were able to exercise control over supplies of prized items like cowrie and conus shells. I've walked on beaches near Lamu and traversed huge piles of abandoned cowrie shells, once a priceless currency far inland, now worthless except as a curiosity. The coastal people also manufactured cake salt from seawater, much prized by subsistence farmers inland. Their ironworkers fabricated finished artifacts for the trade; cotton fabric and other baubles passed inland. The Swahili themselves rarely traveled inland. They relied on local groups, and also on hunters, who provided elephant ivory in exchange for cloth. Gold was harder to acquire, as the sources were far to the south, with dust and nuggets coming from the interior between the Limpopo and Zambezi rivers. Much of it came from gold workings in what is now Zimbabwe. One authority, the archaeologist Roger Summers, has estimated that some 625 tons (567 metric tons) of gold was exported from southern Africa over about eight hundred years, an annual yield of more than 25,000 ounces (709 kilograms).[11] African gold was a major factor in the global economy of the day. The

Figure 8.3 *Stone town architecture at Songo Mnara, Tanzania, with the arches of the mosque in the left of the picture. Songo Mnara is a fourteenth- to sixteenth-century offshoot of Kilwa Kisiwani, on an island just to the south. The quality of the coral-built architecture is notable at the site, and this monumental style is extended to the domestic architecture and a series of very grand houses of the period. Courtesy Stephanie Wynne-Jones.*

first flowering of medieval culture in Europe, with its insatiable demand for gold, ivory, and other luxuries, owed much to the sailors of the Swahili Corridor.

Life along the coast centered around the "stone towns," with their flourishing Muslim congregations, whose mosques almost invariably rose within 1,100 yards (1,000 meters) of the shore, so strong was the coastal orientation, although there was no formal convention. The new architecture was in mud and coral, then, by the thirteenth century, wholly in coral—stone houses, palaces, and other structures forming compact towns, often with courtyards. The switch to coral masonry may reflect the changing focus of the trade away from the Persian Gulf to the Red Sea, where coral buildings were in common use. Mangrove poles formed

Figure 8.4 *The Great Mosque at Kilwa Kisiwani, showing the domed extension built in the fourteenth century. The original structure is incorporated at the northern end (to the right of the picture) and dates to the eleventh century. Courtesy Stephanie Wynne-Jones.*

the ceilings, their length restricting the size of rooms, making small rooms a common feature of coastal architecture.

The "stone towns" were far more than a mere architectural vogue.[12] Their appearance coincided with the growth of an increasingly prosperous class of urban merchants who controlled most wealth and thus had access to political power. Stone town architecture also reflected different groups within Swahili society, with *waungwana*, the oldest and most respected urban families, at the apex. Domestic social structure centered on the types of houses and where they were built, with a progression from the simple thatched hut through the lowest floors of multistory buildings to the pinnacle of society in the upper levels. This was, however, above all an African society, fortunate to be at a great crossroads of the vast global trade networks that relied on the monsoon winds and encompassed a good quarter of the earth. The predictability of the ocean and its winds brought an essential stability to the coastal towns. Swahili merchants could anticipate monsoon wind shifts and predict when dhow fleets would arrive and depart. They could accumulate cargoes in advance, arrange credit and take on debt, become wealthy, comfortable within a stable marketplace. The stone towns reflected this stability, with their fine houses, mosques, and civic buildings.

As coastal society prospered, so Islam took even firmer hold, providing an element of trust between trading partners with the same ethical values. It also provided protection against slavery, as Islam prohibited the enslavement of believers, while also fostering closer alliances with communities in the hinterland, who produced many of the goods handled in the trade. The stone towns became ever more important commercial centers. According to the Portuguese writer Duarte Barbosa, Mombasa was "a very fair place, with lofty stone and mortar houses, well aligned in streets . . . This is a place of great traffic, and has a good harbor, in which are always moored craft of many kinds."[13] For all their wealth, the stone towns remained independent from one another. The linear coast and limited water supplies militated against the formation of a single state. Instead, elite families maintained contact with one another and their trading partners at home and abroad. There were commercial and political alliances, the exchange of gifts, well-timed marriages, and, only rarely, military conflict.

By 1400, the stone towns lay at the edge of a vast network of monsoon trade routes that linked distant lands far over the horizon. Their rulers and merchants were active participants in a far wider world defined and decoded by the predictable monsoon winds. These same winds now brought huge fleets of foreigners into what had long been a polyglot world.

CHAPTER 9

"We Spread Our Cloudlike Sails Aloft"

IN 1414, AN EXOTIC BEAST ARRIVED as tribute from Bengal at the court of the emperor of China: an African giraffe. The unfamiliar creature "had the body of a deer and the tail of an ox and a fleshy boneless horn, with luminous spots like a red or purple mist. It walks in stately fashion and in its every motion it observes a rhythm." An artist, Xendu, drew the animal in the flesh and wrote that the emperor's "virtue equals that of heaven. Its merciful blessings have spread far and wide, so that its harmonious vapours have emanated a ch'i-lin, an endless blessing to the state for many years." So unfamiliar was the giraffe that the Chinese immediately assumed it was of divine origin—a mythic beast known as a *qilin*, or a unicorn, whose "harmonious voice sounds like a bell or a musical tube."[1]

The giraffe had arrived in Bengal aboard a dhow from the East African coast on the wings of the monsoon, a curiosity for a wealthy prince's collection. The Indian potentate sent it on to China as tribute for the emperor in the hands of Grand Director Zheng He, commander of seven expeditions that explored the monsoon regions of maritime Asia and the Indian Ocean in one of the first truly global ventures on the world's oceans.[2]

Grand Director Zheng He commanded these expeditions to what the Chinese called the Western Ocean between 1405 and 1433, three quarters of a century before Portuguese caravels rounded the Cape of Good Hope. Not that he was venturing into unfamiliar seas, for Arabs and Indians had traded across the Indian Ocean and as far as Southeast

Figure 9.1 *Presentation of the* qilin *(giraffe), Shen Du, 1414. National Palace Museum, Taipei.*

Asia and Chinese waters for many centuries. Word of East Africa's valuable commodities had traveled as far as China as early as the tenth century, during Tang Dynasty times. At the time, China was one of the two great economic powerhouses of the monsoon world, the other being the Abbasid caliphate, ruling from Baghdad. More than a million people lived in the imperial capital at Changan (now Xian). Everyone has heard of the Great Silk Road that linked China with the West through Mongolia. The lesser-known monsoon counterpart, sometimes called the Maritime Silk Route, had linked China, the Indian Ocean, and the Persian Gulf since at least the time of Christ. Aromatic woods, exotic coral, fine textiles, and pearls passed eastward. Rolls of silk traveled westward, as did ceramic dishes and plates that served as luxury dinnerware from Southeast Asia to the Gulf, Arabia, and Africa. Arab, Indian, and Persian ships carried most of the cargoes along sea lanes that wound between the islands of Southeast Asia before emerging into the Bay of Bengal and open waters to the west.

Monsoon passages were never easy, but they were especially challenging among the Indonesian islands, where reefs and submerged rocks lurked close to the surface. Hundreds, if not thousands, of heavily laden ships came to grief in these waters over the centuries in narrow, unmarked channels where pirates also lurked. We know almost nothing of these vessels and the contents of their holds, except from a chance discovery of an Arab dhow that sank in the Gelasa Strait between two small islands off southeastern Sumatra during the ninth century C.E., laden with more than sixty thousand pieces of Tang Dynasty gold, silver, and ceramics. Sea cucumber divers chanced on the wreck in 1998, found some bowls, and sold them. A team of divers with no archaeological training subsequently emptied the wreck in shifts in a treasure recovery operation that has raised profound controversy in archaeological circles. A Singapore business subsequently bought the cargo for $30 million.

The cargo in what is called the Belitung or Tang wreck had many sources; most of it was bowls of Changsha pottery from Hunan, in southern China, which were valued as far afield as Persia. These were nested in large storage jars by the hundreds. Inscriptions on some of the vessels date them to about 826 C.E., giving a close date for the wreck.

There were 763 inkpots and 915 spice jars from different parts of China, perhaps special orders. The cargo was almost entirely trade goods, aimed at an eclectic marketplace, some bearing Islamic inscriptions, others Buddhist motifs. The stern yielded richer fare, including a magnificent gold cup and a silver flask adorned with mandarin ducks, again perhaps part of a special consignment.

The square-sailed ship itself, a simple form of Arab dhow, was about 60 feet (18 meters) long, with a raking bow and stern, constructed of African and Indian timber. The sewn-plank hull was held together with what appears to be coconut-husk fiber. Somewhat similar vessels can still be seen in the waters off Oman. Judging from the Chinese cargo, it was probably bound westward, having left a major port such as Canton, in southern China, home at the time to more than ten thousand foreigners, mostly Arabs and Persians. The ultimate destination is unknown but could have been Basra, at the head of the Gulf, close to the heart of the Abbasid world.

CHINA LAY AT the eastern end of a huge global trade network as trade with the West expanded steadily. Nevertheless, there were powerful factions at court who were profoundly distrustful of the outside world. In 878 C.E., shortly after the Belitung ship sank, a rebel leader named Huang Chao burned Canton, slaughtering thousands of foreigners. Much of the trade withered, but everything changed when the Yongle Emperor (1360–1424) of the Ming Dynasty seized the throne in 1402.

The Yongle Emperor was a usurper and consumed with a passion for fame and prestige. He spent much of his reign fighting the Mongols in the far north of his domains, suppressing potential rivals, and devoting much time to preserving Chinese culture. The emperor was far from inward-looking, for he dispatched as many as seventy-two missions to states as far afield as Japan, Korea, Nepal, Tibet, and others in Central Asia. But he reserved some of his greatest efforts in foreign diplomacy for seven great seagoing missions, which visited at least thirty-three countries throughout the world of the monsoon winds. These were no voyages of mere commerce and exploration. The emperor planned his expeditions

Figure 9.2 *Zheng He. His actual appearance is unknown.* © *China Stock.*

on a grand scale to display the wealth and power of China to neighboring countries in Southeast Asia and around the Indian Ocean. In the imperial mind, this involved not mere exploration or trading, but the development of tributary relationships with rulers in these regions. He placed these ambitious ventures in the hands of a trusted eunuch, Zheng He.

A military commander and skilled administrator of uncertain religion, Zheng He (1371–1433) was born in southwestern China, perhaps of Muslim parents, although he was at least nominally a Buddhist in later life. Taken prisoner in a rebellion against the Ming while still a child, he was castrated at an early age. Subsequently, he became a trusted member of Prince Zhu Di's retinue. They campaigned together on the Mongolian frontier. Zheng He also played an important role in the long civil war that brought his master to power as the Yongle Emperor in 1402 and gave him considerable influence at court. Despite his complete lack of maritime experience, this loyal and trustworthy adviser was a logical choice as commander of an expedition on a grand scale that was to display the power and wealth of China. His appointment came after byzantine maneuvering at court. The enterprise was a success for commercial, imperialist, and religious factions who wanted to support and expand Chinese trade in the Indian Ocean, initiatives opposed by Confucians with conflicting values. Over the next twenty-eight years, Zheng He commanded seven Chinese fleets, each known as the Xiafan Guanjun, the Foreign Expeditionary Armada, which sailed as far as the Arabian Peninsula and the East African coast. Part diplomat and part military soldier, Zheng He himself remains a shadowy figure, but the magnitude of his voyaging was stupendous. By all accounts, he seems to have been the ideal man for the command.

The Yongle Emperor "wanted to display his soldiers in strange lands in order to make manifest the wealth and power" of his kingdom.[3] He had no desire to found colonies or to explore unknown lands. The emperor, being the Son of Heaven and ruler of the Middle Kingdom of lands directly under Heaven, considered his expeditions a means of enforcing the Chinese tributary system on the Indian Ocean. Foreign rulers and their ambassadors would come to China and present tribute in local products to the emperor as an acknowledgment of his unique status on earth. In return, they would receive imperial recognition and munificent gifts that included money, silk, and a Chinese calendar as a basis for their communications with the court.

To mount such expeditions was a formidable task, but at least the fleets were not sailing into unknown waters. By taking advantage of the reversing patterns of the monsoon winds, the ships could usually sail downwind, with none of the hazardous sea conditions, typhoons, and headwinds that beset the open Pacific beyond China's eastern shores. Navigation was never a problem. Zheng He always knew he could return home simply by waiting for the winds to reverse. All his remarkable voyages lay within the vast monsoon region, for there was no easy way out of the Indian Ocean. South of Madagascar, the Chinese would have encountered violent storms, which had deterred East African traders for many centuries. Perhaps a few junks did round the Cape of Good

Hope before the Portuguese in 1488—indeed, a Venetian mapmaker reported a sighting of a junk off the southwest African coast in the mid-fifteenth century.[4] But there was nothing south of the Mozambique Channel of use to the Chinese, no peoples with whom they would wish to have dealings.

THE YONGLE EMPEROR organized his expeditions on a grand scale. In 1405, he ordered the construction of an imposing fleet, including some of the largest wooden ships ever built. Sixty-two large junks known as "treasure ships," 225 support vessels, and no fewer than 27,780 men are said to have made up the first expedition. Big oceangoing vessels were nothing new in China by Zheng He's time. When the Venetian traveler Marco Polo accompanied Princess Kokocin to Iran in 1292, he sailed with fourteen great ships, each with four masts. The Islamic traveler Ibn Battuta described large Chinese ships in 1347 that had twelve sails and carried a thousand men, of whom four hundred were soldiers.

Zheng He's "treasure ships" were the culmination of centuries of Chinese seafaring in the South China Sea and were ten times the size of any ship in European waters at the time. Controversy surrounds their size, but the largest may have been up to 440 feet (134 meters) long, with a beam of 180 feet (55 meters). These dimensions seem fantastical, until one remembers that a wooden rudder post excavated from the Longjiang shipyard, at Nanjing, known as the Treasure Ship Yard, supported a rudder of at least 452 square feet (42 square meters), capable of steering an even larger vessel. The treasure ships were lumbering sailing barges, capable of carrying large numbers of people in comfort, as well as enormous quantities of tribute, but they were seaworthy. The sinologist Joseph Needham described an 1848 voyage from China to London by the 160-foot (49-meter), three-masted junk *Keying*. Her mainsail alone had an area of 6,000 square feet (557 square meters) and weighed nine tons (eight metric tons). Her anonymous British captain described her as "a good sea boat and remarkably dry." An unnamed English explorer sailed from Macao in a large merchant ship that was much smaller than the treasure vessels. "These floating bodies of timber are able to encounter

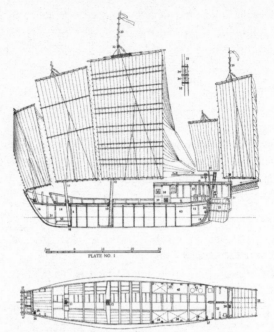

Figure 9.3 *A Chinese junk, a much smaller trading ship than Zheng He's vessels. Chinese ships had no keels. Instead, they relied on external longitudinal timbers near the waterline and numerous internal bulkheads, which served as watertight compartments. The drawing shows the transverse bulkheads and the battened sails. Courtesy the Picture Collection/New York Public Library.*

any tempestuous weather, hold a remarkable good wind, sail well, and are worked with such facility and care, as to cause the astonishment of European sailors."[5]

Ming China was immensely wealthy and more than capable of commissioning a fleet of huge ships that carried up to 28,000 people. Yongle's fleets were maritime juggernauts, designed to intimidate, to collect tribute, and to carry large numbers of soldiers to enforce Zheng He's demands. The pace of each journey was measured and stately, with an average speed that rarely exceeded 2 knots (3.7 kilometers an hour), much like a royal progress that unfolded effortlessly across the open sea. Bad weather or strong winds were no deterrent. The Chinese had supreme confidence in their ships and their sailing abilities, probably in large part because the junk rig, with its battens (stiffeners inserted in sails for better control), could be reduced in size in seconds. The seven expeditions certainly sailed thousands of miles, apparently with few casualties. In 1431, Zheng He and his associates commissioned stone-carved inscriptions for the Temple of the Heavenly Princess, at the port of Liujiagang, on the Yangtze River, in which they boasted of having visited more than thirty countries:

"[We have] traversed over a hundred thousand *li* of vast ocean [and have] beheld great ocean waves, rising as high as the sky and swelling and swelling endlessly. Whether in dense fog and drizzling rain or in wind-driven waves riding like mountains, no matter what the sudden changes in sea conditions, we spread our cloudlike sails aloft and sailed by the stars day and night."

Not that these were necessarily peaceful expeditions. Gifts may have been forthcoming and honeyed words uttered, but the mailed fist was aboard the ships. Then the Liujiagang inscription proudly adds:

"When we arrived at the foreign countries, barbarian kings who resisted transformation [by Chinese civilization] and were not respectful we captured alive, and bandit soldiers who looted and plundered recklessly we exterminated. Because of this the sea routes became pure and peaceful."[6]

Zheng He's seven voyages took his fleet through the South China Sea, across the Bay of Bengal into the Indian Ocean to Sri Lanka, and then to India's Malabar Coast, the Persian Gulf, the Red Sea, and the East African coast. The first three expeditions, between 1405 and 1411, traveled only as far as the Malabar Coast, at the time the world's major source of pepper. The fleet also visited ports on the coast of Siam (Thailand) and along the Malay Peninsula.

On December 18, 1412, the Yongle Emperor ordered Zheng He and his colleagues to go on a fourth voyage "bearing letters to confer rich gifts of silk floss, thin silk gauze, colored thin silk, and other goods, each according to his deserts" on the rulers of several countries.[7] The expedition lasted three years, again comprising sixty-three large ships and a large military force. Zheng He sailed to Melaka and other ports on the

Malay Peninsula, anchoring at Samudera, on the north coast of Sumatra, where the fleet prepared for the crossing to Sri Lanka and India. Zheng He than sailed around the southern tip of India to Calicut (Kozhikode), which one of his interpreters, Ma Huan, described as "the great country of the Western Ocean." The previous three expeditions had made Calicut their western terminus, but this time they sailed north and west, probably to the Maldive and Laccadive islands, on their way to Hormuz, on the Persian Gulf—a crossroads between Arabia, India, and points east. Ma Huan wrote of Hormuz, "Foreign ships from every place, together with foreign merchants traveling by land, all come to this territory in order to gather together and to buy and sell."[8] The Chinese fleet had but one purpose: to display Chinese power to those who traded with her. All of Zheng He's voyages sought to overawe the countries of the Western Ocean and to bring them into the Chinese tributary system. If there was resistance, the ships disgorged troops and overwhelmed rebellious armies on land. The grand director duly slaughtered Chinese pirates in Sumatra and conquered rebellious armies in Sri Lanka.

Zheng He returned to Nanjing in 1415, bringing with him envoys from nineteen countries and all manner of exotica, including the *qilin*. The emperor promptly dispatched him on a fifth voyage, which lasted from 1417 to 1419. He was to return the envoys to their homelands, laden with letters and rich gifts for their rulers. Silk brocade, colored thin silk, fine gauze, and other expensive luxuries traveled on the ships, as well as an inscription for the ruler of Cochin, who had received each expedition and sent tribute regularly. Yongle also conferred the title of State Protecting Mountain on a hill in the prince's kingdom. Once again, Zheng He set out on a carefully choreographed expedition—it was nothing less. After visiting ports on the Malay Peninsula and northern Sumatra, the fleet crossed to Sri Lanka, then Cochin, Calicut, and Hormuz, before anchoring at ports on the Arabian coast as far west as Aden. From there, Zheng He sailed into unfamiliar waters, across to Mogadishu and Barawa, on the Somali coast, before heading south to Malindi, on the modern-day Kenya coast. He may have encountered resistance in Somalia, a country "located where the climate is always hot, and the fields are barren and yield little."[9] Here he acquired ambergris and frankincense, both highly desired commodities in the monsoon trade. Both Mogadishu and Barawa dispatched tribute missions to the emperor between 1416 and 1423, with gifts that included elephant ivory, camels, and ostriches.

Before he departed, the grand director had burned incense at Quanzhou, in southern China, a port with a large Muslim population and an important port for foreign merchant vessels. The offering invoked divine protection for the forthcoming voyage. While in port, he loaded a cargo of porcelain and other goods. Interestingly, Ming porcelain has come from excavations in East African towns. The fleet does not seem to have sailed farther south in Africa than Malindi, which is described in the *Minghsi*, the official history of the Ming Dynasty, as being "a long way from China." It was here that Zheng He received giraffes, from the same location where the first, and sensational, gift of 1414 had originated. By this time, giraffes were becoming more commonplace in China. Both Aden and Mecca sent them as tribute during the grand director's later voyages, but they were probably of African origin. Zheng He's inscriptions identify the native name of the giraffe as *zulafa*, from the Arabic word for giraffe, *zarafa*. Perhaps rumors of imperial interest caused these exotic animals to become desirable commodities in the highly competitive monsoon trade.

Is there evidence, beyond Chinese sources, that Zheng He's ships actually sailed as far as the East African coast? Local oral traditions and folklore tell of Chinese visitors, of a visit by Zheng He in 1418. A storm off the coast may have wrecked one of his ships. Perhaps some of the survivors married local women. For years, there have been archaeological hints—like the fifteenth-century Chinese vases hauled up from the seabed in fishing nets off the town of Lamu, to the north. Then there's the nondescript village of Mambrui, where a circular tombstone in the cemetery has four-hundred-year-old Chinese porcelain bowls embedded in it. Chinese scientists recently took DNA samples from Mambrui villagers to probe for possible foreign ancestry, for some of the locals have subtly Chinese features. When archaeologists from Beijing University teamed up with Kenyan excavators to dig at the edge of the Mambrui cemetery, they unearthed an iron smelter and slag, and also a fragment of an early Ming Dynasty bowl, of a design made only for the royal family at the famous Longquan kilns in eastern China, still famous for their porcelain. The jade-green shard, the base of a much larger bowl, bears two small fish in relief swimming below the glaze. But the most conclusive hint is a small brass coin with a square hole in the center, bearing the inscription YONGLE TONGBAO, known to date between 1403 and 1424. According to the Chinese archaeologist Qin Dashu, only envoys of the emperor Chengzu carried such coins. Zheng He was such an envoy.[10] This tiny find is startling evidence of the global reach of the monsoon trade before European ships arrived in the Indian Ocean.

BY THE TIME the grand director returned to China in 1419, the emperor was preoccupied with military campaigns on the Mongolian frontier. He authorized a sixth voyage in 1421, this time to return sixteen envoys to their countries, accompanied by the usual gifts. By now, the burden of heavy military expenditures both in the north and in Vietnam, as well as the cost of building a new imperial capital at Beijing, weighed heavily on the government. The lavish voyages had produced some tribute, but they were unlikely to have yielded significant profits, given the enormous size of Zheng He's ships. As the expedition set out, the emperor forbade treasure ships from "going to foreign countries," presumably an edict aimed at any future voyages, as Zheng He was already under way.[11] After reaching Calicut, the grand director divided his fleet into squadrons, which sailed on separate ventures while the main body of treasure ships proceeded to Hormuz, thereby using his vessels to cover as much ground as possible. The detached squadrons apparently sailed direct to Arabian ports and to the Mogadishu region, but only to familiar locations, presumably to reinforce the impression left by earlier visits. According to Chinese sailing directions, the passage from India to the Somali coast took twenty to twenty-one days, as if this was a routine voyage. It certainly was for Arab traders.

The squadrons rejoined the fleet in India after delivering their envoys, and the expedition returned home in September 1422 after visiting Thailand. Two years later, the grand director made a much smaller-scale, entirely separate voyage to deliver royal insignia to an official in Palembang, on Sumatra. By the time he returned, the Yongle Emperor had died, and with him the imperial habit of embarking on expensive projects without considering their long-term costs. Despite the changes at court, Zheng He remained in command of his ships and their crews and served as commandant at Nanjing until 1431. His main achievement, executed at enormous cost, was the construction of the great Baoen Temple at Nanjing, a project begun by the Yongle Emperor in 1412 and finally completed under the watchful eye of his successor, the Xuande Emperor, in 1431. One hundred thousand "soldiers, skilled craftsmen and miscellaneous laborers" are said to have worked on the nine-story Buddhist pagoda.[12] Perhaps, but this is conjecture, as some of the funds intended for voyages were diverted to temple construction. It may be no coincidence that the Xuande Emperor, who ruled from 1425 to 1435, gave orders for a seventh voyage as construction wound down and conditions in the north and in troublesome Vietnam momentarily improved.

The imperial decree was succinct: "Everything was prosperous and renewed, but the foreign countries, distantly located beyond the sea, still had not heard and did not know. For this reason, Grand Directors Zheng He, Wang Jinghong, and others, were specially sent, bearing the word, to go and instruct them into deference and submission."[13] Tribute had arrived but sporadically from the countries on Zheng He's regular itinerary since the virtual cessation of diplomatic activity after 1422. Clearly, a display of overwhelming military power was the only way to maintain the kind of tributary relationships the Yongle Emperor had envisioned with Southeast Asia and the Indian Ocean. Given the distances involved, such relationships required massive shows of force that could be deployed only by sea. The monsoon winds made such displays possible. It's a measure of the global reach of the trade networks of the monsoon world that the Yongle and Xuande emperors even considered such enterprises.

Before leaving, Zheng He set up his inscriptions in temples at Liujiagang and at Changle, 402 miles (647 kilometers) away, which are now a major source of information on his voyages. Both honor the goddess Tian Fei, the "Heavenly Princess," whose spirit roamed above the waves wearing a red dress and rescuing drowning sailors. From Changle, where he may have loaded his ships, the grand director sailed west of Borneo and then into the Java Sea, a course that involved some tacking close to the wind rather than running before the monsoon. After a stop at Semudera, "the most important place of assembly [for ships going to] the Western Ocean," the fleet sailed for Sri Lanka, a potentially hazardous passage on account of the vicious cyclones that can develop in the Bay of Bengal.[14] Eventually, the fleet ended up at Hormuz, where several squadrons split off on separate missions, apparently to as far away as the Somali coast.

This time Zheng He also had his eyes set on Mecca. Seven men from a squadron based at Calicut boarded a merchant ship sailing to a port near Mecca. According to the interpreter Ma Huan, it took three months for them to reach the port of Jeddah, from whence they traveled overland to Mecca. Here the people spoke Arabic and the Great Mosque contained the holy site called the Kaaba. He described the Muslim pilgrimage and the rituals of walking around the Kaaba. "There they bought strange gems and rare treasures, as well as giraffes and ostriches for their return." Envoys (probably merchants) accompanied the men on their return, bringing tribute. The emperor "rejoiced and gave them even more valuable gifts."[15]

The fleet reassembled at Calicut and made a faster journey home, averaging about 2.1 knots, a reflection of the stronger southwesterly monsoon driving the ships. By Arab and Western standards, however, these were glacially slow voyages. In 1805, British admiral Lord Nelson crossed the Atlantic with ten large ships of the line, designed for firepower rather than speed, at an average speed of 13.5 knots. Nineteenth-century clipper ships achieved even higher speeds. Back at court, the emperor received the envoys from as far away as Aden. They all "came to court and presented as tribute giraffes (*qilin*), elephants, horses, and other goods." The emperor said, "We do not have any desire for goods from distant regions, but we realize they [are offered] in full sincerity."[16] He firmly rejected attempts by his courtiers to associate the giraffes presented before him as evidence of his virtuous rule. With this imperial pronouncement, China's great voyages ended. The grand director died during or shortly after his return from his seventh voyage.

The end of the seventh voyage, in 1433, coincided with a major shift in Chinese policy as successive emperors focused their attention on threats from the north. The capital remained at Beijing, in the north, as Ming rulers chose an enhanced position in the north over influence at sea. High civil officials opposed to lavish maritime expeditions were in the ascendancy. Furthermore, the Ming elite was consistently opposed to projects headed by eunuchs. They regarded Zheng He's expeditions as little more than examples of imperial extravagance.

Zheng He's voyages never led to a lasting tradition of Chinese deep-sea voyaging. Later emperors did not even create a powerful fleet to protect their own coasts from Japanese pirates. In 1436, the emperor forbade the building of oceangoing ships and foreign trade. China was turning in on itself. Even the records of earlier voyages were destroyed. In about 1475, the Chenghua Emperor ordered a search for documents related to expeditions to the Western Ocean in the archives of the Ministry of War. The responsible official, Liu Daxia, director of the Bureau of Military Affairs, admitted to the minister of war that Zheng He had returned with exotic and precious things, but they were of no benefit to the state, and thus a sign of bad government. The documents were burned, "deceitful exaggerations of bizarre things far removed from the testimony of peoples' eyes and ears . . . Even if the old archives were still preserved they should be destroyed in order to suppress [a repetition of these things] at the root."[17] Liu Daxia was eventually promoted to minister of war. Some historians believe this story is apocryphal, but there is no question that the plans of the treasure ships and documents about the voyages did disappear. By the seventeenth century, Zheng He's voyages were virtually forgotten.

The grand director's momentous voyages dwarfed any previous maritime enterprises in the monsoon world, remarkable not only for their ambitious scale but also for their long reach, thousands of miles across open waters. Zheng He presided over what can only be called a global enterprise, but one that did not endure. Where the Chinese withdrew, others moved in. The ancient rhythms of the highly competitive monsoon trade persisted, as they always had, in the hands of polyglot sailors from all corners of the Islamic world. Melaka, on the southern Malay Peninsula, had been one of Zheng He's major ports of call. After the sultan converted to Islam in 1436, more and more South China Sea and Indian Ocean trade passed through his port. This became the eastern terminus of the huge networks of the monsoon-wind trade once dominated by the Chinese fleets—from the northern regions of Sumatra (what is now the Aceh area) to Sri Lanka, Cochin, Calicut, and the Malabar Coast, Hormuz and Aden, on the Arabian Peninsula, and the stone towns of the East African coast. The same pattern of trade flourished until the arrival of the Portuguese, in 1497, and beyond. Even today, the occasional dhow arrives in Lamu and Mombasa with the northeast monsoon, laden not with exotic treasures but with day-to-day commodities like cement and timber. When loaded, they slip out of port quietly to coast slowly along shores familiar from history, passing gently, almost imperceptibly close off the breakers, using landmarks known to Arab and Greek, Phoenician and Indian, since time immemorial.

TURBULENT WATERS IN THE NORTH

When the wind is from the west
All the waves that cannot rest
   To the east must thunder on
   Where the bright tree of the sun
Is rooted in the ocean's breast.

          —Rumann, "Storm at Sea," c. 700 C.E.[1]

The heaving waters of the North Atlantic formed a symbolic frontier beyond the western shores of Europe, a place where dreaded beasts preyed on sailors and great storms ravaged anyone bold enough to set sail beyond the horizon. The North Atlantic was the most formidable of all seascapes for mariners to decode, as were the English and Irish seas, the North Sea, and the Baltic. There were no predictable shifts to allow an explorer safe passage home from an outward journey. Great storms could erupt any month of the year; pitiless rocks, strong tides, and on-shore winds made pilotage close to land a risky venture even in calm summer weather. These were tough, unrelenting waters, reflected in the faces of the men who fished and traded in the North Sea and farther afield. No one knows when people first ventured offshore here—perhaps across the English Channel or across the North Sea—but it was at least 6,000 years ago. By 2500 B.C.E., passages over open water were relatively commonplace, but probably surrounded by strong ritual associations, sometimes voyages involving the trading of exotic artifacts. Some centuries later, waterborne trade increased significantly, perhaps at a time when hide boats came into use. Such craft were remarkably seaworthy, if slow: witness the epic voyage of Pytheas, a Greek merchant from the Marseille region, who may have sailed as far north as Iceland in about 320 B.C.E. The tempo of offshore voyaging increased after Roman times, with the remarkable passages of Irish monks and the expansion of Norsemen from their northern fastnesses. We describe ship burials, the coastal journeys of the Norse lord Ohthere, who visited the court of King Alfred the Great of England, and *æfintyr*, the restless quality that drove so much Norse exploration of unknown seas. And we show how ancient traditions of seamanship and pilotage under oar and sail survived into the twentieth century alongside the Atlantic liners of the Industrial Revolution.

CHAPTER 10

Seascapes of Ancestors

STAR CARR, NORTHEAST ENGLAND, late spring, 10,500 years ago. The reeds grow anew on the low promontory that projects into the small glacial lake a short distance inland from the North Sea. Dense birch forest presses on the lakeshore, except where the hunters have felled trees and burned off the vegetation to foster new growth and to make a convenient landing place. Generations of foragers have camped here, returning again and again to the same location each spring, hunting red deer as they feed at water's edge. The gray water is mirror-still this calm morning. A man and a woman launch a simple raft of birch logs lashed together with fibers into the shallows and paddle quietly to a nearby spot where they know that pike often rise to feed. As his wife holds the raft steady with a wooden paddle, the fisherman peers at the bottom, dimly visible close below the surface, three-pronged barbed spear poised at the ready. He thrusts with expert timing. Seconds later, an impaled pike flaps helpless on the birch logs. A quick blow with a wooden club and the hunter resumes his watch. Some hours later, husband and wife return to shore with half a dozen pike. With practiced ease, they gut and clean the fish, butterflying some of them to dry by the fire, putting the rest aside for the evening meal. Nearby, close to shore, two men have cut down a straight birch tree. Using stone wedges and flint axes, they split thick planks for a walkway that will lead to water's edge. The distinctive crack of the splitting wood echoes softly over the still water on this quiet spring day.[1]

The Star Carr people hunt and fish in a rapidly changing Northern

European world. More than seven thousand years of irregular global warming separate them from the Ice Age, but their remote forebears, accustomed to sub-zero temperatures and open steppe, wouldn't recognize the landscape of dense birch forests and glacial lakes that hems them in on every side. A satellite image of Northern Europe would reveal dramatic changes from even a thousand years earlier. Massive ice sheets still mantle much of Scandinavia, but they are retreating irregularly northward. Sea levels are still well below modern contours; the Baltic is a brackish sea about to become a freshwater lake as the earth's crust adjusts to the lessened weight of glacial ice. The southern North Sea is a low-lying marshy expanse, with the forerunner of the Elbe River flowing northward into the deep waters of the Norwegian Trench. The Rhine, the Seine, and the Thames run into a wide estuary between England and France that is now the English Channel. This rapidly changing world is a dynamic maze of shallow river valleys, mudflats, and sandbanks, with exceptional biodiversity. Shallow inshore waters, sheltered inlets, and extensive wetlands provide fish and mollusks. It was here, in these cold but bountiful waters, that Northern Europeans first developed a close relationship with the ocean.

As temperatures rose, so descendants of much earlier late–Ice Age hunting groups moved northward from warmer locations in search of new territories. Many of them settled by estuaries, lakes, and rapidly changing Baltic and North Sea shorelines. At Star Carr, for example, the lake was a magnet for human settlement, as much part of the daily landscape as the land was. The same must have been true for groups who fished and hunted by Baltic shores or in the marshlands and estuaries of the southern North Sea, a huge tract of low-lying terrain named Doggerland by the scientists who have probed its depths.[2] Both the Baltic and Doggerland had coastlines that changed by the year, even by the month. Those who dwelt in such environments treated both land and sea as part of their hunting territories. They ventured on water for fishing as routinely as a woman collected plant foods or a man pursued deer in the forest. At the same time, people living by the shallow ocean knew that the settlements of their ancestors often lay beneath the surface. Thus it may have been that the seascape, apart from being

Figure 10.1 *Map showing locations in Chapter 10.*

a convenient larder, was also the realm of the ancestors, of death. The sea, with its sudden gales and unpredictable moods, was a central part of a human existence that placed no artificial barriers between the living and the supernatural realms, exemplified, in part, by the heaving waters close offshore.

Unfortunately, almost all the coastal archaeological sites along northern shores lie beneath today's high sea levels, so we know little of these people. At this early stage in northern seafaring, all the activity was in shallow water, as much on lakes as it was in narrow fjords and sheltered seaways. Decoding the seascape revolved not around open-water passages or deepwater crossings, but around the best fishing spots, places where eels ran in spring and fall, and mollusk beds lay in deeper water. Dugouts and rafts served as platforms for catching and spearing fish such as pike, for laying and servicing tunnel-like eel traps, and for hunting waterfowl with bows and arrows. Such humble craft date back to the end of the Ice Age, perhaps even earlier. Actual examples of dugouts, even finds of paddles, are rare. The earliest known canoe comes from Pesse, near Drenthe, in the Netherlands, and dates to between 7900 and 6500 B.C.E. Fyn Island, in Denmark, has yielded a couple more dating to around 4000 B.C.E. As time moves on, such finds become more common, for dugouts remained in use until at least medieval times.[3]

Short dugouts thrived among coastal wetlands and marshes, with their rich biodiversity. Even with the simplest of hollowed-out tree trunks, hunters could pass effortlessly through otherwise inaccessible terrain. Here fish abounded, waterfowl could be shot and trapped, and game could be hunted among waterways navigable only in the smallest of boats armed with paddle or pole. I've kayaked in such places, deep among thick reed beds, the muddy water sluggish and glasslike, the narrow creek twisting and turning through the featureless landscape, dividing and then dividing again. Time and time again, I've had to decide which way to turn, which direction to take. Sometimes I've ended up in a dead end. Other times, I've suddenly emerged in a small lake where geese are feeding quietly by the reeds. With a sudden whir, they take off, to circle and land some distance away. Such inlets and small lakes were the places where Stone Age hunters of ten thousand years ago learned about fish and water, the vagaries of Baltic and North Sea weather, and the unique seascape they lived in.

Just as in the Aegean, survival would have also depended on interaction with neighbors, on the constant exchange of basic commodities and occasional exotic luxuries such as Baltic amber, prized for its perceived magical qualities.[4] The dugout would have been the vehicle for most forms of trade and communication in this watery world. The distances that exotic artifacts such as polished jadeite axes traveled by canoe were extraordinary—from the Alps far north to Germany, Belgium, and the Netherlands, and across to England. There may be good reasons why

dugout canoe designs are remarkably similar at either end of the Rhine
as early as 4000 B.C.E.

DUGOUTS ARE SMALL craft, capable, at the most, of holding a family.
Load carrying required quite different boats, for transporting game, large
fish catches, mollusks, tents, and people attending summer gatherings—
probably an essential part of the annual round in a landscape where
most bands lived in relative isolation for much of the year. Just as in the
Arctic and the Aleutians (see Chapter 12) hide boats were the only viable option for load carrying in largely treeless environments like those
of Northern Europe immediately after the Ice Age and before birch
forests spread widely during warmer centuries. Such craft have many
advantages—light weight, simple construction, and tough, flexible hulls
that could be built on wooden frames to provide relatively high freeboard, essential in short, steep seas. Alas, the remains of such boats are
unlikely ever to be found, even if there are claims that worked reindeer
bones were used for the frames of hide boats deployed against migrating herds crossing lakes as early as 12,000 years ago.[5]

Theoretically, at any rate, the technology for constructing hide boats
is as old as sewn clothing—both required stout, eyed needles and an
ability to fabricate tailored clothing with waterproof seams. Hide boats
are, after all, a form of tailoring on a much larger scale, but, unfortunately
for the archaeologist, they are organic artifacts, which perish rapidly when
abandoned. Like all working craft, hide vessels would have been short-
lived and often dismantled and partially recycled, another reason why
even their ribs never occur in archaeological sites. Hide boats may well
have been the first vessels used to cross the English Channel and the
North Sea and were widely used for thousands of years. A variation on
such vessels, known as currachs, survived in daily use in Ireland into the
twentieth century.

There was never a time when people living in Britain were unaware of
land across the water. Much of the southern North Sea was a low-lying
maze of marshes and wetlands long after the Ice Age. You could coast
your way along the borders of Doggerland from inlet to inlet in a hide

boat without trouble—perhaps, even, in a dugout in calm summer weather. As with everywhere else, knowledge about the coast, of changing weather conditions and important landmarks, of peoples living along the shore would have been passed from father to son, from one generation to the next. It must have been only a matter of time before someone took a short cut and paddled directly across the North Sea during a period of settled weather. To people used to spending much of their lives on the water, such a journey would have eventually been a straightforward enterprise, undertaken after careful assessment of potential risks. Any hunter is familiar with the heavenly bodies, with the movements of land birds. Those who spend much time on the water were well aware of the subtle clues that invisible coast was just over the horizon. Inevitably, too, the knowledge acquired on such passages—of sea conditions and places for safe landfall—would have passed down the centuries, as would the personal connections acquired by people living on the other side of the sea. In time, too, some travelers would have settled on the far coast, perhaps marrying into local groups, developing contacts to acquire exotic commodities and artifacts. Inevitably, newly acquired kin ties would have strengthened ties across the North Sea and the English Channel.

These contacts may have been sporadic at first, but they acquired increasing importance with the expansion of farming across Northern Europe in about 4000 B.C.E. Until then, hide boats were probably the boats of choice for carrying loads and people, but the emergence of domestic animals may have changed the seafaring equation fundamentally. Hide vessels, with their flexible hulls, would not have been ideal for carrying livestock across wider expanses of water. This may have been the point at which boatbuilders transferred their stitching skills to timber and began constructing sewn-plank boats, using the same thongs and weaves as they used on hide.

To STITCH PLANKS onto the sides of a dugout to increase its freeboard is simple enough for anyone used to splitting planks with stone wedges and polished axes. Later, bronze tools produced thinner, carefully shaped planks and larger boats with enhanced load-carrying abilities. There were no nails, so the builders sewed the planks together with yew fiber, then caulked the seams with moss.

Remnants of ten such sewn-plank boats have come to light in Britain. Teasing together the fragments gives us a portrait of boats built with beveled oak planks, braced with cleats and cross-timbers to make them rigid.[6] Unlike dugouts, these were larger vessels, up to 60 feet (18 meters) long, capable of carrying as many as twenty people, with a slightly higher freeboard than a log boat. All the sewn boats we know come from estuary shores or coasts, which strongly suggests that they were used for longer, open-water journeys. Like early dugouts and hide boats, these large craft were almost certainly paddled. There is no evidence of sails or stout mast steps among the surviving fragments.

Some of the best-known sewn boats come from the Humber River area of northeastern England, which includes a location at North Ferriby where they appear to have been constructed on the foreshore—oak chips lay amid worked timbers. This is the earliest known boatyard in the world. A canoe unearthed at nearby Hasholme has a hollowed-out oak hull, a transom stern with strengthening beams, and a composite bow made in several parts. The builder attached washboards to either side, securing them in place with wooden pegs, presumably to increase the loading capacity and to raise the sides for safety in slightly rougher water. The entire Humber area formed an intertidal wetland with a series of natural harbors that served as a crossroads for trading activities of all kinds—perhaps even for open-water passages across the North Sea.

One of the sewn boats, in the form of a much-eroded plank, comes from Kilnsea, about two and a half miles (four kilometers) north of Spurn Head, at the mouth of the Humber River, and dates to between 1750 and 1620 B.C.E. At the time, Kilnsea was an estuarine wetland, the outermost navigable inlet of the Humber, making it an ideal location both for departing to cross the North Sea and for vessels making landfall.[7] The northern shores of the Kilnsea inlet also supported what appears to have been a ritual landscape. As early as 3800 B.C.E., Stone Age farmers were living there. Their descendants built a small circular monument, known to archaeologists as a henge, between 2600 and 2000 B.C.E. Two circular burial mounds covering individual graves rose on the beach

Figure 10.2 *A reconstruction of the Ferriby boat, from northeastern England. Hull and East Riding Museum: Hull Museums.*

in about 2000 B.C.E.; others are known to exist nearby but have not been investigated. Pollens from the sites tell us that forest with large clearings covered much of the landscape, but why so many ritual monuments lay at this particular location is a mystery.

Most sewn-plank boats were used for fishing, cross-estuary travel, and local load carrying. All were also, theoretically, capable of crossing open water, even the North Sea when weather conditions were favorable. Rapid passages in such craft were certainly practicable. Judging from experiments with a modern reconstruction of one of the Ferriby boats, an expert crew would have taken about twenty-four hours to paddle across to the European coast from Spurn Head, at the mouth of the Humber, in calm water—an average speed of about 5 knots (9.25 kilometers an hour). This is a remarkably fast time and speaks volumes for the efficiency of the sewn-plank boat. Actual speeds would have been lower, especially with heavily laden canoes operating in waves. The maximum load for one of these craft was about 12 tons (11 metric tons). Locally, their cargoes would have been passengers and prosaic commodities such as grain or cattle.

Figure 10.3 *The Dover boat. Canterbury Archaeological Trust.*

Another sewn boat comes from Dover, dating to between 1575 and 1520 B.C.E.[8] Thirty-one feet (9.4 meters) of the boat survive, the planks hewn from straight-grained oaks whose trunks, without branches, were at least 36 feet (11 meters) long, an extreme rarity in Europe today. Two planks carved out of a half log form the bottom, with cleats and rails that allowed them to be jointed to curved side planks sewn with strong and flexible twisted yew stems. The carved wooden bow somewhat resembled that of a modern punt. Beeswax and animal fat caulked the stitching holes, while a second row of planks once lay above the first pair. Pads of moss wadding and thin oak lathes covered the stopped seams. Some of the original tool marks on the bottom were almost worn away, as if the boat had grounded on sand and gravel spits on many occasions.

A GREAT DEAL of effort went into the Dover boat and other such sewn vessels—so much that one wonders why, given the limited advantages of a sewn boat over a hide one. As the archaeologist Stuart Needham has argued, such craft may been used for special purposes, such as the acquisition of exotic objects from afar. To build a sewn boat required much labor, large planks, and skilled artisans, so that the very act of construction may have been a gesture of conspicuous display, denoting that the owner was a member of an exclusive maritime group.

We can only guess at such associations, but by the Dover boat's time a significant number of exotic objects were arriving regularly in England from the Continent. Ceremonial flint daggers from Scandinavia, bronze artifacts of various kinds, jewelry, amber, as well as jet and faience from all manner of locations. Some of these luxuries arrived in the form of regular "tool kits" that appear in elite burials in both England and Ireland. The most famous of these come from lavishly decorated graves under burial mounds near Stonehenge, in southern England. Such interments are a clear sign that, for the first time, society had changed profoundly, with the emergence of prominent kin leaders who formed a wealthy elite. Much of the trade in exotic objects must have lain in their hands in the form of carefully arranged exchanges between fellow kin, often long distances apart. Judging from rich grave offerings, such artifacts, and the beliefs associated with them, accompanied their owners to the grave and beyond, for they were now revered ancestors, often buried in the heart of sometimes elaborate ritual landscapes. One of these may have been the burial mound complex at Kilnsea, on the edge of an ocean that stretched to the eastern horizon.[9]

The North Sea may have become the realm of the ancestors, but its coastal landscapes changed constantly as sea levels rose and fell in response to adjustments in the earth crusts and ever-changing cycles of colder and warmer climates. A few inches could make a significant difference. Footpaths vanished under rising water; low islands disappeared, scoured into oblivion by fast-moving currents; tidal surges nourished by severe gales would burst ashore without warning; shallow canoe passages used for generations would evaporate overnight. As a result, an expanding reservoir of memory surrounded the seascape. The archaeologist Robert Van de Noort believes that the North Sea became an actor in the histories and myths of the people who lived around it over thousands of years of often rapid environmental change.[10] One way of commemorating this was through honoring the ancestors who had paddled its waters in earlier times. Another was by making offerings of valuable stone and bronze artifacts either in encroaching wetlands or in deep water, both under circumstances where they would not be recovered again. At least fifty metal artifacts, including axes, chisels, and weapons such as rapiers and swords, and also a gold torc (arm ring), have come from wetlands associated with the Humber River. Isolated finds are known from much deeper water, including 182 swords, rapiers, and other weapons found 500 feet (152 meters) off the coast near Dover. Perhaps these artifacts come from shipwrecks, but they may equally well have been deliberate deepwater offerings to the gods.

Ancestral burial mounds overlooked the North Sea at Kilnsea. The ancestors under these mounds had once been people of prestige and wealth, whose position in society came both from kin ties and from their ability to command the loyalty of others. Their personal connections must have extended across the North Sea as part and parcel of the continuous and often ceremonial exchange networks that flourished for many centuries, their origins deep in the remote past. We know of these ties because of finds of virtually identical clay, beaker-like vessels on both sides of the North Sea, themselves associated in many instances with the package of exotic objects found in burial mounds.

Between about 2250 and 1950 B.C.E., there was a surge in the intensity of contacts across the English Channel and the North Sea, reflected by an increase in valuable objects and materials such as amber from the Continent. Exchanges in prestige goods between individuals were acts of political, social, and religious importance. Participation in such activities implies access to exotic knowledge and the artifacts associated with it. This would have meant embarking on journeys to other lands—to the Baltic for amber, to the Upper Rhine for bronze artifacts, and so on. Van de Noort believes that this expansion in prestige goods and exotica coincided with the development of sewn-plank boats that could be paddled to the Continent during much of the year. The journeys also allowed the growth of societies where prestige depended on acquiring wealth and social status to create larger retinues of followers. The sewn boat became a political and economic instrument for conducting voyages over open water to distant lands where acquiring contacts was the key to social, economic, and religious success. Out of these often enduring relationships came a pattern of interaction that involved all manner of rituals that engaged communities on either side of the Channel and the North Sea with one another and with the dangerous forces of the ocean. Perhaps—and this is, of course, pure speculation—ritual cups found on both sides of the divide served as symbols of libations and other rituals that surrounded seafaring.

The great European rivers that drained into the two seas, and also the Thames and many lesser streams, extended the maritime routes deep inland. Inshore islands, such as the Isle of Thanet, close to the mouth of the Thames estuary, often had unusual ritual associations. Thanet is rich in burial monuments of all kinds, as are the Orkney Islands, off northern Scotland, and the Ushant archipelago, off northwest Brittany. The Isles of Scilly, to the west of Britain, are well endowed with burial monuments and cairns. Both Ushant and Scilly are in the open sea—portals, as it were, to the open Atlantic and to Ireland and western Britain. There were many crossing routes involving islands, notably the Channel Islands, which were a convenient stepping-stone from Europe to Britain across to the strategic rivers of Wessex, in southern England.[11] The Thames estuary was a natural outlet for trade across the southern North Sea and over the narrows. By the first millennium B.C.E., the waters of the English Channel and the North Sea were thoroughly known and regularly traversed by both sewn-plank boats and hide boats, engaged not only in voyages with powerful ritual undertones but with much more prosaic trade and economic activities of all kinds.

HIDE BOATS WERE the workhorses of Northern European seafarers, for they were capable of long voyages offshore—across the mouth of the English Channel and over the Irish Sea, rough and unpredictable waters at any time of year. Judging from the accounts of classical writers, these boats were commonplace. A sea guide of the sixth century B.C.E., quoted by poet Rufus Festus Avienus in his *Ora Maritima* (*Sea Coasts*) during the fourth century after Christ, refers to tough, proud traders apparently living near Cape Finisterre, in northwestern Spain, or in Britanny, who plied "the widely troubled sea and swell of the monster-filled ocean with skiffs of skin . . . [They] marvelously fit out boats with joined skins and often run through the vast salt water on leather."[12]

During the third century B.C.E., the historian Timaeaus, quoted by Pliny in his *Natural History*, wrote that "there is an island named Mictis lying six days inwards from Britain where tin is to be found and to which the Britons cross in boats of wicker covered with sewn hides."[13] Quite where Mictis was is unknown, but it may have been the French coast. According to the geographer Strabo, writing in the first century, the peoples of northwestern Iberia (Spain) "used boats of tanned leather on account of the flood tides and the shoal-waters."[14] Such vessels were ideal for the fast-running rides and sandbanks of local waters. Even Julius Caesar ordered hide vessels constructed to cross a river in Spain "of a kind that his knowledge of Britain a few years before had taught him" during the Great Roman Civil War.[15]

We have no idea what these hide boats looked like, except for one tantalizing clue. In 1896, an Irish farmer at Broighter, on the shores of Lough Foyle, in County Derry, found a hoard of seven gold objects, including a massive arm ring, two wire necklaces, and two models—one of a cauldron, the other of a boat. The goldsmith depicted what is almost certainly a hide boat of elongated oval shape with a large steering oar at the stern. Nine benches served for the rowers; eighteen oars and oarlocks provided human propulsion. A mast step amidships supported the mast and a yard for a large square sail. The model is only 8 inches (20 centimeters) long, but scaled up, it would probably have been a stout hide boat up to 51 feet (15.5 meters) long.[16] The Broighter boat depicted a tough seagoing vessel, fully capable of handling rough Atlantic seas.

Thousands of Irish currachs remained in use into the twentieth century, and replicas thrive to this day. In 1901, the Irish writer and poet J. M. Synge experienced a hair-raising passage in a currach among the Aran Islands, off western Ireland. It was a stormy morning, but the tide turned at two o'clock and the men thought the seas would be calmer. "The eldest son of the family was coming with me and I considered that the old man, who knew the waves better than I did, would not send out

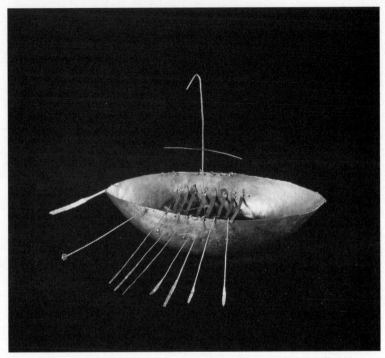

Figure 10.4 *The Broighter boat, probably part of a votive offering to the sea god, dating to the first century* B.C.E. *Length: 7.71 inches (19.6 centimeters). Courtesy National Museum of Ireland, Dublin.*

his son if there was more than reasonable danger." The old man re-marked: "'A man who is not afraid of the sea will soon be drownded, for he will be going out on a day he shouldn't. But we do be afraid of the sea, and we do only be drownded now and again.'" The crew checked the oar pins and braces with sedulous care, then launched the four-oared boat. A small rag of sail carried them over large waves abeam of their course. The steersman used his oar to turn the boat so it was heading toward the largest waves. As the boat fell into a furrow, the steersman let go his oar and clung on with both hands. The oarsmen rowed frantically when the wave was past, only to have the same violent maneuver repeated time and time again. Sometimes the steersman would cry out *"Siubhal, siubhal"* ("Run, run"). The oarsmen would bend to

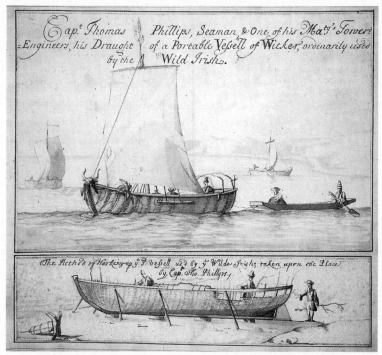

Figure 10.5 *An Irish currach, drawn by Captain Thomas Phillips in the late seventeenth century. Pepys Library, Magdalene College, Cambridge.*

their oars and the boat darted ahead, stern to a large wave, trying frantically to avoid a capsize. "Our lives depended on the skill and courage of the men, as the life of the rider or swimmer is often in his own hands, and the excitement of the struggle was too great to allow time for fear." Incredibly, Synge enjoyed the passage: "Down in this shallow trough of canvas that bent and trembled with the motion of the men, I had a far more intimate feeling of the glory and power of the waves than I had ever known in a steamer."[17]

Hide boats were remarkable for their simplicity, lightness, and seaworthiness. However, seafaring in the northwestern Atlantic required careful timing, for the tides run strong. A favorable stream would speed a laden ship on its way; to set sail in the face of a contrary tide was to stand still, make limited progress, or even drift backwards. Much depended, also, on when one traveled. The spring tides of the full moon brought extreme tidal ranges between high and low and powerful flows; neap tides saw much weaker streams and the minimum range. There were no predictable wind shifts here like the trades or monsoon breezes of the tropics. Gales blew from any direction throughout the year. Winds could rise and fall in minutes, shift from bow to stern in moments. Coasting in these waters required tracking rapidly shifting conditions, especially when a strong onshore wind turned even a hospitable coastline into a hazardous lee shore. For this reason, experienced sailors tended to sail farther offshore into clear water, well away from headlands like Ushant and Land's End, in Cornwall.

Over the centuries, both merchant vessels and warships preferred two major sea routes from Spain and Southern Europe into northern waters. Both took advantage of prevailing westerly winds and as little open-water mileage as possible. A westerly course passed from the Bay of Biscay into the Irish Sea, then northward into the stormy waters of the Hebrides and western Scotland. Britain separated the Irish route from a course that took the voyager through the narrows of the English Channel, then into the often rough tidal waters of the North Sea. The Channel route required careful use of tidal streams but had the advantage of mainly westerly winds that carried one eastward with relative ease.

As was the case elsewhere, most of these routine voyages took place off the radar screen of history. However, in about 320 B.C.E., a Massalian (Marseille) merchant known as Pytheas the Greek went on a voyage into northern waters. He wrote a book entitled *On the Ocean* about his experiences.[18] Alas, his original work is lost, but later writers drew on it extensively, so we have at least a general impression of his explorations. He traveled overland along well-trodden routes from the Mediterranean to the mouth of the Gironde, on the Biscay coast, thereby saving hundreds of miles, then along the Brittany coast, where, among others, the Veneti in the present-day Morbihan region were expert mariners. Their homeland lay in a strategic position, with comfortable anchorages for ships bound northward from the Gironde and Loire estuaries that were about to embark on the much more perilous journey around the Armorican Peninsula, in extreme northwestern Brittany, inshore of Ushant. The entire area was an important nexus of long-distance exchanges, along what is now the French coast and across the mouth of the English Channel to Cornwall, where tin was to be obtained.

From Brittany to the Cornish coast is a distance of about 109 miles (175 kilometers). Northbound, the passage would have been a straightforward run for a hide boat before the prevailing southwesterlies at the mouth of the Channel, perhaps a twenty-four-hour run for a seaworthy sailing vessel with a large square sail. The landfalls along the Cornish coast are relatively straightforward, for there are many conspicuous landmarks and high cliffs, with deep water close inshore, leading to sheltered estuaries like the Fal and the Fowey. The strongest tidal streams run near the Brittany coast, which made for serious navigational complications on the return journey toward a shoreline armored with jagged offshore rocks and with low-lying terrain inshore. A wise seafarer attempted this passage in clear weather so that he could identify landmarks far offshore and make adjustments for the cross-tides inshore in good time.

Pytheas crossed the Channel along a route followed by tin traders. Little remains of their activities, except a couple of shipwrecks. A Bronze Age wreck complete with tin ingots has come from the Salcombe region of Devon, and another from a reef at the mouth of the River Erme. Nothing remains of the ships themselves, just finds of tin ingots once neatly stacked in their holds. From Britain, Pytheas sailed on to the Irish Sea at a time when the waters of Northern Europe were already alive with hide boats. He traveled northward along coastlines where ocean waves broke against rugged cliffs and mountains were close to the sea, perhaps as far north as Orkney. There he would have certainly seen great monuments like the Standing Stones of Stenness, the Ring of Brodgar, and the great burial mound of Maeshowe. The tumulus and towering stone circles were already 3,000 years old in Pytheas's day, parts of a long-vanished ritual landscape designed to be as visible from the water as from land. They commemorated the close links between the living and their ancestors, who inhabited the supernatural realms of the ocean. Pytheas may have heard folk legends of the people who erected these stupendous monuments, and of voyages to remote lands carried out by people of power. He may also have spoken with people who had sailed far northward over the open ocean, to what he called a "congealed sea" and a place called Thule, often assumed to be Iceland, which lay six days' sea time north of Britain.

Did Pytheas reach Iceland and visit the pack ice, said to be a day's sail farther north? As with so much else, the evidence is ambiguous. Certainly the hide boats of the day would have been capable of the journey of more than 500 miles (800 kilometers) if their skippers picked their weather and season carefully. Later writers, familiar with Pytheas's now lost book, tell us that he wrote of days without night. Whether he visited the island is still uncertain, but he probably landed in Shetland, where he would likely have heard stories of a large island far to the north. The Shetlanders would have been well aware of the spring and autumn migrations of birds such as geese and the whooper swan, with its bugle-like call and distinctive V-shaped flying formation, a sign of land over the horizon. These people were farmers and above all fisherfolk, who were used to taking cod in deep water—and some of the best cod-fishing grounds in the North Atlantic are off the southern Icelandic coast. They

Figure 10.6 *Maeshowe burial mound in the Orkney Islands, c. 3000 B.C.E., perhaps seen by Pytheas the Greek.* © *Doug Hamilton/Alamy.*

certainly would have used hide boats to travel there, for trees are rare in this cold and windy archipelago. Pytheas's hosts undoubtedly had the maritime technology and the knowledge of a deciphered ocean to do so.

By Pytheas's time, there were seafarers crisscrossing the North Sea, sailing across the English Channel, and venturing into the open Atlantic long before the Norse burst forth from their northern fastnesses in the tenth century C.E. There is, of course, the great Saint Brendan (?484–577 C.E.), sometimes called the Navigator, famous for setting out into the Atlantic in a currach on a search for the Land of Delight, the Garden of Eden. *The Life of St. Brendan* describes how his party constructed a currach with a wickerwork frame, "as is the custom in their country."[19] They tanned ox hides with oak bark and caulked the seams with pitch, carrying butter with them to grease the hides. Brendan's powerful currach was large enough to carry seventeen people and had a square sail set amidships. The voyage is said to have taken seven years, taking Brendan and his companions to a blessed island covered with lush vegetation. His voyage, probably partly fact and partly legend, has generated speculation ever since. One theory has it that he colonized the Shetland Islands, which were settled by monks at about this time. Brendan returned to Ireland convinced that he had discovered Paradise—and encountered a sea monster on the way. So did his contemporary Saint Columba. According to his biographer, the learned Adomnán, abbot of Iona (627/8–704 C.E.), Columba completed many open-water passages in seagoing currachs with oars and a square sail set on a center mast.

But even in Pytheas's day, new ship designs were transforming human knowledge of the ocean. As we have seen, Pytheas stopped among the Veneti of Brittany, where he may have seen and even traveled in their strong wooden ships, developed over many centuries. Three centuries later, Julius Caesar encountered and defeated Venetian ships in a memorable sea battle in Quiberon Bay. He admired their design, perfectly adapted to local waters:

"The . . . ships were built and rigged in a different way from ours. Their keels were somewhat flatter, so they could cope more easily with the shoals and shallow water when the tide was ebbing; their prows were unusually high, and so were their sterns, designed to stand up to great waves and violent storms. The hulls were made entirely of oak to ensure against any violent shock or impact."[20]

Massive cross-beams and iron bolts "as thick as a man's thumb" held Venetian ships together. Their anchor cables were of iron chain, and their sails of hide or soft leather. Caesar described ships admirably suited for local conditions, easy to heave to offshore, where they would ride out even a violent gale in relative comfort. If caught near the shore, their flat bottoms enabled them to lie on the bottom at low tide in shallow water, even on rocky shores. Venetian ships had developed over many centuries in response to the often savage weather conditions of the Brittany coast, where 25-foot (7.6-meter) tidal ranges are commonplace and the tides run strong. It was for this reason that their sailors carried iron chain for their anchors: sharp-edged rocks on the bottom would soon wear through a fiber cable. From these and other skillfully crafted wooden boats evolved the magnificent Norse ships of later centuries, described in Chapter 11.

CHAPTER 11

"Storms Fell on the Stern in Icy Feathers"

"WILL HE ROUND THE POINT?" The famed Danish artist Michael Ancher's painting mesmerized me. A fierce gale blows from the southwest at Skagen, a fishing port where the North Sea meets the Kattegat, the strait that separates Norway and northern Denmark. The rain has stopped, but a tremendous sea rolls into the outer harbor. Ancher painted a cluster of fishermen standing at breaker's edge during an 1879 storm. Their eyes are fixed on the sea. One man points as they watch an unseen vessel driving helplessly toward shore. Silently, they stare unflinchingly into the biting wind, their faces as hard and unrelenting as the force of the storm. These were tough men, bred to the sea, who knew no other life. Even as recently as the 1950s, four hundred fishing boats still left Skagen every twenty-four hours, crewed by fishermen who thought nothing of playing cards around a red-hot stove while a North Sea winter gale blew up above.

Another Ancher painting shows two Skagen fishermen leaning against a boat and gazing into the teeth of the wind. Their bearded, weatherbeaten faces are stern and unyielding, the land at their backs. Only the turbulent Kattegat is their company. You know, looking at these paintings, that these were men apart, with the very meaning of the ocean etched in their faces.[1]

To their medieval forebears of a millennium ago, the ancestors of Skagen fishermen and other such sailors along the Atlantic coast, the western coasts of Europe were the frontiers of the earth. The sun set in

Figure 11.1 *Michael Ancher,* Vil Han Klare Pynten *(* Will He Round the Point?*). Private collection: akg-images.*

an unknown, watery abyss, peopled by savage beasts and capricious waterspouts. Here, the terrible monster Leviathan lurked in the depths, ready to consume men's souls and drag them down to Hell. Leviathan was a force of chaos, conquered only by Faith: "It was You who drove back the sea with Your might, who smashed the heads of the monsters in the waters. It was You who crushed the heads of Leviathan, who left him as food for the creatures of the wilderness."[2] The Atlantic shore was a symbolic frontier between the heavenly firmament of the land, with its life-giving freshwater that sustained Christian existence, and the salty ocean. Those who sailed even its inshore waters took their lives into their hands every time they went afloat.

The Atlantic occupied a powerful place in both English and Irish lore. A short Anglo-Saxon poem, "The Seafarer," preserved in a tenth-century book in Exeter Cathedral, writes of the loneliness of life afloat, of a frigid place devoid of human company:

Figure 11.2 *Michael Ancher,* To Fiskere Ved en Bad *(Two Fishermen Beside a Boat). Staten Museum for Kunst. SMK Foto.*

There I heard nothing save the harsh sea
And ice-cold wave . . .
Seafowls' loudness was for me laughter,
The mews singing all my mead-drink.
Storms, on the stone cliffs beaten, fell on the stern in icy feathers.[3]

Generations of scholars have argued over "The Seafarer." Is it an allegory, a symbolic journey like that of life, or an early recognition that the English as islanders would one day be forced to make their living from the deeper waters that were their turbulent neighbors? Perhaps it represents a record of ocean sailing; we will never know. But it does reflect the loneliness, even powerlessness, of life at sea. The verses don't allow us to decipher the poet's intent.

The Atlantic was a feared wilderness, but, inevitably, dread and superstition gave way to a greater familiarity with open water. By the ninth

Figure 11.3 *European locations in Chapter 11 and the Epilogue.*

and tenth centuries, Irish monks led the way. They sailed northward from western Scotland to the Orkney and Shetland islands, then to the Faroes. A few even settled in Iceland, solitary folk in quest of hermitlike seclusion where they could devote themselves to God. Early histories tell us they traveled in strong hide boats braced with wooden frames. Such was their faith in the afterlife that they cared little about the hazards of the open ocean. Piety does much to conquer fear of the unknown. Soon afterward, Norse and other sailors with more pragmatic objectives followed in their wake.

THE OLD NORSE word *æfintyr* means "venture," a word that implies a strong element of risk, and the fear and excitement of facing the unknown and unpredictable. Open water was no place for the ordinary traveler, who crossed the North Sea or the Bay of Biscay with fear and trepidation, at the mercy of shipwreck, storms, or pirates. But the spirit of adventure and excitement was irresistible to those who enjoyed voyages in well-built ships. Such voyages gave power, prestige, and mobility—the ability to move across the known world and to its edges like gods and chiefs. The ship often became a kind of mobile church that carried its crew through stormy waters. Ultimately, it was *æfintyr* that turned coasting Norse into offshore explorers. Having been compared to one's stormy and often troubled passage through life, or the living emblem of Hell, the Western Ocean now became a prosaic, matter-of-fact part of existence for those who lived on its shores and possessed closely held knowledge of its secrets.

The voyages that took Norse sailors to Iceland and beyond in the late tenth century were the culmination of centuries of coastal trading. Coastal distances were relatively short, crossings like that of the North Sea often a matter of little more than a day at sea. By Roman times, tramping was routine, from the Bay of Biscay to the Baltic and along the Norwegian coast.[4] From the earliest times, a wide, and little-known, diversity of watercraft paddled these waters, reflecting the great variety of coastal environments. In Ireland, where beaches were often small and exposed to Atlantic swells, light, flexible hide boats were ideal, for they were easily hauled above the high-water mark. Elsewhere, the log boats of earlier times, their freeboards raised by sewn planks, slowly gave way to more sophisticated planked vessels, which ultimately became the ancestors of Norse ships and other boatbuilding traditions.

Planked ships were well established in the dangerous tidal waters of Brittany by 56 B.C.E., when Julius Caesar observed the planked vessels of the Veneti there. Their builders used iron nails to fasten the planks to the frames, constructing the framework first, then adding the planks, a sharp contrast to the northern practice of building the hull, then adding the frames. The dominant technology, however, was still the expanded dugout, which, with its gently curved shape, was more at home in smoother water—just as such canoes were in the Pacific Northwest. Centuries of experience building expanded dugouts provided the basic shape and internal structure of the later Norse ship. A number of fundamental changes took hold: The builders shifted from softer to harder, straight-grained woods like oak and pine, which were easier to split and more durable. Most northern ships began with a straight-grained tree trunk, to which were added split planks—carefully thinned and carved to save weight, then fitted together with cleats and lashings. Gradually, iron fastenings replaced stitched fastenings for overlapping planks. Perhaps most important of all, paddling gave way to rowing. (Oars, with their fixed pins or oarlocks attached to the side of the ship, provide much better leverage and better boat speed, especially in heavier vessels and against headwinds. It is not known when they first came into use.) Mercenaries serving in Roman fleets on the Danube and Rhine may have introduced some of these ideas to the north.

As always, we know of these innovations only from archaeological shreds and patches, from abandoned working boats and shipwrecks. One spectacular discovery, dating to the early seventh century C.E., provides a fascinating portrait not only of contemporary boatbuilding but also of burial customs associated with the sea. In 1939, the farmer turned archaeologist Basil Brown excavated a wide trench across a burial mound at Sutton Hoo, in eastern England, part of a complex of at least fourteen tumuli on a bluff overlooking the nearby River Deben.[5] He soon found five iron ship nails, all that survived of long-vanished planking buried in the mound, and suspected at once that he had come across a funerary boat. Using trowels and brushes, he and his workers cleared the bow and eleven frames of an Anglo-Saxon vessel, then exposed a sealed bulkhead. Wisely, he called for expert professional help, realizing the task was beyond his expertise. The Cambridge University archaeologist Charles Phillips, an expert on ancient timber structures, took over. He followed gray discolorations in the mound soil and traced the lines of the boat and planked burial chamber that lay amidships. Phillips recovered the treasure buried with the long-vanished body of a nobleman, which included metal cauldrons, bowls, spears, axes, bottles, and thirty-seven coins dating to about 650 C.E. The long-vanished

Figure 11.4 *Sutton Hoo, Mound 2: the day of burial. An artist's reconstruction. Drawn by Victor Ambrus. Courtesy British Museum Company.*

body was perhaps that of Anglo-Saxon king Rædwald, of the kingdom of the East Angles, who ruled c. 599–624, but the identification is tentative. In recent years, brilliant survey and excavation work by Martin Carver and his research team have greatly refined our knowledge of the burial and associated cemetery.

The burial ship was 89 feet (27 meters) long; thirty-eight oars propelled it. We have only the ghost of the hull to work with, but enough to establish that it was double-ended, with high bow posts and sternposts. The builders split nine narrow planks for each side, constructing the hull in clinker-built style, which means the planks overlapped one another, and were fastened not with cleats for lashing but with iron nails. There was no keel, but there was strengthening at the stern, as if a steering oar was mounted there. Nor was there a mast step or any signs of rigging, so the Sutton Hoo ship was apparently designed for rowing, not sailing. The mourners hauled it laboriously from the nearby River Deben nearly a mile (1.5 kilometers) to the summit of the bluff to form a final resting

Excavations at Sutton Hoo, England

Nine years of state-of-the-art archaeological excavation and survey, spread out between 1983 and 2001, under the direction of Martin Carver, a consummate excavator, revealed a great deal more about the Sutton Hoo cemetery. The project involved a three-year evaluation, followed by six years of excavation. The research began with surface survey and remote sensing using subsurface radar to identify the full extent of the cemetery area. The cemetery area turned out to be 2.5 acres (1 hectare) in extent, so large-scale area excavations were decided upon to identify and map its features. As result, Carver was able to show that Sutton Hoo had been occupied from before the Bronze Age, more than 4,000 years ago, during Roman times, and by the Anglo-Saxons.

The excavations investigated what was a prestigious cemetery for those of high status from the late sixth to the late seventh century C.E. Early burials were cremations, placed in bronze bowls under burial mounds. Later burials were inhumations, one of them a woman. Apart from excavating further in the classic burial mound, Carver investigated so-called Mound 17, one of only two tumuli in the cemetery, which had survived intact but was barely visible above the surface. Two burials survived under the mound, one of a high-status man in his twenties, buried with a sword, shield, cauldron, and horse harness, the other of his horse.

By carefully scraping and excavating large open areas, Carver used postholes and other subtle clues to show that the cemetery remained in use until the tenth or eleventh century, long after the royal burials. The excavators found numerous lower-status burials clustered around another mound at the eastern end of the cemetery. Only fragile, sandy outlines of the dead survived, identified with meticulous care. The outlines revealed that those buried in these graves had been brought to Sutton Hoo to be executed, many of them decapitated, others hung. The remains of a gallows came to light at the eastern end of the cemetery. Many of these excavations may date to the time of the royal burials.

> Sutton Hoo, with its human sacrifice and ship burial, was a pagan cemetery, with ties to Scandinavian beliefs at the time, the kingdom perhaps formed as a response to the emerging Christian empire of the Merovingians, which had already subjugated southeastern England.

place for its owner. A modern half-size replica constructed by a yacht builder, tested under oar and sail, proved fast and maneuverable in sheltered water. She sailed fast downwind and on a broad reach with a square sail but, having no keel, was hazardous to sail close to the wind. Under a double-reefed square sail, she was stable and safe in a strong wind, but she was difficult to tack and made no progress to windward. Whether the original ship was sailed still remains an open question.[6]

WHY DID NORTHERN peoples, Anglo-Saxons and Norse alike, engage in time-consuming ship burial?

Shield was still thriving when his time came
and he crossed over into the Lord's keeping.
His warrior band . . .
shouldered him out to the sea's flood,
the chief they revered who had long ruled them. . . .
They stretched their beloved lord in his boat,
laid out by the mast, amidships,
the great ring-giver. Far-fetched treasures
were piled upon him, and precious gear. . . .
And they set a gold standard up
high above his head and let him drift
to wind and tide, bewailing him
and mourning their loss.[7]

The early lines of the ninth-century epic poem *Beowulf* describe the funeral of the mythic chieftain Shield Sheafson (Scyld Scëfing), carried over the horizon in a funerary boat. Shield's burial rites were more elaborate than most, but boat burials were relatively commonplace during the first millennium c.e.[8] The reasons for boat burial elude us, for such coffins were far more than convenient repositories. Hollywood, with its beloved "Viking funerals," has wrongly condemned all Norse boats to serve as convenient firewood. Some ships were burned, but by no means all. Perhaps they were vehicles for carrying the dead to the next world or were symbols of power or of control over trading activities. Nor do we know how long such interments were fashionable. Almost certainly the custom goes back far into prehistoric times. A handful of spectacular ship burials in later times, such as the famous Gokstad and Oseberg ships, in Norway, and, of course, Sutton Hoo, testify to the wealth and splendor lavished on the funerals of prominent individuals in the late pre-Christian era. By no means all of them honored men. The Oseberg ship, with its magnificent wood carvings and textiles, commemorated a high-ranking woman with close ties to cults of fertility and death.

For all the lavish adornment of a few burials, the objects in them did not necessarily commemorate wealth and power but had much deeper symbolic meaning, now lost. Many boat graves without spectacular adornment may have reflected the role of the deceased in society, something that became clear with the excavation of the Slusegaard cemetery, on the southern coast of Bornholm Island, in the central Baltic. Two coastal sandbanks yielded 1,395 graves from between the first and fourth centuries c.e., most of them identified from impressions in the sand. Of the burials, one stood out, that of a man laid out with his weapons in a 17-foot (5-meter) boat set in a 20-foot (6-meter) trench. A second, upside-down boat served as a vaulted lid over the first. While the size of the ship clearly reflected the importance of the deceased, the myths of pre-Christian cosmology may account for boat burials. The ship was an icon for *Skidbladnir*, Old Norse for "assembled from thin pieces of wood," a mythic craft built by the gods and made of parts so small that it could be folded into a bag or unfolded to provide transportation for the gods on their voyages—always, of course, with a fair wind. The three gods Njor, Freyr, and Freya were the center of the cult of fertility and the passage of the seasons and also presided over safe navigation and good fishing. These busy gods further supervised the cycles of human life and death.

The most spectacular graves, like Sutton Hoo and Oseberg, come from the seventh to tenth centuries, when Christian beliefs threatened the ancient cults behind traditional power structures. The ship was a powerful icon, the vehicle for the deities that perpetuated the cycles of day and night, summer and winter, life and death. Early Scandinavian kings claimed descent from the god Freyr and other ancestral deities. The Danish archaeologist Ole Crumlin-Pederson believes that individuals who were *godar*—helpers in the fertility cults—had their names marked on ships or were buried in them. No one believed they would use the vessel to travel to another world, but it symbolized their role in society during life.

THE SUTTON HOO ship and other such craft were distant prototypes of the Norse ships of later centuries. Most famous among them is the so-called longship—fast, powerful, and a lethal assault weapon for marauding raiders. We don't know when they first came into use, but King Alfred, Christian king of the West Saxons, may be able to take some credit. A near-mythic figure in English history, he fought at least twice against Danish "sea-rovers," according to the *Anglo-Saxon Chronicle*, which also says Alfred's ships were "almost twice as long as the others, some with sixty oars, some more."[9] They also stood higher out of the water than their enemies' boats, being apparently more slender, double-ended vessels that were arguably the prototypes for the celebrated Norse warships of later centuries. However, Norwegian vessels may have been broader and higher on account of the difficult sea conditions off their coasts.

Hedeby, in Jutland's Schlei fjord, close to the northern German city of Schleswig, was one of the great medieval harbors of the Baltic region. The port was a desirable place and was attacked on at least three occasions, then sacked by the Norwegian king Harald Hardrada in 1051. The remains of a Danish longship from Hedeby suggest a long vessel, 98 feet (30 meters) in length—built, so tree rings from the timbers tell us, around 985 C.E.[10] She must have moved fast in calm water, for she was about eleven times longer than she was wide. The excavators recovered much of the port side and discovered that the ten-to-twenty-year-old ship had been burned down to the waterline along its full length. She was filled with brushwood, then set afire and cast adrift on an easterly wind to drift down into the harbor defenses. The fire ship passed into the inner harbor and sank against one of the piers. Written records are sparse, but it seems most likely that the attack took place in 999 or 1000. At the time, Hedeby had a semicircular earthen defense wall on the landward side and a large wooden harbor palisade, the entrance defended by wooden watchtowers built on piles. This may have been why the Norwegians took a relatively new, captured Danish ship, more suitable for shallower, more sheltered waters than for their rugged coast, to set the watchtowers aflame.

We tend to think of Norse ships in terms of the longships, favorites of Hollywood Viking funerals, but Norwegians used all manner of vessels large and small. Their ships traveled familiar maritime trade routes that followed coasts from the Bay of Biscay to the North Cape, throughout the North Sea, along Irish and Scottish coasts, and far into the Baltic, many of them dating back to Roman times and even earlier. Like most such ventures, the voyages were unsung, far from the limelight, but engaged thousands of humble ships over the centuries. Just occasionally, we learn something of these enterprises. Sometime between 871 and 899 C.E., Ohthere, a wealthy foreigner from Helgoland, in what is now northern Norway, visited the court of King Alfred. A man of substance, Ohthere was a landowner and farmer who kept reindeer and cattle and went whale hunting on occasion. He is said to have killed sixty small whales, or perhaps walruses, in two days. The visitor had traveled widely, as far north as the North Cape and the Kola Peninsula and deep into the Baltic Sea, but whether he was a merchant or engaged in diplomatic missions is uncertain. Alfred welcomed interesting visitors, which may account for Ohthere's presence at his court, perhaps during a trip to other parts of the country, such as Viking York. He enthralled the king with an account of his voyages, which has come down to us in the form of a stilted question-and-answer session. Nevertheless, this provides us with some valuable information on coastal passage making at the time.[11]

Ohthere's ship was probably a large sailing-and-rowing vessel, with a crew of perhaps thirty to forty men, sufficient both to row long distances and to fight off pirates. We can be almost certain that his voyages unfolded during the sailing season, from April to September. Frequent gales precluded most winter sailing. Wind, cold, and darkness militated against voyages of more than two days during these months. As much as fifteen hours of summer daylight allowed uninterrupted passages of several days, for it is never totally dark at midnight in these waters. The worst days for night sailing would have been those during moonless periods. These are waters of unpredictable weather and constantly changing wind directions, so much so that Ohthere and his contemporaries would have made every possible use of fair winds.

We don't know exactly where Ohthere lived, but his home lay somewhere near or north of the island of Kvaløya, near Tromsø. He described three voyages to Alfred's court, one from his home, north into unknown waters around North Cape, as far east as the Varzuga River, and around the Kola Peninsula, in modern-day Russia. He also described the familiar waters southward along the Norwegian coast to Kaupang, in southern Norway, a distance of about 1,128 miles (1,815 kilometers) if sailing outside the islands. This voyage, said Ohthere, could be completed in a month if one camped at night and each day had *ambyrne wind*—favorable wind. His third sail took him from Kaupang down the Swedish coast, then across through the Schlei fjord to Hedeby, in Denmark, a passage that took him five days, apparently under favorable conditions.

A North Cape voyage was another matter. Ohthere and his men sailed "as far as he could sail" when the winds were favorable, with the sea on their port side. The six-day journey would have been stressful, for numerous small islands lie off the coast that would have been hard to see in poor visibility. At North Cape, the land "turned east, or the sea into the land, he did not know which of the two." In a few hours, they left the terms of coastal reference they had used from childhood, for the mainland, fortunately devoid of offlying islands, now lay to the south.

He waited for "a wind from the west and slightly north . . . [then] sailed east along the coast as far as he could sail in four days." Then the shoreline turned south and he had to wait for a north wind. When the wait ended, Ohthere sailed "in a southerly direction as far as he could sail in five days." They turned into a large river, "because they dared not sail on past . . . because of hostility." So he turned around and made for familiar waters.[12] If his accounts are to be relied on, Ohthere averaged between 48 and 95 miles (78 and 154 kilometers) a day, even sailing extremely cautiously and waiting for favorable winds.

Seafaring along Europe's coasts and across the English Channel, the North Sea, and elsewhere required hard-won knowledge of tides and currents, of landmarks, conspicuous and inconspicuous, along the way. Coasting ships and fisherfolk navigated across shallows and deeper waters, over vistas of featureless waves, but with subsurface landscapes identified by lead-and-line, that became like second nature to them. As a North Sea fisherman remarked in the 1880s, "There's nothin' in the world can be easier, when you've learned your lesson, than to pick your way about in the North Sea just with nothing else to guide yer than the depth o'water an' the natur' o' the bottom." The *Seebuch*, a fifteenth-century German guide to northern waters, refers again and again to the colors of mud and shingle brought up from the bottom by lead-and line. The same must have been true in Ohthere's day, as it was right into the early twentieth century. "They pride themselves upon carrying the art of navigation in their heads," remarked the German humanist Georg Joachim von Lauchen of a Prussian skipper in 1540.[13] Scores of small boats and traders threaded their way through narrow channels in eastern England, in the Danish archipelago, and in Swedish waters with only their local knowledge and a lead-and-line to help them. The days of navigation beacons and buoys were long in the future.

LIKE EASTERN MEDITERRANEAN trade routes, the courses taken by tramping vessels changed little over the generations. For many centuries, Northern European merchants conducted their business with oar power. Oars also propelled warships. Both raiders and settlers crossed the North

Sea in longboats under oars as early as the fifth and sixth centuries. Some two centuries later, Scandinavian seafarers developed sailing vessels that enabled them to undertake much longer voyages. Many of these passages were coastings like Ohthere's, taking them along familiar routes deep into the eastern Baltic and also up navigable rivers into the heart of continental Europe. Their Atlantic trading extended from the White Sea, in the far north, to the Mediterranean, in the south, the salt trade from the Noirmoutier area of the Bay of Biscay being especially lucrative, given the burgeoning demand for salted fish of all kinds for consumption both at sea and on holy days ashore.

According to Crumlin-Pedersen, Nordic mercenaries may well have observed sails in use on the Danube and the Rhine, but sailing had few immediate advantages. A rig of any size required large quantities of expensive leather or sailcloth as well as numerous long ropes of different sizes. Furthermore, Norse ships carried large crews to defend their cargoes against pirates and raiders. The same crew served as oarsmen for both coastal and river passages, giving the ship enough moving power to make headway against currents and strong contrary winds. By rowing in shifts, the crew could continue their passage throughout the day without interruption.

Converting an oars-only longship into a combined sailing-and-rowing craft required considerable modifications of the hull design. Apart from developing hulls with long, straight keels and curved, steeply raised ends that differed from the raked stems of earlier ships, the builders had to strengthen the hull to accommodate the stresses engendered by the rig. Numerous experiments went into sail shape as well, until seaworthy and efficient sailing vessels developed. They assumed various forms, from the fast longships used by raiders and warriors, through multipurpose ships (the Gokstad ship in Norway, from about 895 C.E., is an example), to stout *knarrs*, designed predominantly as merchant ships and load carriers.

The refinements in seagoing vessels led to an explosion in Norse seafaring, much of it in the form of raids across the North Sea and as far as Ireland.[14] Monasteries were a primary target, for they were often repositories of valuables for the surrounding countryside in times of trouble. The Norse marauders had no compunction about ravaging and destroying religious houses and killing their monks, for they were of a different faith. In fact, however, regular trade assumed far greater importance in Norse seafaring. Numerous merchant ships sailed out of centers like Hedeby. Ribe, on the western shore of the Jutland Peninsula, and Kaupang, in southern Norway, became major, organized trade centers. At Ribe, for example, founded as early as 710 C.E., the Norse, with their clinker-built open-water ships, traded with Frisians from what is now the Netherlands, who arrived in shallow draft vessels. Excavations in the port have uncovered huge piles of cattle dung, for live beasts were apparently traded by ship from Norway and landed here in exchange for quern stones and luxury items such as jewelry from inland. Ribe even had its own mint and was also a major center for trade between Denmark and England for many centuries.

These trading centers were cosmopolitan communities, where Norse rubbed shoulders with Anglo-Saxons, Franks, Frisians, and Slavs, and even perhaps with some people from the Middle East. These were safe havens, neutral places in a wider world beset by political conflict, highly fluid alliances, and violence. Commerce and raiding coexisted. Meanwhile, Norse fleets grew and raiding became more organized, even as far south as the Mediterranean. Instead of small raids led by chieftains, rulers and princes now organized larger expeditions, anxious to establish settlers under their political control across the North Sea, especially in the British Isles and in Normandy. As far as settling in northeastern England was concerned, the newcomers could have farmed and fished in environments that shared many common features with their homelands. In Ireland, the Norse maintained strongholds such as Dublin for centuries. From these, they provided mercenaries to warring Irish kings, and they developed trades that were exported along with slaves to Britain and the Franks.

By the ninth century, a full-fledged maritime culture based on the Norse tradition of ship construction flourished across Northern Europe from the Baltic to Ireland, along western Scotland, and as far north as Shetland and the Orkneys.[15] During the eleventh century, King Cnut the Great presided over a "North Sea Empire" that encompassed not only his English domains but also Denmark, Norway, and parts of central Sweden. After Cnut's death in 1035, war broke out between King Svein Estridsson of Denmark and King Harald Hardrada of Norway. Hardrada burned down Hedeby and attempted an invasion of England in 1066 but was defeated at the Battle of Stamford Bridge, in Yorkshire. Shortly afterward, Duke William of Normandy invaded England from the south and changed history.

Hardrada's ships failed to penetrate Roskilde fjord, near modern-day Copenhagen. Fortunately for science, the fjord's defenders sank a barrier of merchant vessels and a warship, combined with a barrier of wooden stakes that kept the invaders out. Thanks to years of careful excavation and reconstruction work, we know a great deal about the Roskilde ships, especially the stout *knarrs*, which were the workhorses of Norse trade and exploration. The so-called *Skuldelev* 1 ship is a medium-size Norwegian *knarr*, 54 feet (16.5 meters) long, built of pine planks felled in western Norway in about 1030. This hardworking vessel, probably designed for the eastern Baltic trade, was repaired three times with new oak planks. It had a half deck fore and aft, high sides, and a full bow with well-developed tumble-home planking that enhanced seaworthiness. The ship could carry a load of between 20 and 25 tons (18 to 23 metric tons), a perfect capacity for coastal trading, with stone ballast added as necessary. The Danes have reconstructed a full-size replica with traditional methods to study its seaworthiness and sailing abilities. *Ottar*, named in honor of Ohthere, has sailed from Hedeby to Gdansk, in Poland, and also crossed the North Sea to Edinburgh.

While sailing in Tahiti some years ago, I chanced upon a Norwegian replica of the same ship, which was in the process of circumnavigating the globe. She was bound for Fiji in a few days. I did not envy the crew, who ate, slept, and lived entirely in the open. The passages cannot have been comfortable, even with a modicum of modern comforts at their disposal. Sea trials with a replica of another Roskilde ship, *Skuldelev 3*, a small, 46-foot (14-meter) coastal trader probably used by a farmer to go to market, show that Norse ships could tack against the wind at an angle of sixty degrees, giving them a speed of about 1 to 2 knots (1.8 to

Figure 11.5 Skuldelev 1, *a replica of a Norse* knarr. *Courtesy Viking Ship Museum, Roskilde, Denmark.*

3.7 kilometers per hour) against the wind. Their remarkably flexible hulls allowed them to weather rough seas when offshore. Downwind, they could achieve impressive speeds of 8 knots (15 kilometers per hour) or more.

Largely because of the Roskilde finds and well-preserved ship burials, Norse shipbuilding tradition, as opposed to later medieval boatbuilding, tends to dominate the archaeological literature, but we know from pictures and occasional references that there were, in fact, many vessel forms, especially merchant ships. Cogs, known from a wreck near Bremen, were bulk carriers used extensively by Hanseatic merchants in northern waters, designed with straight sides and a single square rig to transport heavy loads such as barrels of salted fish or wine. (The Hansa, or Hanseatic League, was an economic alliance of trading cities in the Baltic and North Sea region that flourished between the thirteenth and seventeenth centuries.)

Flat-bottomed cogs sailed in the waters off the Low Countries and in the Baltic, especially after the adoption of a stern rudder during the late twelfth century. They sailed as far north as Bergen for salted cod and eventually on occasion westward to Iceland. There were hide boats and flat-bottomed barges, too, but the cog was the dominant merchant vessel, eventually superseding the Norse-style ships, with their limited crew protection. Cogs were fully decked, whereas Norse ships had half decks and open holds. *Knarrs* and other Norse vessels had light hulls that enabled them to land on beaches. Their flexible hulls were uncom-

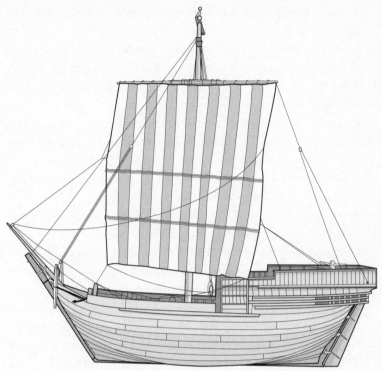

Figure 11.6   *A Hanseatic cog. Drawing by Steve Brown.*

fortable alongside quays or in formal harbors, where their neighbors could bump them. Cogs prevailed in the end not because of their carrying capacity but on account of economic realities. Hanse merchants had access to much more capital than Norse skippers did and benefited from the lucrative monopolies over trade in salt and salted cod, which operated as far north as Norway. Eventually, perhaps in response to timber shortages and cost cutting, another little-known vessel known as the hulc superseded the cog. It was faster, rode better in estuaries and harbors, and could carry more per foot than the earlier cog.

DECIPHERMENT OF OCEANS is, in many senses, inevitable, triggered as much by events on land as by human curiosity. Thus it was with the open

Atlantic. The Orkney and Shetland islands, north of Scotland, had attracted land-hungry Norse settlers by the ninth century, conveniently located as they were as bases for raids and other voyages southward to Scotland and beyond. To the north, Norse ships carrying farming households had by 800 C.E. colonized the Faroe Islands, uninhabited except, perhaps, for a few Irish monks. As far as we can discern, Iceland was a known, but shadowy, presence in the northern sea during earlier centuries, even if no one had settled there. In about 860 C.E., Scandinavians arrived in Iceland, where, once again, they found traces of Irish monastic settlement. Permanent settlers soon followed, so many that they had taken up all available arable land by 930. Perhaps an Irish monk guided a *knarr* northward from the Faroes, using experience gained on an earlier voyage in a hide boat. Part of the explanation may lie in the complex political situation in the settlers' Norwegian homeland, accentuated by a shortage of farmland and pasturage. Perhaps just as important was the spirit of restless curiosity—*æfintyr*.

The journeys across open water relied on skills honed over many centuries of coastal voyaging and crossings of the rough waters of the North Sea and much farther afield. Those who set out northward from the islands or westward from the mainland knew that easterlies prevailed in early summer. They also knew that prevailing westerlies would carry them back home if they found no land—precisely the same strategy used by the Pacific Islanders when probing unknown waters on the other side of the world.

The Norse sagas contain much valuable information about passage making in the open North Atlantic. During the fourteenth century, monks set down long-established oral traditions based on the experiences of many voyagers over four hundred years. "Wise men say that from Norway, from Stad, there are 7 days sailing for Horn on the east coast of Iceland" is a typical example.[16] These crude directions mention the place of departure, the destination, the course from one to the other, and the expected sailing time. To return, one simply reversed the directions.

Norse pilots lacked compasses. Instead, they sailed from east to west and back using what is called "latitude sailing." The navigator followed a track where the altitude of a chosen celestial body remained constant at the meridian during the entire voyage. Sailing direct from Norway to Greenland, a passage of more than 1,500 miles (2,400 kilometers), a Norse skipper would keep north of the Shetlands but have the islands just in sight, then sail south of the Faroes, at a distance of about 40 miles (64 kilometers), at which point the cliffs were mostly obscured. Then the course passed south of Iceland at a point where "the sea-birds and whales can be seen." This is the edge of the krill-rich continental shelf some 60 miles (97 kilometers) offshore. From there, the ship passed into open water across the Denmark Strait until Greenland's mountains came into sight. Depending on ice conditions, the crew now steered southwest and rounded Cape Farewell at the southern tip, before heading for the settlements on the other side. Latitude sailing was commonplace in many waters until the nineteenth century, when chronometers for calculating longitude became cheaper and more widely available.

Some form of latitude sailing was highly effective, provided one could see the heavens. In northern waters, the stars are of little use during high summer, so the Norse probably relied heavily on the sun. They are known to have used some form of sun compass, a circular board with a gnomon (an upright on sundials that casts a shadow) in the middle floating in a bowl of water. Before leaving, the pilot would measure the length of the shadow, then steer so that the shadow had the same length at noon throughout the voyage. With the sun's declination being minimal in midsummer, the navigator would know that he was too far south if the shadow was shorter, or to the north if it was longer. But what if the skies were cloudy, as they often are in these stormy waters? The Norse sagas refer to "sunstones," which are now thought to have been calcite crystals that depolarized light and allowed a pilot to detect the concentric rings of polarized light around the sun even through cloud.[17] No one has yet found a sunstone in a Norse archaeological site, but a replica made from Icelandic spar, a rock familiar to the Norse, set in a wooden device that beams light onto a crystal through a hole, allowed scientists in France to track the sun throughout a cloudy day. We do not know, of course, whether the Norse actually used such devices, but one possible stone has come from an Elizabethan wreck in the English Channel.

The Norse had the ships, as well: stout merchant vessels capable of transporting cattle and sheep, as well as families, farming implements, and sufficient provisions to support them both on passage and once ashore. Once colonization was successful, the same hulls would carry locally made trade goods back to the mainland in exchange for iron tools and other goods needed from home. The *Skuldelev I knarr*, with its half decks fore and aft, a well-proven trading vessel, was probably like many of the anonymous ships that made deepwater crossings from the northern islands and the Norwegian mainland to Iceland. These were never easy journeys, for severe gales can arrive suddenly, even in high summer. Confronted with such weather, the *knarrs* would have lowered sail and lain ahull, the crew lying in the bottom of the boat, perhaps for days. This was when ships vanished without a trace, never to arrive at their destinations. High casualty rates were a fact of life.

Volatile factionalism splintered the new Icelandic society, as is inevitable in isolated communities headed by men with strong, often violent, personalities. Thus it was in the late tenth century that quarrelsome, redheaded Erik the Red became enmeshed in a feud. Blood was shed; he was exiled for three years. Boldly, he sailed westward to explore some mysterious islands sighted by a drifting ship captained by a relative about half a century earlier. Soon he sighted high mountains, skirted the land, and landed in the sheltered fjords of what he called Greenland. Twenty-five ships followed the persuasive Erik to colonize the newly discovered land. Only fourteen reached their destination. Sometime after 985, Leif Erikson, the son of Erik the Red, followed up on reports of forested land to the west. Norse voyagers soon reached Labrador and Newfoundland, as well as a region they named Vinland on account of its wild grapes.

With these voyages, North America entered the consciousness of Northern Europeans. The *Icelandic Annals*, a manuscript dating to about 1300 but obviously based on earlier sources, wrote of the north, "To the south of Greenland lies Helluland [possibly Baffin Island] and then Markland [Labrador], and from there it is not far to Vinland, which some people think extends to Africa."[18] Long before Christopher Columbus crossed to what he called the Indies in 1492, the Norse had deciphered the hazardous waters of the North Atlantic without elaborate technology or advanced navigational devices. They were taciturn people, careful with their knowledge, close to the ocean in ways we cannot imagine. The sea was their company, fathers mentors of their sons. We can imagine a *knarr* pitching midway between Iceland and Greenland on a brilliantly clear day. The skipper stands by the mast, a May easterly of early summer filling the great square sail overhead. His twelve-year-old son listens by his side as he recites an ancient saga and points to the distant glaciers and mountaintops that are the signposts to the ice-bound land on the bow. No books or written sailing directions were at hand, just the carefully accumulated knowledge of fathers and grandfathers stretching back generations into the past.

THE PACIFIC TO THE WEST

> The most reliable indications by which they could fore-
> tell the weather for the next day, were the sunset and
> the dawn, by which those who knew were able to tell
> without error what sort of a day was to follow. They
> observed changes in the sky with such an intensity that
> this, in their expression, was known as talking with the
> sun and sky.
>
> —Ivan Veniaminov, 1840[1]

The Pacific seems boundless from American shores, unbroken water
extending to the horizon with no hints of invisible land within reach.
Fogs often mantle much of the long coastline; the Aleutian Islands seem
suspended amid stormy, rain-lashed seas; huge swells break ashore without notice, generated by storms thousands of miles offshore. As in the
North Atlantic, there were no predictable wind reversals here. The prevailing northerly and northwesterly winds along much of the coast made
paddling in those directions impracticable for any significant distance.
Chapters 12 to 14 describe societies that mastered the waters that were
close at hand and usually in sight. With the notable exception of smaller
numbers of Andeans, who sailed northward from the South American
coast to Central America in balsa rafts, no one went offshore, and only
very rarely did they go out of sight of land. This was a story of maritime
societies who made the inshore seascape as much a part of their lives as
the landscape was. In the case of the Aleuts, the Northwest Indians, and

the Chumash people of Southern California, the people were just as much at home afloat as they were ashore, for much, if not most, of their subsistence came from the ocean. The roots of these societies go back deep into the past. The ancestors of the Aleuts had settled islands far out in their island chain by at least 7000 B.C.E. Here, wide boats and kayaks ruled and were so effective that Russian fur traders adopted them for their sea otter hunts: they were far more seaworthy than their heavy wooden vessels. The Northwest Coast is a tapestry of islands and narrow channels, where straight-grained timber abounded, making for a canoe-building tradition that goes back thousands of years into the past. To Northwest peoples, inshore waters were an arena not only for fishing but for trading, social interaction, and warfare, for this was an environment where canoes were the only means of load carrying and ready communication. Like the Chumash of Southern California, with their unique planked canoes, coastal peoples in the Northwest traded for centuries over long distances, handling commodities of all kinds—in the case of the Chumash, acorns and shell beads. Far to the south, the decipherment of ancient Maya script allows us to appreciate the complex relationships the Maya and other Native American societies enjoyed with the ocean. To the Maya, the sea was a Fiery Pool, a place of terrifying forces, which they skirted in dugout canoes along well-trodden trade routes. Much of this trade was in sacred objects such as stingray spines and conchs, and also the shells of the spiny oyster, spondylus, valued not only by Maya lords but also by Andeans, who traded them far inland from what is now the Ecuadoran coast. Such was the demand for these shells that South American traders sailed northward in large balsa rafts, bringing copper metallurgy to the Maya realm. Judging from what we know about the Maya relationship to the Fiery Pool, these voyages had important spiritual undertones.

CHAPTER 12

The Aleutians: "The Sea Becomes Very High"

THIRTY MILES PER HOUR (48 kilometers per hour) of northwesterly wind scoured our faces with driving snow. The temperature hovered near zero even before you added in the windchill factor. Far from ideal conditions for archaeological fieldwork, one would reasonably assume, but there we were, looking at ancient house pits and a midden overlooking a small bay on Kodiak Island, at the root of the Aleutian Islands, in the far North Pacific. I imagined kayaks and larger hide boats landing on the beach—but in this wind? "Certainly, if they could navigate the breakers safely," my Native American host told me. As I gazed into the teeth of the gale, I remembered the gentle winds of Southeast Asia and the warm anchorages of the Aegean, and I shuddered.

Kodiak lies at the mouth of the Cook Strait, an hour's flight or so from Anchorage. The turbulent waters of the Shelikof Strait separate the island from the nearby Alaska Peninsula, a channel narrow enough to be considered a wide river by the local people. From Kodiak, it's a two-week kayak journey out to the Aleutian Islands, a 1,200-mile (1,930-kilometer) arc of windswept volcanic peaks spanning a huge tract of ocean. Some of them, including active volcanoes, tower high above the Pacific. Others are no more than a few feet above sea level. Savage winter storms pound the islands. Relentless ocean swells break against abrupt and deeply in-dented shorelines. These are pitiless waters with rare clear days. Moist, relatively warm southwesterly winds flow northward over the progressively colder water of the northern Pacific, restricting visibility seriously for up to a third of the time. This is a gray world where islands appear and disappear in drifting gloom. The British Admiralty's *Ocean Passages for the World*, the ultimate in sober maritime authorities, reports that "over the greater part of the zone the weather is very cloudy and foggy," and the authors are not exaggerating.[1] The Aleutians were a death trap for sailing ships. Nineteenth-century Arctic explorers heading for Point Barrow and the Arctic Ocean would sail far northwest to Kamchatka, in Siberia, rather than risk a passage through the Aleutians, where one false navigational decision or poor dead-reckoning move could put them ashore in the gloom. They were wise to play it safe. The last time I had

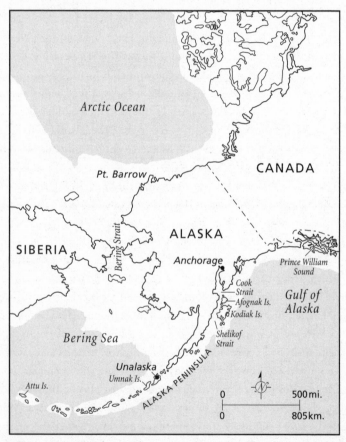

Figure 12.1 *Map showing locations mentioned in Chapter 12, including the extent of the Bering land bridge.*

passed through the Aleutians, we saw nothing except clouds hovering close to the surface. You could have been mere yards from the rocks before sighting land.

The Aleutians are forbidding terrain, set in the midst of a gray, stormy ocean. But there are compensations—generally relatively moderate temperatures by subarctic standards and ample freshwater, much of it in lakes on higher ground. The water is remarkably pure, so much so that the nineteenth-century ornithologist Lucien Turner remarked, "I much doubt if water from any part of the globe makes better tea."[2] There are plenty of sheltered inlets and beaches where small craft can land safely through the surf in good weather. Above all, the outer Alaska Peninsula, Kodiak, and the Aleutians teem with marine life—with seals and sea lions, whales, and fish of every kind, including the staple catches of cod and halibut. Most of the food consumed by the ancient Aleut communities came from the ocean and from the rivers that flowed into the Pacific. Such was the bounty close inshore that they could live in the same locations for many generations, something that few land-based hunters could ever do. With such plenty in the waters at their doorstep, the peoples of the peninsula and the islands developed some of the earliest completely maritime societies on earth, not only because they were expert sea mammal hunters and fishers, but because they also mastered the art of moving through an environment where men—and many women—spent most of their lives afloat. This mastery came not only from their understanding of the marine environment, but also because of their extraordinary watercraft.

A GERMAN NATURALIST, Georg Wilhelm Steller, was one of the first Europeans to describe the Aleuts. He sailed through the islands with the explorer Vitus Bering in 1741. Opinionated, quarrelsome, and stubborn, Steller is remembered not by a strait named after him, like his captain, or even by an island. No one liked him enough to endow a landmark in his name. But he's commemorated by just as durable a memorial: living things—a sea lion, a sea cow, and a jay, the first of which played a central role in Aleut life. He also left us the first description of Aleutian boats, their baidarka kayaks: "The American boats are ... pointed towards the nose but truncate and smooth in the rear ... The frame is of sticks fastened together at both ends and spread apart by crosspieces inside. On the outside, this frame is covered with skins, perhaps of seals, and colored a dark brown. With these skins, the boat is covered flat above but sloping towards the keel on the sides ... About two arshins [56 inches (1.4 meters)] from the rear on top is a circular hole, around the whole of which is sewn whale guts having a hollow hem with a leather string running through it, by means of which it may be tightened or loosened like a purse." Each Aleut propelled his craft with a "stick a fathom long, at each end provided with a shovel, a hand wide." Alternate paddle strokes on either side maneuvered the kayak "with great adroitness even among large waves."[3] Steller watched in admiration as the paddlers landed effortlessly through high surf that defeated Russian oarsmen in their heavy skiffs, then picked up their boats with one hand and launched them once more.

By the time Steller came along, the Aleuts had been paddling their way happily through the islands for a very long time. They were not the first human settlers in the far north. Some fifteen thousand years ago, handfuls of Siberian hunters crossed from extreme northeast Asia into Alaska. At the time, sea levels were as much as 300 feet (91 meters) lower, so they crossed what is now the Bering Strait dry-shod. The Bering land bridge was an inhospitable tract of shrub-covered steppe tundra, swept by Arctic winds. Even during the brief summer, thick, jostling pack ice would have ravaged its low-lying shores. Great ice floes must have piled one upon the other. These would also have been stormy waters, with strong offshore winds and intense windchill factors adding to a forbidding maritime equation. We don't know, of course, whether any of the first Americans arrived by sea, but the chances are that they did not. If they did, they might have been able to exploit inshore kelp beds.[4] Thousands of years may have passed before anyone paddled in these hazardous waters, even in high summer. When they did, they must have stayed close to shore in the simplest of hide boats, there being no trees for dugout building.

About ten thousand years ago, temperatures rose rapidly and sea levels climbed, soon inundating the land bridge. Both water temperatures and ice conditions would have moderated sufficiently for hunters to take to the ocean. Whether there's a connection between rising waters and regular maritime travel is a matter of conjecture, for any ancient settlements near the coast that might tell us lie many feet below modern sea level. As far as we can tell, however, full-fledged maritime societies did not develop along Siberian and Alaskan coasts until much later, around 3500 to 3000 B.C.E. Seafaring began much earlier to the south along the indented shores of the Alaska Peninsula, on Kodiak Island, and far out along the Aleutian chain—at least as early as 7000 B.C.E.

No one knows when fishers and sea mammal hunters first paddled out, island to island, from the mainland deep into the Aleutians. This may have been a harsh and unforgiving environment, but it was paradise by the standards of the far north. Ice conditions were less severe in this linear environment, where you could paddle from island to island using line-of-sight navigation on clear days. Plentiful fish and sea mammal stocks lay within easy paddling distance, readily taken with bone- and ivory-tipped spears that worked equally well on land and afloat. Over at least 9,000 years, the people of the Alaska Peninsula and the Aleutians developed enduring maritime cultures that changed little over time, except for an increasing sophistication in art, culture, and ritual.

About 9,000 years ago, some remote ancestors of the modern Aleuts lived at Anangula, on an islet 1.5 miles (2.4 kilometers) long, off the western shore of Umnak Island, far out in the central Aleutians.[5] Here, a small community dwelt in houses partly dug into the ground, which were entered through the roof. These fishers and sea mammal hunters lived in a treeless environment where the only raw materials for boatbuilding were driftwood when it could be found, sea mammal bones, and sea lion hide. Their ancestors must have traveled from island to island along the archipelago in hide boats capable of carrying entire families, which were the prototypes of the much more refined watercraft of later times.

To paddle hide craft in these waters required not only remarkable qualities of seamanship but also an understanding of subtle equations of ocean, ice, and changing weather that would have been unimaginable in the benign waters of Southeast Asia. Above all, there was the cold—not only that of air, damp, and wind but also of frigid ocean waters. Anyone dunked into water only a few degrees above freezing point suffers from virtually instant hypothermia. Immersion hypothermia occurs within minutes in Arctic waters, because water draws away body heat much quicker than air. Your skin becomes cold and paler; you shiver intensely until your body temperature drops below 90 degrees Fahrenheit (32.2 Celsius). As your temperature continues to fall, your speech slurs, your muscles become rigid, and you are soon disoriented. In Arctic waters, hypothermia is a virtually instant killer, which can be kept at bay only with highly effective protective clothing.

No sane hunter would venture even into shallow, sheltered waters in layered furs. Reindeer- or caribou-skin parkas may work on land, but, once wet, they are dead weight on the body and could soon swamp even a strong swimmer—if he survived long enough in the cold water. The well-being of the paddlers depended on the skill of their wives as seamstresses. Aleut women used fine bone needles to sew sea lion or seal intestine parkas that reached to the ankles, lashed tightly around the head and wrists, and were often decorated with feathers and sometimes human hair. They would also sew parkas from bird skins; between thirty and forty cormorant or puffin skins went into a single garment, which lasted about two years. The seams were completely waterproof, the garment tied around the cockpit hatch to make the paddler and his kayak a single waterproof unit. Their sea-lion-hide boots had soles made from the scaly skin of the fore-flippers, which provided a rough surface for traction on rocks. On their heads they often wore fiber hats with rims, or bentwood helmets with long visors that shaded the eyes from glare and protected the face from spray, rain, and wind. They adorned these with sea lion bristles and other tokens of the hunt and also with images of whales and other prey. A hunter's hat imbued him with symbolic power and gave him a close relationship to his quarry.

Efficient clothing is all very well, but it's useless without seaworthy boats. Unfortunately, archaeological sites rarely preserve hide and wood, and often not even bone, so we can only guess intelligently at the earliest watercraft used by the ancestral Aleuts in this treeless world. In more recent times, Arctic watercraft had bone or driftwood frames, lashed

Figure 12.2 *Cod fishing from a baidarka, Captain's Island, Alaska. The paddler wears a waterproof anorak. William Henry Elliot, 1872. MS 7119, Inv. 08594900. National Anthropological Archives, Smithsonian Institution.*

together with sinew to form flexible skeletons for hull coverings fashioned from seal, or preferably sea lion, hides. Fairly large hide-covered boats were, without question, the earliest Arctic watercraft, seemingly fragile, but in fact their hulls resisted the shock impact of an ice floe to a far greater degree than one might expect, thanks both to the form of the boat and the traditional way of constructing larger skin vessels. Historical builders never attached the hide rigidly to the frame, as one might expect. Rather, they secured it rigidly at the gunwales and at either end, and only loosely to the frame. As a result, a hard blow could distort the skin cover considerably. At the same time, the bone or wooden frame would have been flexible, the transverse frames having relatively slack lashings. The same qualities of flexibility gave large hide boats the ability to weather even quite rough seas in comparative safety. Just like Norse ships, with their planked hulls (see Chapter 11), they flexed with the swell and the waves. Presumably simpler, much earlier hide boats enjoyed the same qualities.

Hide-covered hulls are light, which allows the crew to remove the boat from the water and carry it over icy obstructions. Such craft could also be hauled with some ease. Driftwood would have been in short supply along Siberian and Alaskan coasts, so the use of wood must have been kept to a minimum, making hulls light and flexible relative to the size of the boat. This also allowed the crew to carry heavy loads in watercraft constructed with a minimum of raw materials.

Our hypothetical early prototypes must have been remote ancestors of the Eskimo umiak (a large hide boat) of much later times, for the qualities of these sturdy craft were exactly the same as those sought by the first paddlers in the Aleutians and perhaps in Bering Strait waters thousands of years before. The first essential quality was speed that enabled a crew to cross open water rapidly and sometimes to paddle ahead of impending bad weather. An umiak never achieved the velocity of a kayak, but even a small crew could paddle one efficiently. Seaworthiness is a remarkable attribute of umiaks and must have been just as important in earlier times, in a region with frequent and unexpected summer storms. Like umiaks, earlier prototypes must have had flat bottoms and flared sides that allowed them to carry heavy loads without a dramatic increase in draft, as well as making them ideal beach craft.

The historical umiak may have been the successor of much earlier seagoing craft in the north, as was the Aleutian kayak, the baidarka. Both came in many forms, for the secret of navigating and hunting off northern shores was to adapt your boat design to local conditions. For instance, a heavily laden skin boat will make little progress when paddled against high waves and strong headwinds. When confronted regularly with such conditions, the builders duly reduced the flare and the height of the sides to decrease wind resistance. There was no such thing as a fixed boat design, for the variations on the common theme of a large skin boat were infinite, even within a few miles.

The large hide boat was the prototype of the baidarka. The ornithologist Lucien Turner collected oral traditions on Attu Island, at the extreme western end of the Aleutians, which record plausible stories of much

Figure 12.3 *An Eskimo umiak setting off to hunt whales in the spring from Barrow, Alaska. Aleutian hide boats would have looked much the same.* © *Accent Alaska.com/Alamy.*

older kayak designs that were like larger hide boats, but with broader beams and upturned bows and sterns. Like modern-day umiaks, this boat had no coverings—a family boat in which people paddled along the shore looking for food, almost a floating dwelling. According to the same traditions, such vessels came into use before rivalries and warfare broke out between neighboring groups. Then the chief elder decided that women and children should no longer accompany the men in smaller boats. Now the design changed as the paddler moved to the center and decks extended to the cockpit. The beam narrowed to allow easier and faster paddling; the sheer of bow and stern became less pronounced. According to Attuan oral tradition, the kayak came into use as both a hunting and offensive weapon. The larger hide boat, in which women and children traveled, became a load carrier.[6] Meanwhile, the baidarka, one of the most effective and refined hunting conveyances ever developed, evolved through hard experience with local conditions over many thousands of years.

I FIRST ENCOUNTERED an Aleutian baidarka in a wooden-boat show at Mystic Seaport, Connecticut, on a hot June day, in a radically different environment from that of its homeland. This kayak was no original: the few that survive are prized museum exhibits. This was a faithful replica, built from a kit of wooden frames, lashings, and rolls of synthetic cloth instead of sea lion skins. Sleek and apparently tippy, it floated just off the beach, ready for a quick excursion. I climbed in cautiously and stretched out my legs inside the cockpit, digging the paddle into the sand to stabilize the hull. My every movement flowed through the baidarka—the slightest muscle twitch, a shifting of one's weight to get comfortable. I seemed destined to a capsize in short order. But as I started to paddle, the kayak came alive in my hands. Each paddle stroke drove it fast and straight, oblivious to the wash from passing motorboats. The baidarka was like a thoroughbred: restless, itching to take off at a gallop. All I had to do was paddle smoothly and let the boat do the work. I have never felt so well looked after by any watercraft, large or small. I soon acquired a healthy respect for the baidarka and the Aleut paddlers who lived in them from childhood.

Aleut men spent much of their lives in their baidarkas. Fathers would place their six- or seven-year-old sons in the kayak with them and teach them how to paddle. Soon they would make them hold small paddles, launch the baidarka into large waves breaking on the shore, and watch them handle rough water. At first, the elder would attach a line to the child so he could haul him in if the boat overturned, but soon the boy was on his own. While afloat, boys also learned how to shoot accurately with the harpoon stowed on board.

Baidarkas took months to construct. Just collecting the driftwood for the keel and ribs was a prolonged task—especially the longer pieces for the keel, which was assembled in several pieces and was up to 21 feet (6.4 meters) long. The Russian hydrographer Gavril Sarychev wrote in 1802, "To this they fasten, by means of split whalebone, ribs of willow and alder-branches, on the upper extremities of which they place a frame with crossbars . . . Over the whole they stretch the hide of a sea-lion . . . leaving on the top a round but smallish opening, in which the rower sits."[7] Commander Joseph Billings, who served on Captain Cook's last voyage and then entered the service of Catherine the Great of Russia, admired the baidarkas, "made smoothly to the severest symmetry of ship construction." He noted that the bows were shaped like "the head of a fish with opened upper and lower jaws."[8] A thin rod placed across it kept seaweed from entangling the bow. The jawlike bow provided less water resistance and contributed to the remarkable speeds achieved by paddlers.

The upper frame, with its whale-baleen binding, contributed to speed and seaworthiness, but the most important component of all was the sea-lion-hide covering. The battle-toughened outer hide of the Steller sea lion's throat provided the covering—a raw material also used for waterproofing boots. The builder placed the carefully trimmed, wetted hides around the frame, then drew them on from stem to stern like a form of stocking, a demanding task that took several people. Then the women would sew the top seam from stem to cockpit with fine sinew, pulling tight and close-stitching it to ensure a completely waterproof fit. As the hide dried, it contracted and bound together the entire boat.[9]

These, then, were the watercraft that carried Aleut hunters from island to island, and sometimes far out to sea, in all kinds of weather. The baidarka's seaworthiness was impressive. Eli L. Huggins was a U.S. Army lieutenant, sent to Fort Kodiak in 1869, who spent many hours in baidarkas propelled by Aleut paddlers with muscular arms and shoulders. He likened the kayaks to "a mammoth cigar," so flexible in the water that one was never seasick.[10] In 1869, he traveled for eight hours to Afognak Island with a group of baidarkas, riding effortlessly on the open-ocean swells and breakers that surrounded the island. The paddlers approached a narrow passage between the surf, paused for a moment within a few yards of the rocks, and then darted rapidly to the beach on the crest of a carefully timed wave. In rough conditions, when caught in open waters, the Aleuts would tie their kayaks to one another like a kind of raft, taking care that the hulls did not touch, then try and steer them with their paddles while at the mercy of the wind.

Baidarkas were, above all, hunting craft. The Aleuts depended almost entirely on birds, fish, and sea mammals for their diet, especially after about 2500 B.C.E., when archaeological sites document a steady population increase. This was the moment when intensive exploitation of seacoasts came into its own after thousands of years of experience acquired by much smaller hunting populations. By this time, most settlements of domelike, semi-subterranean houses lay on open coasts, near sea lion rookeries and other places where fish, shellfish, and sea mammals could be taken in abundance. Longlines with bone or wood hooks cast from kayaks brought cod and halibut to the surface, where a hard blow with a heavy club dispatched them. Most communities depended almost entirely on their ability to hunt in the open sea. All hunting equipment had to be light enough to be stowed within easy reach on deck. Bows and arrows were useless afloat, so the hunters relied on bone- and stone-tipped spears or harpoons, propelled by hooked throwing sticks, steadying the baidarka with the paddle in one hand while casting with the other. The toggle harpoon was a particularly effective weapon against sea mammals in expert hands, for the swiveling head buried itself in the prey and could not be dislodged. Hunters now used razor-sharp slate lance heads against sea mammals as large as whales, which they pursued in both larger boats and kayaks; elaborate rituals surrounded such hunts.

Arguably, the most important prey of all was the Steller sea lion. *Eumetopias jubatus* is among the largest of the pinnepeds. Light brown to blond in color, Stellers thrive in the cool coastal waters of the North Pacific, consuming enormous quantities of fish, squid, and shrimp. In June and July, they come ashore to mate and give birth in rookeries. These large animals are aggressive beasts, the males weighing up to 1,500 pounds (680 kilograms). Most were killed by Aleuts while ashore in their rookeries, for they were usually inaccessible when at sea. But they were essential quarry. Without Stellers, the islanders couldn't have constructed their baidarkas and hunted their most important staples. When sea lion populations collapsed suddenly, as happened on several, still poorly documented occasions over the millennia, the effects were devastating. The last collapse, about 1,200 years ago, brought rapid changes in Aleut life.

Archaeological surveys chronicle an ancient tradition of settlement along open coasts, as one might expect of a people fishing in deeper waters. Then, suddenly, after 650 to 750 C.E., the large coastal villages disappear.[11] Most communities now settled along the banks of major salmon

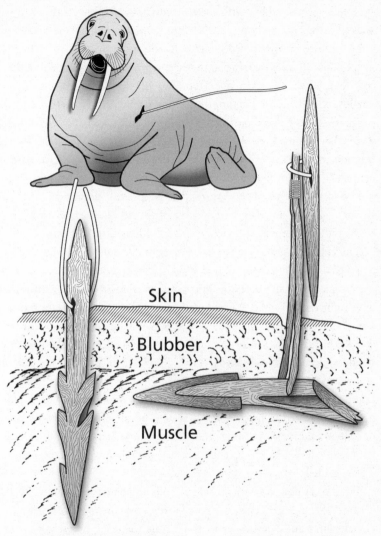

Figure 12.4 *How a toggle harpoon works. The harpoon head swivels once it has penetrated the hide, making it virtually impossible to disengage.*

streams, especially those with sockeye runs. The ensuing centuries were ones of turbulence and sporadic warfare, so much so that people lived in large, multiroom dwellings, perhaps for defensive reasons. Eventually, the population collapsed; the large settlements gave way to much smaller communities of a few extended families, villages of only a few dozen inhabitants. Then, once again, the situation changed. By 1450 C.E., the population was rising rapidly and people moved back to open coastlines, where they resumed the old pattern of sea mammal hunting and fishing. By 1600, more than eleven large village sites lay along the western Alaska Peninsula, with probably more people living there than at any other time over the previous 4,000 years. The people still dwelt near sockeye streams—hardly surprising, since some of the runs in rivers like the Nelson and the Bear today still yield nearly a million salmon a year.

The culprit may have been changing seawater temperatures that triggered changes in marine productivity. The Aleutian low-pressure system has a major influence on both climate and marine productivity throughout the northeast Pacific. When the low is strong, it strengthens the pumping of nutrients from the subarctic gyre (rotating current) toward the coast. Throughout most of the millennia since the Ice Age, the low was strong and marine productivity was high. However, between about 800 and 1200 C.E., during the global Medieval Warm Period, the ocean circulation changed dramatically, the low weakened, and warmer water temperatures resulted in much lower marine productivity. Productivity rose once more during the ensuing, much cooler Little Ice Age. Another such major shift took place as recently as 1860, with fluctuating ocean warming since then.

What has this to do with Steller sea lions and baidarkas? A great deal, it turns out. In recent decades, populations of Steller sea lions have declined significantly over much of the region, the result, in large part, of changed circulation patterns and warming. A recent study by the Alaskan archaeologist Herbert Maschner and his colleagues has documented similar events over the past 4,500 years that always coincide with ocean warming. Stellers were the primary source of the hides that covered baidarkas. A kayak builder used between four and six sea lion skins to cover its frame, and each cover had to be replaced every year. These figures pale beside the statistics for the larger skin-covered boats that each community used to carry loads and people: each hull needed between fifteen and twenty skins to cover it.

The link between Steller sea lion populations and climate change is so compelling that there must have been a connection between the ability of hunters to exploit coastal and offshore waters and the availability of sea lion hides to cover their boats. Maschner and his colleagues observe that a brief warming period during the 1860s and 1870s came during a period of intense sea lion hunting, which was necessary to cover the hundreds of baidarkas used in commercial sea otter hunts. A combination of changing ocean circulation and intense hunting resulted in such scarcities that some villages became stranded because of the collapse in sea lion populations. Russian Orthodox priests and Alaska Commercial Company agents actually imported sea lion skins from California so that the Aleuts in the western Aleutians could build enough baidarkas to go hunting.

Climate change, marine productivity, and human history were closely intertwined in the islands, where the hunter maintained an intimate relationship with the inshore and offshore environment. This relationship and the ways in which paddlers thought of the ocean permeated the inner recesses of Aleut and Kodiak society.

ALEUT SPEECH IS a nuanced directory to the ocean. Their vocabularies include dozens of words for the wind alone—strength, direction, and characteristics. Every crossing of open water required careful preparation and a clear understanding of what the next day's weather would bring. Wrote the Russian bishop Ivan Evseevich Veniaminov, who often traveled in baidarkas: "The most reliable indications by which they could foretell the weather for the next day, were the sunset and the dawn, by which those who knew were able to tell without error what sort of day was to follow. They observed changes in the sky with such an intensity that this, in their expression, was known as talking with the sun and sky."[12]

Any passage over open water was made in company, so that if rough weather came up and your cockpit covering was torn off and your kayak half-filled with water, there was someone who could come to your help. As we have seen, when caught out, the paddlers would bring their kayaks alongside one another, forming a simple raft, paddling carefully to maintain a steady angle to the waves. Everything depended on the seamanship and skill of the paddlers. With their bent gait, from habitual paddling, they may have been clumsy ashore, but afloat was another matter. In 1827, the Russian admiral Fyodor Litke visited Unalaska, in the central Aleutians, where he saw an Aleut "bent forward with crooked legs, waddling like a duck, and then alone in his *baidarka* . . . steering in the middle of huge waves with extraordinary dexterity and nimbleness." He had trouble believing it was the same man.[13]

Baidarkas were so seaworthy that the Russians used them for many purposes. When a smallpox epidemic killed around three thousand Aleuts in the summer of 1838, Dr. Edward Blaschke had the task of administering vaccines to 1,400 patients living in twenty-two villages and nomadic settlements on Unalaska. He traveled in a three-person kayak, accompanied by two others, one of which carried his supplies, including tobacco, tea, sugar for gifts and barter, and also "several bottles of rum." The doctor spent long hours afloat, as many as sixteen hours at a stretch on occasion. We owe to him estimates of paddling speed—an average of four and a half knots on long passages and up to six or more on shorter stretches where there was no need to conserve the paddler's strength. A paddler in a single-hatched baidarka acted as his guide from one settlement to the next, often in rough seas. Blaschke was astonished at his guide's adept boat handling as he vanished from sight, then reappeared, carefully avoiding breaking waves that could have capsized the kayak. He also noticed that the paddlers painted their faces with traditional designs, the paint being a mixture of oxide pigments and whale-fat ointment that protected their skin from the effects of seawater. Meanwhile, the skin peeled off Blaschke's face during his journey.[14]

Blaschke's Aleut guides never took unnecessary risks. Every paddler knew the times of high and low tide, for they were well aware that the tidal streams were decisive when crossing narrow straits. As every small-boat sailor knows, a strong current or tide flowing against even a moderate wind can throw up nasty overfalls, in which steep-sided waves tumble in every direction. A well-found, decked fishing boat or small boat merely experiences pounding discomfort, with water flying in all directions. A baidarka would capsize or break up in the turmoil. Crossings were timed for slack water or for when wind and current flowed in the same direction.

Every morning, the elders observed the sunrise. If they proclaimed that conditions were dangerous, no paddler set out. Whatever the circumstances, an Aleut paddler had to be self-sufficient, always ready for an unexpected problem. On one occasion, Blaschke was paddling in company when his servant's baidarka was holed. Water poured in. The servant sat awkwardly on the three-man kayak while his paddlers upended the damaged craft, found a two-inch (five-centimeter) hole near the keel, and quickly patched it with some raw whale blubber that they always carried with them. The journey resumed without further incident.

The French ethnologist, linguist, and adventurer Alphonse Pinart was another long-distance baidarka traveler, paddling from Unalaska to Kodiak Island in September–October 1871.[15] The journey involved a passage along the exposed southern shores of Umnak Island, where the wind started to blow strong from the southwest. "The sea becomes very high; the wind raising a deep foam which covers all the sea and falls again in a sort of rain." The Aleuts tied the baidarkas together in pairs. The paddlers tried to keep them on course, but eventually they had to lie to at the mercy of the wind. After eleven hours, they managed to land through high surf at the north end of Otter Cove. Pinart covered about 35 miles (56 kilometers) that day. It was late in the paddling season, and the paddlers had to fight headwinds most of the way. Fortunately, the Aleuts knew every landing place, identified by oral knowledge passed from one generation to the next. By this time, most Aleuts were Christians, so crucifixes marked difficult crossings.

From Pinart, we learn something of the full extent of Aleut knowledge of their home waters. His notebooks contain dozens of Aleut words for different kinds of wind, knowledge acquired by the paddlers from hard experience on the water. On this particular journey, Pinart covered more than 1,150 miles (1,852 kilometers) in sixty-four days, many of them spent ashore, stormbound. Much Aleut passage making was by line of sight, from one island or rocky outcrop to the next. On occasion, however, they made longer journeys that took them out of sight of land, or they would be afloat on days when fog or low clouds obscured landmarks. Bishop Veniaminov observed how the paddlers would find their way to an island over the horizon by using the set of an imperceptible swell or the flight of birds to and from unseen land. On occasion, they also dropped whitened sea lion bladders attached to long, stone-weighted lines, setting them in a line within sight of one another— or they used whitened kelp bulbs for the same purpose.

EVEN BEFORE THE Russians arrived, Aleutian paddlers made long journeys from island to island, sometimes venturing out of sight of land but apparently never far offshore. Then came the fur traders, and everything changed. The Russians soon found that baidarkas were vastly superior to their own slow-moving wooden ships and forced Aleut hunters to obtain furs. The founding of the Russian-American Company in 1799 gave the owners a virtual monopoly over the lives of the Aleuts. The ruthless merchant Alexander Baranov organized huge fleets of as many as seven hundred kayaks, forcing the paddlers to cross the dangerous wastes of the Gulf of Alaska to Yakutat, on the mainland coast, for the hunt. "They have to endure hunger on the way and often perish in stormy seas because this coast offers no adequate shelter," he wrote calmly.[16] Tlingit warriors, traditional enemies of the Aleut, were a constant threat, so large fleets offered a measure of protection. Many of the kayaks fell apart on the return journey as their covers rotted in the damp. In 1805, 130 kayaks returning to Kodiak after wintering at Sitka learned of an impending ambush by Tlingit warriors, who had destroyed the Russian fort at Yakutat. All but thirty elected to travel nonstop across the Gulf of Alaska to Kayak Island in Prince William Sound. Fortunately, the ambush never materialized. Those who stayed behind rested undisturbed, then resumed their journey. Those who elected to travel nonstop perished, to a man, in a sudden storm.

Many centuries of constant refinement in a demanding environment produced hide-covered baidarkas that were ideal for hunting and paddling relatively short distances from island to island, even in rough conditions.

The Aleuts were remarkable seamen, with an intimate knowledge of their home waters. There were always casualties in these demanding waters, but nothing like the death rates sustained when the Russians forced the paddlers offshore. It's a tribute to indigenous seamanship and local knowledge that so many of the paddlers survived passages for which their experience and watercraft had never prepared them. Baidarkas remained in common use until World War II, when they finally succumbed to competition from diesel engines. But the lessons of this ancient maritime world survive in the Aleutian communities of today.

CHAPTER 13

Raven Releases the Fish

Princess Louisa Inlet, British Columbia. I pondered the insignificance of humanity as we sailed here. Black and gray cliffs dwarfed our boat. They fell sheer into the deep, still waters of the fjord. You could sail up and touch the rock without going aground. Deep glacial valleys bisected the towering rock, long devoid of the ice that had carved them thousands of years in the past. Dense forests crowded the sandbanks and channels of fast-flowing rivers; bears foraged along deserted beaches. Mile after mile, wilderness pressed on our senses, with no sign of people along the shore or afloat. When we encountered a fishing boat, it was an event. The tides run strong here, at speeds up to 16 knots (30 kilometers per hour) in some narrow inlets, where a wise canoe or small-boat skipper passes through during the brief minutes of slack water between ebb and flood. Here tides run strong in narrow defiles. I've felt nearby islands shake during spring tides. We waited for two hours above the narrow Malibu Rapids, at the entrance to the inlet, until the current slackened and the steep overfalls subsided. Then we quickly slipped through into the deep water a few hundred yards beyond. The scale of the coast and the distances dwarf even modern-day cruise ships and ferries; in ancient times, it must have been even more daunting. We anchored in a bay like glass, our shadow mirrored in the still, ink-black water, high cliffs on every side. A distant wolf howled at the full moon high above us, where the cliffs gave way to snow-clad peaks. Then total, absolute silence fell, the silence of wilderness. We were an insignificant dot in a much larger cosmos.

Forested islands, gray cliffs, their tops lost in gathering clouds: North

America's Northwest Coast is often a brooding place. Innumerable channels, large and small, wide or as narrow as a creek, thread their way from
what is now Alaska through British Columbia, then south to Washington
State's Olympic Peninsula.[1] Rare sunny days are glorious; ferocious
storms roil normally sheltered inlets and fjords with steep-sided waves.
Along this formidable, intricate coast, high mountains and virtually impenetrable wilderness crowd onto river valleys and islands where Indian
communities flourished for thousands of years. Fjords penetrate deep inland, some of them home to major rivers. The Stikine, Skeena, Fraser, and
Columbia, and also the Klamath—clogged with salmon runs in spring
and autumn—connect the land and the Pacific. For those who lived here
in the past, there was almost an unspoken distinction between the world
of the ocean and the forbidding, often virtually inaccessible interior, with
its menacing predators, fast-flowing rivers, and narrow forest paths. The
interior was for solitude. The coast was a paradise for hunters and fisherfolk and a region of remarkable cultural and linguistic diversity—eleven
language families and thirty-nine different languages.

The Northwest Coast offers a dramatic contrast to the windswept
Aleutians, to the north. The coast is a linear maritime world about 1,300
to 1,400 miles (2,100 to 2,250 kilometers) long, which begins in Alaska's
Alexander Archipelago, where the modern cities of Sitka and Juneau lie.
Ironbound, swell-battered coasts face the open Pacific, protected in places
by low-lying glacial islands, exposed by retreating Ice Age glaciers. Dense
forests cover the mainland, passing into a landscape of inlets, estuaries,
and rocky islands. This is today's Inland Passage, traversed effortlessly by
cruise ships and ferries. In ancient times, Native Americans fished and
hunted along its shorelines, in its river estuaries, and in its relatively sheltered deeper waters. The ocean beyond the islands and toward the sunset
was a fearsome place, inhabited by dangerous supernatural beings. For
the most part, only whale hunters ventured on the open Pacific.

Until Europeans arrived, no one raised sails here. The Indians paddled
in dugout canoes, large and small, carved from abundant straight-
grained timber. The forests came soon after the Ice Age. By 6000 B.C.E.,
the Northwest Coast had become a strip of green, forested landscape that
stretched from the mouth of the Copper River south to the Klamath

Figure 13.1 *The West Coast of North America.*

River in Northern California. Cedar, Douglas fir, hemlock, and spruce swathed the rugged coastal landscape. Mile after mile of rich intertidal habitats combined with estuaries to create rich fishing grounds and mollusk beds. For the native people, there were no incentives or compelling social reasons to explore the broad expanses of the North Pacific. The skippers whose canoes paddled these waters were excellent seamen. They had to be, for they needed an encyclopedic knowledge of tides and currents, of safe beaches and natural landmarks. They relied on speed, seaworthiness, and an ability to forecast impending bad weather, often on short notice, to make safe passages in heavily laden canoes through a landscape of gigantic proportions. Over many centuries, the sheltered waterways of this long coastline became the home of communities large and small, a maritime world that was crowded yet deserted. One could paddle for miles without seeing anyone, then enter an estuary and find a series of villages teeming with people to whom the water and its creatures were life itself.

Everywhere in the Northwest, the water seems alive with subtle moods. This is a magic world for the modern-day kayaker, where mirror-calm bays and inlets seduce you. Your paddle dips into black water, drips from your stroke falling like raindrops onto the surface. The bow wave forms ripples that bisect the calm. The shadows from surrounding cliffs darken the inlets, and puffs of wind create ovals, stipples, and zigzags. From my kayak I've watched light play on the sea, creating patterns and fleeting images, restless impressions. Soon after coming ashore from my first excursion, I visited the University of British Columbia's Museum of Anthropology and its magnificent artworks. Here the endless change and restlessness of the ocean came alive in carvings and engravings, in painted tracery on boxes, masks, totem poles, and, above all, on canoes. The water and its creatures profoundly shaped the maritime world of the Northwest.

A workplace and a highway, the Northwest Coast was, above all, a seascape where the dugout canoe reigned. Here the sea was a marketplace, a mosaic of jealously guarded neighborhoods where one was careful to observe social protocol before landing in a strange place. The coast was the front doorstep where visitors were welcomed. This was why the Nootka greeted Captain Cook off Vancouver Island standing up in their canoes, throwing feathers and red ocher into the sea and delivering orations, followed by a song. "After the tumultuous oration had ceased, one of them sung a very agreeable air, with a degree of softness and melody which we would not have expected."[2]

The main harvesting season lay between early spring and autumn, when different foods abounded at widely scattered locations, usually accessible only by water. Such dispersed abundances created a world of constant, carefully scheduled moves from one location to another to maximize salmon harvests and other seasonal events. For example, the Coast

Tsimshian spent their winters in large towns in the modern-day Prince Rupert area of British Columbia. By late February or early March, they were on the move to the mouth of the Nass River, 30 miles (50 kilometers) north, for a eulachon (candlefish, prized for their oil) run that they controlled. By early summer, salmon were running in the Skeena River, and the community settled into summer camps by the estuary. In early fall, they would return to winter camp. These seasonal movements persisted for many generations and were relatively simple compared with those of some groups, who would move as often as sixteen times throughout the year. Five or six moves was the norm, but some communities, lucky enough to live in strategic places near salmon rivers, never traveled at all.

Households, or sometimes individuals, owned food resources of all kinds, including salmon runs, which supplied their basic needs. No community was completely self-sufficient, so coastal waters became a huge emporium. After 5000 B.C.E., a veritable jigsaw puzzle of exchange networks linked village with village. Nephrite for adze and ax blades, ever-popular obsidian for knives, seashells, dried fish—these were but a few of the commodities that passed along well-established trade routes.[3] For many centuries, the Coast Tsimshian exchanged eulachon and their oil with the Haida, Tlingit, and interior groups for such items as buckskins, small canoes, and copper. Finished products changed hands, too, many of them ceremonial items such as copper plaques, pendants, and masks.

The coastal waterways were far more than just marketplaces. They were streets where gossip was exchanged, public places where friends met, enemies fought, and all kinds of social transactions, such as marriages, were arranged. Here people loitered in their canoes, enjoying a public arena and indulging in small talk. Early European visitors traveled in local canoes, expecting fast passages, but were often disappointed. In 1852, colonist James Swan bought a 46-foot (14-meter) dugout from the Quinault Indians in what is now Willapa Bay, in southwestern Washington State. Swan soon became frustrated with progress in the hands of his Indian crew. "When in the canoe, all hands will paddle vehemently, and one would suppose the journey would be speedily accomplished, the canoe almost seeming to fly. The speed will be kept up for a hundred rods, when they cease paddling, and all begin talking." (A rod is 5.5 yards or 5 meters.) Someone would spot something; a piece of gossip from the village they had been visiting would come to mind; a legend associated with a rock or tree would have to be passed from the elders to the attentive young. Then the steersman would utter the word "hurry" and the paddling would resume, only to cease a short distance farther along.[4]

Above the water, humans transacted their daily business from their canoes, their watercraft as much a part of their lives as their houses on land. Beneath the surface, mythic beasts such as Komogwa, an octopuslike creature, lurked. Rich in red-hued copper, a color associated with salmon, this dread figure with prominent beak and nose and all-seeing eyes dragged canoes underwater. Killer whales were his familiars in a cruel and unrelenting seascape teeming with menacing powers. The Tlingit of the Yakutat region of Alaska believed that the sky touched the ocean at the horizon, the end of the earth lying even farther away. Strange things could arrive "from the edge of the world, perhaps from islands out of sight of land, or from the mysterious realm beyond the barriers of the horizon."[5] These exotic objects included driftwood, bamboo, and flotsam carried by the Japan Current. A Tlingit legend tells of a man from Sitka who tried to visit the place where these objects originated. He drifted out of sight of land and came to an island, where he lived among sea otters. A year later he returned, having apparently lived close to the edge of the world.

EVERYWHERE, CANOES ASSUMED huge importance, not only for their carrying abilities but as social instruments in an environment where many personal dealings unfolded over the water.[6] Northwest canoes came, and still come, in many sizes. Small inshore fishing canoes were part of every household, while much larger freight and hunting craft required the services of specialist builders. Anyone could fashion a small dugout. Every man knew how to cut and split wood—he had to build houses and other structures on a regular basis. Larger canoes were a much more serious matter. Old-growth western red cedar trees between three hundred and eight hundred years old were ideal, selected carefully for their straight grain. The builder would perform purification rituals, communicate with the spirit of the tree, and perhaps listen for the chopping sounds of a supernatural assistant already working on the trunk. The woodpecker was often the dream spirit associated with canoe building. Finally, the builder would try to select a tree that was close to a beach, river, or lakeshore. If it was farther inland, he would fell and rough-shape it, then leave the trunk to cure before enlisting the assistance of family and kin to haul it nearer to the water. I've seen rough-outs from long ago abandoned in the forest, bow and stern chopped to approximate shape.

After felling the tree with chisels or by controlled burning, the canoe builder would shape and block out the hull shape before steaming it, the most crucial part of the operation. Wooden pegs drilled into the bottom sides ensured a uniform thickness, usually of two or three fingers. He would heat rocks red-hot in a nearby fire pit, then pour water into the hollowed-out hull and use the rocks to heat it. As heating proceeded, the builder and his assistants splashed water up the sides to accelerate the softening process. Mats placed over the sides helped the steam soften the timber. Then the builder lashed the thwarts into place between the softened sides to form the final shape. Finally, the builder would heat dogfish oil and coat the inside and outside thoroughly. The result was an elegant, relatively light canoe with raised bow and stern and flared sides, capable of navigating quite rough water. Elaborate carvings adorned many canoes, often depicting legendary figures and spirit beings associated with the water. The largest craft used for freight and in war were up to 60 to 70 feet (18 to 21 meters) long. One eighteenth-century war fleet consisted of forty canoes, each carrying twenty warriors. Most canoes were much smaller, in the 18-to-35-foot (5.5-to-10.6-meter) range. They drew about 3 feet (0.9 meter), which enabled the paddlers to operate in shallow water and also to land on convenient beaches, where the canoe could be pulled above the high-water level. The Northwest canoe in its many iterations was a brilliant adaptation to a rugged coastline, where most water was relatively smooth. Fast paddling speeds were imperative in deteriorating weather.

The dugout canoe was a vehicle for trade, exchange, and war and, above all, for fishing. Canoes were platforms—for landing enormous halibut, for hooking cod in deep water, for raking in shoals of herring so numerous that they could be gathered by the thousand. Northwest

Figure 13.2 *Northwest dugout canoe, showing the characteristic raked bow and stern.* © *David A. Barnes/Alamy.*

canoe captains were as adept as their Aleut neighbors far to the north; their watercraft were of superb design and quality, ideally suited to a maritime world of inlets and coastal channels. But they were not seafarers in the sense that Polynesians were; nor, apparently, did they revel in the rough, open waters so readily traversed by the Aleuts. Theirs was a narrower, more circumscribed world where the hard experience of fishing and coastal trading passed from one generation to the next, virtually unchanged, over many centuries.[7]

AT NINSTINTS, OR SGang Gwaay Llanagaay ("Red Cod Island Village"), in the southern Queen Charlotte Islands, a deserted Haida village lies at the back of a sheltered tidal beach where canoes once came ashore. The houses once lay on a ridge above the high-tide level, marked now by a smattering of carved totem poles where there was once a veritable grove of them. A few still stand upright, others lie at an angle, green saplings sprouting from the cedar. Large numbers of them were removed to the Royal British Columbia Museum, but fortunately not all of them, for the Haida believe that the poles, commemorating ancestors, should revert to the forest from which they came. Ninstints is a deeply moving place, more so than other abandoned villages, for there are more poles here. Walking among them on a windy day, with rain drifting across the bay, you can sense just how Haida life was defined by their close relationship with land and ocean, between the realms of the living and the supernatural. Northwest art reflected this dark, sometimes menacing world, where people moved through landscapes rippling with malevolent power.

The inshore waters of the Northwest Coast may have been a neighborhood used by all, but deciphering them meant far more than reading the colors of the water, the fretting of rising wind on deeper waters, and the careful adjudication of fast-running tides. Anyone traveling a significant distance had to know the complex social and political relationships that fractured the coastline in an ebb and flow of alliances and rivalries. Today, most of the great villages of a century and a half ago or more lie abandoned, marked only by collapsed house foundations and sometimes a few weathered totem poles. Most of what we know about their inhabitants

Figure 13.3 *Haida totem poles at Ninstints, Queen Charlotte Islands, British Columbia.* © *Gunter Marx/Alamy.*

comes from archaeology, oral traditions, and the research of early anthropologists such as Franz Boas. They depict a convoluted human world, intensely competitive, with factionalism running rife. Chiefs and commoners alike lived in an atmosphere of fluid alliances and volatile quarrels, which could erupt into punitive raids and war at the slightest provocation.

More than 250,000 Indians lived along the coast when the first European ships arrived in the late eighteenth century. Over thousands of years, the degree of social complexity along the coast varied considerably, depending in part on the abundance of locally available foods. Much of the time, there were such abundances that the people could draw on large reservoirs of stored food, much of it derived from harvesting salmon runs.

However, the abundance varied from one area to the next, creating a volatile atmosphere of competition and profound suspicion among local groups, fueled both by living at close quarters and, for many smaller communities, the opposite—isolation for much of the year.

Kin groups lived and worked together and considered themselves the exclusive owners of land and fishing grounds. Each autonomous local group had its own leader, its own set of privileges that included personal names and crests, dance ceremonials and songs. These were societies that placed a high premium on prestige, social position, and wealth, but one acquired respect and stature not by hoarding food and precious commodities but by sharing them.

If one's household was productive and rich, then one could participate fully in local and regional exchange and in that most celebrated of coastal institutions, the potlatch, or ceremonial feast. Potlatches were dignified ceremonies, given by a chief and his kin group, who entertained other chiefs and their kin. They usually marked an important event like a marriage or the assumption of the right to a title or crest. Elaborate

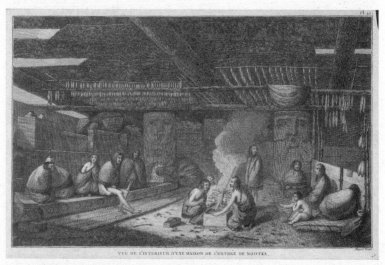

VUE DE L'INTÉRIEUR D'UNE MAISON DE L'ENTRÉE DE NOOTKA.

Figure 13.4 *Interior of a Nootka planked house, Vancouver Island, at the time of Cook's visit in 1778.* © *Mary Evans Picture Library/ Grosvenor Prints/Image Works EMEP0183197.*

ceremonial protocol surrounded the potlatch, with everyone wearing their formal regalia. The hosts dispensed their wealth in food, clothing, and ceremonial objects, for generosity enhanced personal and lineage prestige. From a social perspective, potlatches ensured that wealth was distributed through society and provided a strong unifying force among fellow kin in a social environment where there was every temptation to acquire wealth for oneself.

The masks and regalia worn by chiefs, dancers, and others commemorated ravens and whales, halibut and salmon—denizens of a mobile space full of meanings, portents, and menacing hazards. The motifs and the flowing style in all these conventions evoked dark water, reflections in calm inlets where even a feather of wind would create endlessly moving designs—claws, dismembered eyes, dorsal fins of killer whales. The light played on the water, and the artists used its changing reflections to create parts of traditional narratives as old as society itself. These narratives were a critical part of deciphering the ocean, as was the legend of Raven from Southeast Alaska. One day, Raven spotted a box floating in the ocean, close inshore. After gathering the people on the beach, he dragged the box to shore as they played drums and sang. Then he opened its several doors. Small fish came out from one side, eulachon and herring from another, then salmon from a third. Finally, he pushed out cod, flounder, and halibut. "Just the way he opened the doors, is just the way they come every year . . . And Raven was satisfied, he released all the fish to go around this world."[8]

GIVEN ITS MARITIME geography, the Northwest Coast was an inward-looking world, endowed with much abundance, yet dark and restless, where life was always changing, just as mythic beings transformed themselves into animals and humans. There were no social imperatives to sail away across the horizon. For all the factionalism and suspicion, there was plenty of food and space for new settlements. Only rarely did larger canoes venture into the open Pacific, and then only when fishing or hunting whales. A Spanish ship once sighted a large dugout more than 40 miles (64 kilometers) off Vancouver Island, but such excursions were rare on an open ocean where large swells and steep wind waves were common-place. It was mainly whales that lured canoes into the open ocean, and only to kill their prey and bring it to shore.

South of Cape Flattery, on the Olympic Peninsula, the shoreline turns southward, with no islands to protect the coast. Here the Makah tribe regularly hunted whales in large dugouts. Whale hunters were prominent members of society, who inherited their skills from earlier generations.[9] When a village spotted a pod close offshore, the hunters would set out in eight-man dugout canoes. As they paddled out toward the pod, the whale hunter would invite the whales—"noble ladies"—to come and be caught. Silently, the canoe would paddle to a position above and slightly to the left of the unsuspecting whale. As his prey blew and submerged, the hunter, perched in the bow, would cast his razor-sharp mussel-shell-bladed harpoon. For hours, the paddlers would follow their wounded quarry, pursuing the sealskin floats on the harpoon line. As the whale tired and surfaced, the hunter would approach carefully and kill it with a deep lance stroke behind the flipper. It could take hours to tow the carcass back to the village. The entire community would butcher the car-cass, the meat and blubber being distributed according to rank.

Every whale hunter was well aware of the limitations of his canoe in exposed waters. So were the large Indian dugout captains, who oper-ated out of the Klamath River in extreme Northern California during the mid-nineteenth century. Local headmen set up a transport service for white settlers between the river and Crescent City, 22 miles (35 kilo-meters) to the north. They even occasionally transported loads as far south as Humboldt Bay, 80 miles (129 kilometers) away.[10] The skippers would regularly shoot the rapids and surf at the mouth of the Klamath, but they picked their weather carefully. They had to, because of the low freeboard of their canoes. By paddling close inshore at night and during the calm morning hours, they provided a more reliable service than the heavy European sailing ships that spent hours each day becalmed or battling strong headwinds. But the crews were careful to avoid the hours when the northwesterlies blew, as well as periods of stormy weather.

SOUTH OF THE Klamath, more than 1,250 miles (2,000 kilometers) of Pacific coastline face the open ocean, much of it backed by coastal mountain ranges and rugged terrain.[11] There are major estuaries, often with formidable river bars and extensive wetlands, the largest being San Francisco Bay and its inland delta regions, where fish, mollusks, and waterfowl abound. This coastline is beset by often fierce southeasterly gales in winter and days on end of strong northwesterlies, especially in summer. Large swells break on the shore, generated by storms thousands of miles to seaward. Landing, even on a calm day, can be hazardous unless there is a deep bay or estuary into which one can paddle.

For thousands of years, hunter-gatherer bands lived off game and plant foods along these shores, also taking mollusks and fishing, often in quite deep waters around offlying rocks. Most people lived in small groups, hunting and foraging within territories anchored by streams or near the coast, close to wetlands, where the highest populations were to be found. Few band members traveled far from home. A nineteenth-century oral tradition tells of one Mono woman who lived her entire life in California's Central Valley, within five miles (eight kilometers) of her birthplace. In the San Francisco Bay area, coastal groups subsisting off fish, mollusks, and waterfowl used small canoes made of tule reeds, and also dugouts, but they probably did not pass through the Golden Gate, with its fast-moving tides.

The offshore waters south of the Klamath were not a place for frail craft or simple dugout canoes. There was never a maritime highway here, navigated by heavily laden canoes pressing ever southward in search of new homelands. It is not until one has passed along the Big Sur coast of Central California and rounded Point Conception—the westernmost, and often extremely windy, headland on the West Coast—that one finds people who decoded coastal waters as part of their daily lives.

No one knows when Native Americans first settled along the Central and Southern California coasts, but it seems likely that early settlers visited the shore to search for mollusks and perhaps to hunt sea mammals as early as 12,000 years ago, if not earlier. South of Point Conception, the dynamics of coastal waters change completely. The Santa Barbara

Channel extends east and west from Point Conception, protected to the south from the worst Pacific swells by the barrier of four of the Channel Islands. Here, cold water from the seabed wells upward and transports rich nutrients to the surface. This natural upwelling attracts millions of anchovies and a bounty of other fish; dense kelp beds abounding in marine life grow along island and mainland shores. This is one of the richest fisheries in the world, rivaled only by other areas of upwelling, such as those off the Peruvian and Namibian coasts. Here, Indian populations reached unusually high densities, with permanent mainland villages supporting hundreds of people ruled by headmen and chiefs who both controlled wealth and enjoyed unusual supernatural powers.

These were the Chumash, diverse groups of shore-based and inland hunters, foragers, and fisherfolk who lived both on the mainland and on the Channel Islands, some 24 miles (39 kilometers) offshore. Unlike the Northwesterners, whose lives revolved almost entirely around the ocean, the coastal Chumash maintained close, and constant, ties with the near and far interior. Acorns and exotica such as turquoise flowed to the channel from as far inland as Zuni country, in the Southwest; seashells and shell beads passed in the opposite direction. The people of the coast and the interior could not live without one another in a world of uncertain, seasonal rainfall and sometimes violent El Niños that brought storms and pelting rains. Here, a deciphered ocean was part of daily life, connected directly to economic, political, and social developments on land.

When the first Spanish explorers visited Chumash villages, they were impressed by the ordered authority. One traveler, Juan Crespi, observed in 1769 that "all the towns have three or four captains, one of which is head chief." A few of the men wore bearskin capes, which marked canoe owners and captains. These were individuals of wealth and influence who possessed remarkable vessels—*tomols*.[12]

Tomols were planked canoes, fabricated by expert builders from driftwood laboriously collected over many months. Unlike in the Northwest, a boatbuilder here had no straight-grained logs at hand, unless a trunk drifted ashore from hundreds of miles away. Common folk fished in the kelp from reed canoes constructed of bundles of indigenous tule reeds or from small dugout canoes. These were fine for calm inshore waters, but

Figure 13.5 *A Chumash Indian canoe in the Santa Barbara Channel, Southern California. Santa Barbara Museum of Natural History.*

they lacked the freeboard needed to navigate comfortably in any sea—reed canoes become waterlogged in a matter of days even when coated with the tar found on local beaches. Thus it was that the Chumash or their ancestors turned to planking stitched together from pieces of driftwood, the planks built up from a keel that was basically a dugout canoe. The double-ended *tomol* had a high bow and stern that helped it perform in waves, just like Northwestern dugouts. The sides flared slightly, to keep water outboard. *Tomols* averaged about 12 to 30 feet (3.7 to 9 meters) long, with a beam of about 3 feet (0.9 meter), enough to carry between three and six people and a modest load. Building a canoe took many months. Once it was complete and caulked with fiber and tar, "they put it into the sea and rowed it about, seeing if there is anything wrong with it . . . They check for leaks and whether or not the canoe is lopsided or sinks too deeply into the water."[13] The master builder himself would ballast the canoe, for considerable inboard weight was needed to achieve stability.

Stability they needed, for these are foggy and sometimes turbulent waters. Sometimes a band of dense fog hovers off the mainland, outside the kelp beds. One moment you can see for miles, and the next, visibility is only a few yards. I once sailed with no engine toward Santa Barbara after an all-night trip from Anacapa Island. It was brilliantly clear all night, with a slight land breeze. We ghosted along until a mere two miles (three kilometers) from the harbor. Suddenly the wind died with the dawn, and the fog descended. We could barely see our hands in front of our faces, drifting blindly in the blanketing silence. After a couple of hours, the groundswell became more pronounced and steep-faced. We rolled violently with slatting sails, completely lost except for the increasingly violent motion that warned of shallow water ahead. Just as we prepared the anchor, the fog lifted, showing breakers only a short distance away. We turned on our tail for deeper water, blessing the few breaths of land breeze that carried us to safety.

Tomols were open boats, but fast and seaworthy in the calm seas and light winds that often prevail in the Santa Barbara Channel. Each man sat on a pad of sea grass, paddling with an even rhythm, using his shoulders to do the work, just like modern-day kayakers. A skilled crew could keep up the pace all day, paddling to the accompaniment of a canoe song repeated again and again. Experiments with replicas have shown that experienced paddlers can maintain a speed of 6 to 8 knots (11 to 15 kilometers per hour) with a following sea and an 8-knot (15-kilometer-per-hour) breeze. But if the same wind blew from ahead, progress virtually halted.

Prisoners Harbor, Santa Cruz Island, 1700 C.E.: The calm water is rose-colored from the setting sun, the steep ridges of the island razor sharp in the growing twilight. Three heavily laden *tomols* paddle silently close inshore. Their captains skirt the kelp at the foot of the steep cliffs as they enter the wide bay, the canoes rocking slightly in the gentle swell. They steer for the lowest point on the land, where delicate trails of woodsmoke from the village climb vertically into the clear sky. As the canoes approach land, they hear dogs barking, the soft sounds of leisurely conversation, the *scrape-scrape* of grindstones preparing the evening meal . . .

The next morning, a howling northwester keeps the *tomols* ashore as they prepare to return to the mainland, laden with seashell beads exchanged for mainland acorns. The captains climb to higher ground and ponder the channel—not so much the wind, which will drop at sunset, but the swell. They decide to wait for three days, not that conditions at sea are dangerous once the wind dies down—they are not—but because they will be unable to land safely at their destination, which is exposed to the westerly swell. Even when they do close with the shore, they proceed with great care, rapidly paddling for the beach just after the crest of a breaking wave that carries the *tomol* high on the sand, its precious load intact. Like seamen everywhere, the skippers have learned the ways of the ocean from oral traditions, rote memorization, and hard-won experience.

Tomol skippers timed their voyages for calm days—often more common in winter—and for morning hours. Most island passages began in the area near Point Hueneme, where the passage to Anacapa Island is but 12 miles (19 kilometers), an easy paddle. From there, a canoe could island-hop to nearby coves on Santa Cruz Island and from there as far west as the windy shores of San Miguel Island, where mollusks and sea mammals abounded, provided the paddlers chose the calm hours of day to go to a place where the winds can shriek from the northwest at 45 miles per hour (75 kilometers per hour) for days on end.

Even on quiet days, there was always a danger that the wind would rise without warning, bringing steep waves. Oral traditions tell of catastrophic voyages, including one of a party of canoes that left San Miguel Island on their way south. The wind came up, and not one reached home. More than sixty people drowned. Rough seas were no place for open canoes. No *tomol* boasted of outriggers; all were relatively low in the water, especially when heavily laden. They required experience and nice judgment to handle properly in even moderate conditions. Modern replicas paddle to the islands with escort boats, the crews wearing life preservers. No such amenities were available in ancient times, but just as in other places, the risk was accepted as part of life and compensated for by conservative behavior on the water, and with spiritual beliefs.

For many centuries, there were sporadic crossings to the Channel Islands, where human populations remained small. The canoes carried acorns from the mainland, then returned with shell beads, which were manufactured on the islands and traded extensively into the interior. Sometime after 650 C.E., these interconnections intensified as canoe owners, always influential members of society, now played a central role in a burgeoning trade. They manipulated social contacts with the islands, managed information about fisheries offshore, and controlled a rapidly growing trade in olivella shell beads made with stone drills.[14] Canoe skippers were wealthy, ritually important members of society who controlled the logistics of moving cargoes across open water, using kin ties and other social nuances to develop what was effectively a monopoly. The leaders of this ancient society interwove specialized crafts, cross-channel trade, and marine travel. Their style of leadership, their emphasis on major rituals, and their sophisticated means of promoting both personal advancement and interdependency forged a society without rigid social ranks, warriors, or slaves. It was a brilliant solution to living in an unpredictable, sometimes violent world of climatic extremes, and the Chumash flourished until Europeans decimated their society with exotic disease and forced missionization.

The Northwest Indians and the Chumash were unusual in their deciphering of coastal waters, but they never ventured eastward into deeper waters to the west, where the sun set. They developed sophisticated relationships with the ocean, but always relationships with pragmatic ends—food, intervillage communication, trade, and all manner of social exchange. And underlying these maritime connections lay deeply felt spiritual links with the supernatural forces of the water—both close inshore and out to the horizon and beyond—which, unfortunately, are lost to us. Fortunately, as we shall see in the next chapter, the decipherment of Maya script has given us insights into just how complex these spiritual relationships could be, even in societies whose main focus was centered on land.

CHAPTER 14

The Fiery Pool and the Spiny Oyster

"THERE IS NOT YET ONE PERSON . . . Only the sky alone is there; the face of the earth is not clear. Only the sea alone is pooled under all the sky . . . It is at rest; not a single thing stirs." Then there are murmurs and ripples as Sovereign Plumed Serpent, the creator, glitters blue-green in the dark waters. He consults with the Sky God and they decide: "Let it be this way . . . This water should be removed, emptied out for the formation of the earth's own plate and platform, then should come the sowing, the dawning of the sky-earth." Then "the earth arose because of them" and the elaborate process of creation began.[1]

Such is the beginning of the *Popol Vuh*, the Quiché Maya legend of creation, which tells of the watery arena that was the infinite realm of the ancestors. Deep, often opaque water was the domain of the ancestors in many ancient societies, but it is only rarely that we can learn of the complex but intangible relationship between ancient societies and the ocean. Such relationships were an integral part of both their understanding of and their decipherment of inshore and offshore waters. We can often figure how our remote forebears found their way across hazardous waters, and sometimes why they did so, but almost never do we gain an understanding of the powerful supernatural beliefs behind such ventures. The ancient Maya provide us with a unique insight into a society where the ocean played a central role in human life, even far from water's edge.

The *Popol Vuh* tells us that Maya life began in the limitless waterways of the Underworld, as opaque as the Eastern Sea, where the sun rose.

This was K'ankh' Nahb, "the Fiery Pool," the shimmering realm where the sun rose in the Caribbean and set in the Gulf of Mexico. The Maya knew little or nothing of the Caribbean islands beyond the horizon, even if occasional canoes from the Greater Antilles washed ashore. One arrived in 1539, we are told, bringing naked strangers "to eat men," but these voyagers pass anonymously into history.[2]

The Fiery Pool, in its elaborate radiance, dominated much Maya thought and daily life. They believed that their world, the low-lying Yucatán Peninsula, floated like a turtle on the limitless waters of the ocean. Each morning, the sun rose over the Eastern Sea from a chaotic and violent realm. Here, great cosmic battles raged between gods and sea serpents as the ocean turned red. The saline taste of seawater evoked the taste of the blood that colored the ocean red at sunrise and sunset, whence the "Fiery Pool." Surrounded by this threatening realm, the Maya clung to the turtle's carapace, which cracked and shook when earthquakes struck or floods descended on the fields.

A huge body of water supported the ground and coursed through great underground rivers, a pulsing artery that flowed west from the eastern Caribbean Sea. Like many other ancient societies surrounded by the ocean, the ancient Maya thought of the sea, rivers, clouds, and all sources of water as one, a vital medium that sustained humanity and the foods they ate. The Fiery Pool was a domain of awesome powers that generated hurricanes and violent rainstorms, the birthplace of the sun, the creator of clouds and wind. Here dwelt a huge mythic crocodile, whose limbs extended to the cardinal points that defined the square Maya world. Water cascaded from his extremities—the cosmic flood. Here the rain god Chaac dwelt in timeless waters that were the source of light, abundance, and riches.

Most Mayans lived far from the ocean, but the sea was ever present in their thoughts. Supernatural power came from the Fiery Pool and from the Underworld, so great lords commissioned architecture and monumental sculpture as backdrops for displays of human and divine authority. Pyramids and plazas, the stelae commemorating different rulers: all were symbolic depictions of the Maya world. At Copán, in modern-day

Figure 14.1 *Major Maya sites and other locations mentioned in Chapter 14.*

Honduras, an elevated stage, perhaps a reviewing stand for public performances, depicts the rain god Chaac emerging between two giant conch shells, as if he is at water's edge. Two enormous, apelike wind gods frame the stage. Below in the plaza, three slabs depict the maize god K'awiil, holding the glyph for yellow maize, for he will rise out of the sea through a crack in the tortoise shell.[3] At Calakmul, in Mexico, a 665-foot (203-meter) wall, the "Calakmul place pool wall," turns a nearby plaza into a sea known as Chiik Nahb. Waterbirds and layers of blue paint commemorate the bounty of the watery realm. These and other monuments were the stages for religious narratives set by the ocean or near lakes or marshes.

Nobody was allowed to forget that the menacing ocean, with its dangerous creatures, hovered at the frontiers of Maya life. Artists codified and defined the threat; conch shells from distant shores, used in public ceremonies as conch trumpets, helped center even the largest cities in a much wider universe that included the sea. Both strombus, the conch, and spondylus, the spiny or thorny oyster, played a central role in both Maya and Andean efforts to decipher the ocean.

THE STROMBUS, OR CONCH, forms a natural trumpet, easily fashioned by cutting off the spine and grinding out a mouthpiece. Conch trumpets are part of humanity's musical history.[4] The Greek fish-tailed sea god Triton was said to control the waves by blowing his conch trumpet. An ancient Hindu text, the *Bhagavad Gita* (Song of God), describes how Lord Krishna and the prince Arjuna blew conch shell horns as they rode into battle seated in a giant chariot pulled by white horses. The U.S. Coast Guard even lists conch horns as a legitimate sound-making device in its official Navigation Rules.

The Maya considered conchs sacred. Queen conch shells from shallow water bounding the Eastern Sea traveled far inland to Tikal and other Maya cities. Artisans fashioned them into trumpets, inkpots, and pendants that sometimes bore depictions of ancestors peering down at the living world from the clouds. The conch symbolized the Moon Goddess, night, darkness, and connections with the Underworld, the place where the moon died and was reborn. When conch trumpets sounded, they symbolized rebirth, and also timeless wisdom. One conch shell fragment shows a sitting priest named Jewel-Jaguar smoking a long, thin cigar and wearing a deer headdress. He gestures toward a conch, where a serpentine head appears to embody the voice of the shell. Conch trumpets sounded at great public ceremonies, announced approaching visitors, played important roles in the hunt and in war. These versatile instruments had many symbolic voices, were pregnant with numerous associations. Together with stingray spines, coral, pearls, and objects made of spondylus shell, they evoked the watery Underworld in the tombs of important people.

Conchs thrive in shallow water, which makes them easy to collect. In contrast, another sacred mollusk, spondylus, the spiny or thorny oyster,

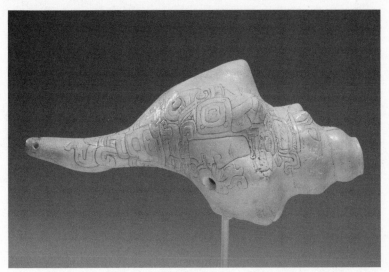

Figure 14.2 *A Classic Maya conch trumpet depicts a floating ances-tor, c. 250–600 C.E. Diameter: 11.5 by 5.25 inches (29.3 by 13.4 cen-timeters). Kimbell Art Museum, Fort Worth, Texas/Art Resource, NY.*

clings to warm-water reefs between 20 and 60 feet (6 to 18 meters) below the surface of both the Gulf of Mexico and the Pacific Ocean. Collect-ing these deepwater mollusks required expert free diving. Those who sought them soon became prone to hearing loss. Spondylus shells had strong associations with the rain god Chaac, and also with the wind god Ik' K'uh, the deity of the east, the ocean, and rain. Like the conch and other shells, the spiny oyster had strong links to the music that was a central part of ball playing, dancing, and other public performances. Pendants tinkled as their users moved; snail-shell bells, drums, gourd rattles and rasps, and clay flutes and whistles all made music, as did copper bells when they came into use in later times. The Eastern Sea, with its seashells and their wavelike sounds when held to the ear, may have been the abode of music. Public performance and ritual played such an important part in Maya life that there was an insatiable demand for both spondylus and strombus. Both defined the complex relationships

Figure 14.3 *A carved bone from Burial 116, Tikal, Guatemala, 734 C.E., shows the maize god (at center) traveling through life in a canoe, heading toward the moment of death. Aged paddler gods paddle on the platforms at bow and stern. Drawing by Annemarie Seuffert. University of Pennsylvania Museum of Archaeology and Anthropology, Philadelphia.*

between the Maya and the ocean—and the trade in objects of great spiritual importance that traveled in their canoes.

DESPITE THEIR COMPLEX spiritual relationship with the ocean, the Maya never traveled over the horizon. They lacked the right kinds of watercraft and also lived in terror of the supernatural powers that lurked in deeper water. The conch and the spiny oyster, as well as other exotica and more prosaic commodities, traveled to cities far inland through a maze of pathways over land and sea. Much of this extensive trade traveled by canoe, and for good reason. Spaniard Hernán Cortés, who overthrew Aztec civilization in one of the most audacious military campaigns in history, wrote of the Yucatán that "there was not a single road to be found anywhere in the whole country, nor any evidence to show that it had been trod by human feet, because the Indians travel only by canoes on account of those great rivers and marshes."[5]

A generation earlier, none other than Christopher Columbus, on his fourth voyage, in 1502, encountered a large trading canoe off the Bay Islands of northern Honduras. His son Ferdinand wrote, "There arrived a canoe full of Indians, as long as a galley and eight feet wide . . . and all of one tree." Twenty-five men paddled the heavily laden vessel. A huddle of women and children with their possessions, and valuable trade goods, sheltered from the sun under a palm-leaf canopy amidships. An astonishing range of luxury goods was aboard, among them copper axes and bells fabricated in Tabasco and crucibles for fashioning other artifacts. There were multicolored quilts and embroidered tunics, probably from the Yucatán, long wooden central Mexican swords, their edges bearing razor-sharp obsidian blades, and bags of cacao beans, so valuable that the crew hastily picked up loose beans "as if an eye had fallen from their heads."[6]

Just this one encounter speaks volumes about the closely integrated maritime trade networks that linked widely separated areas of the ancient Central American world.[7] This particular canoe carried prestigious and much-prized luxuries, none of the basic commodities that passed the length and breadth of Maya domains. Raw cotton, honey, maize, salt, and slaves were the unspectacular staples of the maritime trade, many of them transported to a ring of coastal settlements, such as Uaymil, on Yucatán shores. Islands off the coast, such as Cozumel and Wild Cane Cay, in what is today Belize, had relatively small populations, but they were important distribution points for a steady stream of luxury objects and commodities that passed up rivers and trails into the interior.

The canoe encountered by Columbus had traveled at least 20 miles (32 kilometers) over open water from Guanaja Island, but it was almost certainly island hopping. Even a passage of this length was risky for laden dugouts in any weight of wind. Such crossings required careful preparation and more than a few hours' calm winds and flat water, as well as offerings to the powerful deities of the ocean. To take one example, a relatively short 11.5-mile (18.5-kilometer) paddle from the mainland to Cozumel was considered notoriously dangerous. To embark on such a crossing at the wrong time would unleash the fury of the supernatural beings in the Fiery Pool. When the conquistador Francisco de Montejo, who was to pacify much of the Yucatán and founded the city of Merida in 1542, tried to cross with ten soldiers, he was warned off "because the sea was angry." He insisted on departing. Nine soldiers were drowned, and the tenth killed after his return to the mainland, perhaps to propitiate the furious deities. According to a seventeenth-century Franciscan historian, Diego López de Cogulludo, the local people performed rituals before making this crossing. Conquistadores passing Cozumel reported seeing bonfires atop the shrines and also at other, often remote locations along the shore.

These may have been places where fishers and canoe crews made offerings to the gods and to the ocean itself.

There may have been larger canoes in earlier times, but if so they were certainly log canoes, which do not handle well in rough water. Most Maya craft were much smaller, used for the most part in rivers and creeks and close inshore. But anyone on a longer journey faced submerged coral and other hazards. Experienced seafarers would have known every coral head, landmarks large and small. On the inshore side of the Bay Islands, off the northern coast of Honduras, I've taken a small dinghy through narrow channels lined with seemingly impenetrable mangroves, the defiles shadowed by thick branches overhead. The water is black and still, disturbed only by rising fish and the occasional waterfowl. I forgot that the ocean was close by, for no swell rocked our small boat. We passed side channels and small villages tucked into the swamps, fishing boats working the shallows. It was as if we had paddled back centuries to a time when Maya dugouts paddled and poled through the same swampy creeks carrying exotic goods from afar to distant lords living in magnificent cities over the horizon.

Over many centuries, networks of coastal trade routes linked with riverine ones. The British Mayanist J. E. S. Thompson described a seagoing route that started at an Aztec trading center at Xicalango, in the Laguna de Términos region, at the eastern root of the Yucatán, then skirted the coast of the Yucatán, then went on to what is now Costa Rica and the Panama Canal region.[8] Obsidian, metalwork, and fine pottery were the staples of this trade, probably carried in larger canoes like that encountered by Columbus. Obsidian traveled in enormous quantities by canoe from southern Guatemala north along the Belize coast, and then around the Yucatán Peninsula before traveling to major centers inland. The broad reach of Maya trade brought turquoise from the North American Southwest, gold from lower Central America, and obsidian from central Mexico to form polished mirrors, ear spools, and other ornaments. Much commerce traveled by sea, unifying art styles and symbols of all kinds over the Maya realm and farther afield. But spondylus may have traveled the longest distances—from South America across the open Pacific to western Mexico. The Andeans lived in what must have been as complex a spiritual realm as that of the Maya, but they traveled boldly across open water in ways unimaginable to people in fear of the Fiery Pool. With them they carried sacred seashells, symbols of at least some loose spiritual connection.

Figure 14.4 *A clay vase shows the maize god traveling in a canoe with a sack of maize on his shoulder. Beneath the canoe, a watery serpent is about to consume the god. © Jorge Pérez de Lara.*

CHAVÍN DE HUANTAR, the Andes foothills of Peru, 800 B.C.E. Steady rain mingles with woodsmoke and incense above the plazas and terraces of the ancient shrine. Hidden passages inside the Old Temple sound and thunder with fast-flowing water in the calm morning air. A watching crowd stands in silence, oblivious to the damp. Suddenly a conch trumpet sounds and sounds again. A dancing, masked shaman appears, deep in a hallucinogenic trance. He chants, sings, utters the pronouncements of the revered oracle, and then vanishes into clouds of smoke and into the depths of the shrine as suddenly as he appeared.

In the year 1520, Rodrigo de Albornoz, a royal accountant in the capital of New Spain, wrote to His Majesty about preparations for a planned expedition southward from Zacatula, near the mouth of the Rio Balsas, in western Mexico. Two ships were under construction to follow up on reports from Indians of islands to the south that were rich in gold and pearls. Their fathers and grandfathers remembered large canoes that had arrived from islands to the south, carrying "exquisite things which they would trade for local products." When bad weather prevented their departure, "those that had come would stay for five or six months until good weather occurred and the sea became calm."[9]

Six years later, one of Francisco Pizarro's ships, under the command of his main pilot, Bartolomé Ruiz, sailed south of the equator and sighted a vessel on the horizon "which presented a great bulk, resembling a lateen sail." Ruiz came up to a large raft "with crosspieces and underbody of some poles as thick as pillars, lashed together with line made of what is called henequen [agave fiber], which is like hemp. The upper works were of other thinner poles, also lashed with line, on which people and merchandise rode so as not to get wet, since the lower part was awash." The raft had a "quarterdeck, small huts, rudders, sails, rigging" and also carried boulders that served as anchors. Another observer, Miguel de Estete, noted that the balsa logs that made up the raft were "as soft and light on the waters as a cork." They were, he added, "very safe vessels, because they cannot sink or capsize, since the water washes through them everywhere."[10] The conquistadores helped themselves to the cargo: "They brought many pieces of silver and gold for the adornment of their persons and for exchange with those with whom they went to trade." The inventory included all kinds of ornaments and copper bells and also cotton and wool garments and emeralds. "All this they brought to trade for some seashells of which they made red beads like coral (the reddish colour) and white, that they had the boat nearly full of them." Hundreds of spondylus shells lay aboard.

OCHROMA PYRAMIDALE, the balsa tree, is large and fast-growing, sometimes as tall as 100 feet (30 meters). Native from southern Brazil and Bolivia to southern Central America, it is a lightweight timber with a lower density than cork. When dry, the wood is buoyant and strong, its logs ideal for constructing rafts, especially when coated with asphalt.

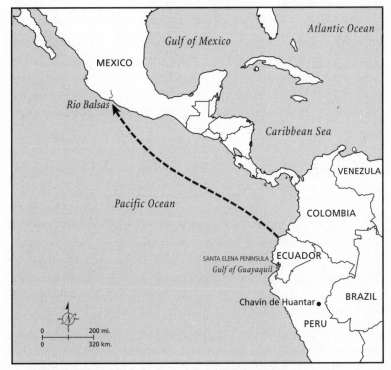

Figure 14.5 *Map showing the hypothetical route of Ecuadoran canoes to Mexico.*

Coastal Indians in what is now Ecuador used such rafts for fishing and much longer passages that took them as far as western Mexico, a hazardous passage even when taking advantage of seasonal winds.

Assuming a speed of about four knots (seven kilometers per hour) and twelve hours of travel a day, a raft would take between six and eight weeks to complete the northward voyage, leaving in early December and arriving in late January, a period when both winds and currents were favorable.[11] By leaving for the south in late March, the rafts would avoid the rainy season, but they probably also waited out the hurricane period. Modern-day engineering analysis confirms that these balsa rafts were seaworthy, easily handled vessels, controlled by centerboards at the bow and stern.

Why would coastal Indians in Ecuador undertake such long and potentially hazardous passages to an unknown land? I believe that spondylus holds the key. The center of the Andean spiny oyster trade was the Santa Elena Peninsula, on Ecuador's south coast, where it began as early as 3000 B.C.E., expanding massively some two thousand years later. And it was from here northward that balsa rafts flourished. Along this stretch of coast, wrote the sixteenth-century Italian traveler Girolamo Benzoni, "the Indians are great fishermen. The craft which they use both for fishing and navigating are a form of raft made of . . . very light logs formed in the shape of a hand."[12] At some point, perhaps coasting or sailing much farther offshore, some of these fishermen turned traders carried spondylus and other exotica as far north as Mexico.

We can imagine a landing after many days of slow progress out of sight of land. The skipper of the laden raft has watched the coast carefully as he sailed inshore. A group of curious villagers stand on the sandy beach, silently watching as he selects a landing place and the crew paddle laboriously to shore. The much-waterlogged raft grounds ponderously in the low breakers. Quickly the paddlers unload their carefully packed cargo and carry it above the high-water mark. Then they cut the fiber lashings and drag the heavy logs ashore to dry in the sun, for they know that they will remain here for many months, until the winds shift to the north. The locals are reluctant to approach, despite gestures of friendship, until the skipper blows a conch trumpet. The strombus provides

Figure 14.6 *A drawing of a Guayaquil sailing raft in 1748. The cartouche shows: (A) bow; (B) stern; (C) the shed or house; (D) set of sheers that serves as a mast; (E) bowline; (F) guares (centerboards); (G) oar that serves as a* guare *and rudder; (H) the galley; (I) water jugs; (K) backstays or stays; (L) the platform or deck. Courtesy Regents of the University of California.*

common ground, a sense of unspoken spiritual connection, even if no one has a common language.

Strombus and spondylus were as important in Andean belief as they were in Maya religious thinking. At least twenty sonorous conch shell trumpets have come from Chavín de Huantar. Modern acoustic experiments have produced resonant sounds in Chavín's underground chambers. A priest's blasts would have amplified supernatural effects and codified the power of water rushing through hidden defiles in the temple. Spondylus also figured prominently in Chavín rituals, as it did elsewhere, across both highlands and lowlands, in later centuries. Andeans used its shell as inlay for fine jewelry and other ornaments. Spiny oyster shell appears in elite tombs, was offered to the gods, and appears clasped in the hands of divine figures.[13] No one knows why the Andeans valued this mollusk so highly. Perhaps it was a symbol of agricultural fertility. We know that in later times lords offered spondylus shell dust to the gods to avert drought. The spiny oyster's red colors linked it to blood, females, and sacrifice. It may also have symbolized spiritual transformation, the ability to move from the realm of the living to that of the ancestors, an important and ancient practice in Andean shamanism.

Spondylus flesh is seasonally toxic, so much so that the Quechua Indians of the highlands called it the "food of the gods," for their myths proclaimed that only deities could consume it safely. When toxic, the meat has hallucinogenic qualities that could induce shamanistic trances. The precious flesh could have been smoked or dried on the coast before being transported inland by llama caravans. Thus, spondylus served as a conduit between the human and supernatural worlds. The "food of the gods" was one way of feeding the appetites of the ancestors, who controlled water sources and the future of human existence. Spondylus was far more than a valued possession; it was a symbolic bridge to life itself in both Andean and Maya society.

Why did Ecuadoran rafts carry spondylus over such long and hazardous distances? Did long-distance raft voyages between Ecuador and western Mexico begin because local spondylus supplies ran short and new sources were needed? Or, perhaps more likely, was the spiny oyster trade so lucrative and prestigious that open-water passages began? The answer may simply be a deeply ingrained desire to trade, honed inland and along the coast for many centuries, an urge to expand trade networks into much broader arenas, for the rafts carried far more than sacred mollusks. We know this because the rafts brought a major innovation to the Central American world of the north: copper metallurgy.

The Andes are one of the two areas in the ancient world where such metalworking began. (The other is the Middle East.) Andean metalsmiths fabricated both cold-hammered hand tools and ornaments such as tweezers and rings and also used the "lost wax" method, wherein molten copper or bronze replaced wax in a prefabricated mold, a sophisticated technique subsequently used in Mexico to make small bells.[14] All of this technology, from smelting the ore to making finished artifacts, would have required long apprenticeships, which is why it's significant that Spanish sources talk of prolonged stays by people who had arrived from the south. Andean metalworkers would have had to live for considerable periods in metal-rich areas like Jalisco and Colima to teach their hosts their skills—and the equally important ritual associations of the metal and finished artifacts.

THUS DEVELOPED SPORADIC contacts between the Andes and the realm of the Fiery Pool that endured for many centuries. The balsa raft journeys from the south did not involve the probing of an infinite ocean, for those who piloted these surprisingly nimble craft knew well that a long coastline lay over the eastern horizon. Their crews transported artifacts and raw materials of enormous economic and symbolic value far beyond the confines of a single kingdom or the purview of one powerful lord. They brought arcane skills with them, and also spiritual beliefs that may have—superficially, at any rate—shared many common features with those of people living close to the Fiery Pool. Most likely, the raft journeys had powerful ritual underpinnings that transcended the passage of short generations.

The situation was somewhat similar to that of the Maya of the Eastern Sea, where dugouts traveled across a Fiery Pool that was a cauldron of awesome supernatural forces. Here, too, powerful spiritual beliefs may have turned journeys on the open ocean into quests along supernatural pathways that endured for centuries. Those who plied these waters traveled across a trackless waste as ruthless in its storms and moods as the Fiery Pool, guided by ancient and long-held spiritual precedent, embodied in the sacred objects in their holds. And they knew that, at the other end, there awaited Maya lords, priests, and merchants, who also lived out their lives in a world of equally powerful supernatural meanings. Finally, they were aware that those who greeted them also believed that the exchange of spondylus for other exotics was far more than a quest for prestige. It was the essence of human existence in a world fraught with spiritual pitfalls.

Epilogue: Of Fish and Portolans

One of the greatest blessings the oceans bestow upon man is a sense of everlasting permanence. The oceans *do* change, but they take their time about it and a thousand years is only an interval. Time apparently stands still for the oceans—the light and play of liquid, the sounds and scent of salt air, and the inhabitants are basically the same as they were long ago.

—Ernest K. Gann, *Song of the Sirens*, 1968[1]

THE AMERICAN CAPTAIN JOSHUA SLOCUM WROTE, "To know the laws that govern the winds, and to know that you know them, will give you an easy mind . . . otherwise you may tremble at the appearance of every cloud."[2] Slocum is one of the immortals of ocean voyaging, a man who was more at home afloat than he was on land. He was a New England sea captain who crammed enough adventure for ten lifetimes into his time at sea. He learned his seamanship aloft in the rigging, in the hard school of Cape Horn and in the Southern Ocean. Experience brought confidence and respect for the ocean, and also an incurable wanderlust. Unemployed and at a loss, he rebuilt a derelict sloop, which he named *Spray*, and sailed her around the world between 1895 and 1898, a voyage of just over three years. Others had circumnavigated before him, but Slocum was the first to perform this now commonplace feat alone. The

37-foot (11-meter) *Spray* had no engine and no labor-saving devices.
"There were none," Slocum remarked, just a heavy paddle to maneuver
her in port, a well-used sextant, and a battered alarm clock—plus a vast,
calm experience of the ocean. Slocum made some astonishing passages
in *Spray*, which had remarkable self-steering qualities. The sloop sailed
for forty-three days from the Juan Fernández Islands off South America, of Robinson Crusoe fame, to Nuku Hiva, in the Marquesas, then
another twenty-nine days to Samoa, without stopping. "For one whole
month my vessel held her course true . . . The Southern Cross I saw every
night abeam. The sun every morning came up astern; every evening it
went down ahead. I wished for no other compass to guide me, for these
were true. If I doubted my reckoning after a long time at sea I verified it
by reading the clock aloft made by the Great Architect, and it was
right."[3] Slocum relied heavily on dead reckoning and the heavenly bodies. His landfall on Nuku Hiva after forty-three days was within an astonishing five miles (eight kilometers) of his intended landing.

Five miles after forty-three days at sea—Slocum's maritime target
seeking seems eerily precise, given the tools at his disposal. I once made
landfall on a 38-foot-high (11.5-meter) rock in the British Virgin Islands
after twenty-four days at sea from Madeira within a mile (1.6 kilometers), but I had computerized navigational tables aboard—and we had
checked our position with a passing oil tanker a day earlier. We rejoiced
at the landfall, but it pales into insignificance beside that of a maestro
equipped with a decrepit alarm clock. I realize now that Joshua Slocum
had truly deciphered the ocean over many years at sea. I'm, at best, a
bare-bones navigator who has barely begun to understand the sea, even
after many years of sailing. And the skills that I painfully acquired are
rapidly fading into extinction. Like the skipper of the oil tanker off the
Virgins, we recreational sailors have learned how to push buttons instead of relying on a sextant and a chronometer.

I don't like the things, but I carry one—a small GPS receiver nick-
named Hieronymous that can tell me where I am anywhere in the world
within a few feet. A few times, I've blessed its convenience, the reassur-
ance it gives me on a foggy day or when we're heavily reefed down and
trying to make landfall. A few button pushes, and a flashing cursor tells

you exactly where you are. The satellites that fix your position care not for weather conditions on earth; their signals are accurate even in the midst of hurricanes. Only a few months ago, we were hurrying inshore from the North Sea toward the treacherous sandbanks and narrow channels of the Thames estuary. The northeasterly wind hurled precipitous showers at us, clouds of torrential rain so thick we could barely see 100 yards (90 meters) ahead. The gloom would clear abruptly as the rain passed. Even distant marks shone out in sudden blasts of sunlight. Ships converged on us from every side—large and small, heavily laden and in ballast. These were challenging conditions for any navigator, but especially for my mentors of half a century ago, who had nothing to rely on but dead reckoning, quick compass fixes of small navigational markers taken from a heaving deck, and their experience of local conditions. We had Hieronymous to guide us instead. I sat at the chart table below, tracking our course from mark to mark, suggesting minor changes to the helmsman, gauging the effect of the tide on our position in what was becoming a narrower, ever more congested channel. Come evening, we anchored in the lee of a sandbank in a small creek sheltered from the strong wind. As we enjoyed a quiet glass, I looked over our course on the chart and was unashamedly thankful that Hieronymous was aboard. He made a complex, potentially dangerous passage almost as easy as driving down a freeway.

But what would have happened if Hieronymous had developed a fit of what the Victorians called the vapors and malfunctioned? How would we have fared if we couldn't locate the three satellites that told us where we were? None of us aboard had the depth of experience that my mentors had acquired over a lifetime of sailing in these waters. Time and time again, I watched them bring us into narrow creeks in fair conditions and foul without even using a compass or a depth meter. They used the color of the mud- and sand-roiled water, the state of the tide, the movements of clouds to decide where to anchor and for how long. They in turn had acquired their knowledge from long-passed experts, many of them fishermen, who had worked these waters year-round with oar and sail.

Much of the art of seamanship—of working boats large and small in tidal waters, in busy harbors, and out of sight of land—is vanishing before our eyes. The loss is immeasurable. Many years ago, in the 1930s, an English yachtsman named Maurice Griffiths lay at anchor off Shotley Spit, near what was once the ancient port of Harwich, in eastern England. Dozens of sailing barges sheltered nearby, on a windy night with squalls shrieking in the rigging. Come dawn, the wind dropped. Griffiths wakened to the *clink-clink* of windlasses lifting anchors and watched as the crowd got under way. "Mainsails were unfolding like stage curtains at a theatre, tops'ls were rising jerkily to mastheads . . . as each barge payed off . . . while anchors dripping black mud, rose to stemheads."[4] Fully a mile of barges hurried to sea on the last of the ebbing tide before using the flood and the fair wind to carry them southward and up the Thames. There was not an engine among them. Some of the barges had been there for days, patiently waiting for wind and tide. Even back then, Griffiths knew that he was witnessing a vanishing history.

We forget just how dependent coastal societies were on freight carried by sea, even a century ago, much of it in small, unspectacular vessels now long forgotten. The knowledge that carried these humble craft on their anonymous voyages was as old as seafaring itself. Their crews may have feared the sea and been accustomed to savage winter storms that could wreck hundreds of merchantmen in hours with massive loss of life. But they knew no other life.

FERNAND BRAUDEL ONCE described the Mediterranean as "an immensity of water." He remarked of the sixteenth-century ocean that "great stretches of the sea were as empty as the Sahara," except where a quick passage over open water was possible, as from Rhodes to Alexandria before a favorable wind.[5] Most sailors followed the coastline, just as their ancestors had for thousands of years, passing from rock to rock, from headland to islands, and from port to port. The Italians of the day even had a word for such coasting: *ciosteggiore*, to hug the shore or to go slowly. For all the perils of storms and lee shores, like that which wrecked the Uluburun ship, with its priceless cargo, off southern Turkey, most of the time, sailing along any coastline—whether off China, Southeast

Asia, the Mediterranean, or the Atlantic shore—was hardly different from navigating a river, as familiar as village paths. It was when one ventured offshore, over the horizon, that deciphering the ocean acquired entirely new, unfamiliar dimensions.

Sailing over the horizon, with no land in sight, began soon after canoes and rafts paddled into deeper water. The earliest open-water passages began in Southeast Asian waters at least fifty thousand years ago, when favorable weather conditions and predictable monsoon wind shifts allowed people to explore land offshore, with a guarantee, based on their knowledge of the seasons, that they would be able to return. Hunters from the Asian mainland paddled or sailed to New Guinea and the arid reaches of what is now Australia. They relied almost entirely on line-of-sight navigation, which was, in the final analysis, the most logical way to acquire familiarity with waters away from one's home base. Their Lapita successors sailed from island to island over an enormous span of the southwestern Pacific for millennia, often traveling for some days out of sight of land to hitherto unexplored islands. Lapita decipherment of the vast reaches of the offshore Pacific depended on a variety of skills, all of them acquired through long experience. Outrigger and double-hulled canoes were essentials. Such craft covered the ground fast and sailed effortlessly while carrying substantial loads. Then there were the foods needed to sustain life at sea for days—readily stored cultivated plants and domestic animals like dogs and pigs. Finally, there were the navigational skills that allowed canoe pilots to sail to tiny landmasses hundreds of miles over the horizon and to return safely having found, or not found, them.

There's no mystery about the way in which the Micronesians and Polynesians deciphered remote Oceania. We know from surviving Micronesian and Polynesian navigators that pilots served long apprenticeships before they were allowed to skipper a canoe, acquiring experience in the school of hard knocks and through demanding oral instruction that included memorizing star courses and other esoteric information. Perhaps most important of all, they developed an intimate knowledge of the ocean, of its swells, bird life, and changing winds. Pilots acquired this information almost from birth in societies where the Pacific was as much part of daily life as the land—a universe respected and feared, but one where they could find their way around with the requisite knowledge. The knowledge itself was tightly held, but perpetuated in such a way that voyages were made and completed, and people returned to tell the tale and to speak of new lands over the water. In Micronesia and Polynesia, apprentice pilots learned from practical experience at sea and also from constant tutoring. They learned recitations that described the passage of heavenly bodies, acquired oral traditions that told of long passages offshore, and, above all, received privileged knowledge from older navigators, themselves trained the same way. Years passed before they became pilots on their own. North Sea fishermen spent their lifetimes afloat in all kinds of weather, not necessarily going far afield but acquiring an intimate knowledge of fishing grounds, of weather, tides, and conditions on the seabed from years as deckhands before they became skippers in their own right.

Why, then, did humans sail deep into Polynesia, to the minute specks of land that are Micronesia, and as far as Rapa Nui and Hawaii, perhaps even to the Americas? We can discount curiosity or a lust to explore the open ocean, for these qualities were rarely found among people who believed that the sea was peopled by malign spiritual forces or was a place of the ancestors. In many cases, the reasons may have been almost entirely social, such as among societies where land and other possessions, as well as status, passed to the oldest sibling. This led to quarrels, and probably to voyage after voyage as younger brothers and other relatives sailed over the horizon to find new land that they could pass on to their own descendants. I believe the exploration of the Pacific was an intensely social process, driven as much by personal ambition and social necessity as by other, more prosaic causes such as trade, although we know that valuable commodities like obsidian passed over enormous distances.

The Pacific and the vast compass of monsoon-swept waters between the South China Sea and East Africa and the Red Sea were the two major open-water arenas for decoding before the Norse sailed into the Atlantic about eleven hundred years ago. The South Asian monsoons reversed direction with predictable regularity, so a sailing vessel could voyage from India or the Persian Gulf to East Africa and the Red Sea and back within twelve months. The secrets of the monsoon winds were familiar to sailors of the Persian Gulf and the Malabar Coast of India from the beginnings of urban civilization, some five thousand years ago. Hundreds of small, battered ships coasted along the arid shores of Arabia, Iran, and north-western India to the Indus River and beyond, long before Christianity.

Quite when Arab or Indian skippers learned to sail direct from the Red Sea or the Gulf to India and back without coasting is unknown, but they had deciphered the intricacies of this passage long before the Greek skipper Hippalus wrote of them in the second century B.C.E. By the time Vasco da Gama arrived off Mombasa, in East Africa, in 1498, the monsoon routes linked China, India, the Gulf, and the Mediterranean, as well as Africa, in an enormous global trade network that had ebbed and flowed for centuries. However, as *The Periplus of the Erythraean Sea* reminds us, most monsoon voyaging followed familiar coastlines, traveled by skippers who spent most of their lives on the water, sailing a few hundred yards off the breakers. It was an anonymous trade, involving ships large and small, some beautifully maintained, others ramshackle in the extreme. Every member of the crew traded, and sometimes smuggled. Dhow captains had friends and trading partners in every port, sometimes wives as well. This commerce of infinitely varied cargoes flourished far under the radar of historical events along coastlines that had changed little for centuries.

The decipherment of the Mediterranean, like that of the monsoon waters, was very largely a matter of coasting, for here, as elsewhere, bulk cargoes traveled most readily by water. Coasting—or tramping, proba-bly a more accurate word—dates back to the earliest days of seafaring, based on navigational lore that passed from father to son as they worked humble merchantmen under sail and oar. One can imagine a boy at the steering oar off the Lebanese coast in 2000 B.C.E., a gentle wind blowing from astern. His father stands watchful as they approach a low head-land. He glances constantly behind the ship, prepared for a sudden gust. He says little but occasionally makes a suggestion, heading the boy's course slightly farther offshore to allow for a current that sets inshore off the headland. He has passed this way dozens of times; his son will do the same in future years.

Constant mentoring, hard-won experience gained in all types of weather, navigational directions painfully memorized day after day—these were the only effective ways of transmitting unwritten expertise down the generations. Most coasting voyages were short—along, say, Baltic shores or on the classic counterclockwise route taken by the ill-fated Uluburun ship and thousands of others. Every voyage was a passage of fits and starts, of weeks spent waiting for favorable winds or taking refuge from pirates who lurked near lucrative trade routes. Cargoes changed completely from one end of the voyage to the other, in an endless process of buying and selling. Ships were like traveling stores, bazaars where shoppers bargained and skippers took advantage of price differentials from one port to the next. Earlier, I called these coastings part of a perpetual-motion machine. Braudel terms them "slow-motion shipping," almost processions. It is no coincidence that villages throughout the Mediterranean lay a day's sail apart.

As Braudel once remarked, this tramping was "more than a picturesque sideshow of a highly colored history." It was "the underlying reality," the way in which life over much of the world unfolded in the days before fossil fuels, diesel engines, the automobile, and the steamship.[6] We tend to be seduced by the romance of large ships—by Viking warships and *knarrs* plying the high seas, or King Henry VIII's magnificent warships, known to us from the spectacular recovery of the *Mary Rose* from the tidal waters of the Solent, off the Isle of Wight.[7] But for all the larger vessels, the troop carriers, royal barges, and bulk wine carriers, there were a great deal more smaller, humbler craft that spent their lifetimes sailing from port to port or fishing in some of the most hazardous seaways in the world. Pytheas the Greek's voyages in leather boats, the open-water passages of Irish monks, Hanseatic cogs and hulcs—all are part of a rich legacy of inshore commerce that linked people living hundreds of miles apart. In Europe, the tradition of such voyages goes back at least three or four thousand years, to Bronze Age planked dugouts, if not earlier, to a time when trade across the ocean was a journey across the realm of the ancestors, an undertaking imbued with social prestige and powerful ritual undertones. From such voyages were born more prosaic enterprises that supplied Cornish tin to Brittany, salt from the Bay of Biscay to the Low Countries, salted fish from Bergen to France.

This was a world of working boats, strongly but roughly built, often with recycled lumber from earlier vessels. Like the Kyrenia ship from Cyprus, such craft had hard, relatively short lives, perhaps of a decade or so. Working boats were like dilapidated houses—artifacts that were mined for useful parts, then thrown away and forgotten, which is why we know so little about the humbler craft from before the nineteenth century. But such vessels were of momentous historical importance, for they quietly shaped history, satisfying commercial or religious demands as part of their daily work. The Hanseatic cog was one such vessel. Cogs transported people, livestock, and general merchandise—between 10,000 and 25,000 tons of salted herring alone each year at the height of Hanse power in the Baltic during the fifteenth century. Behind these sturdy vessels lay an ancient tradition of tramping that linked larger ports with tiny villages lying behind shelving beaches. Thousands of vessels participated in this inconspicuous trade. Even more exploited the rich fishing grounds of the Baltic, the North Sea, and the British Isles, for, thanks to the religious, the fish trade was big business.

In about 530 c.e., Saint Benedict of Nursia, in Italy, founder of the Benedictine Order, promulgated his famous rule for monastic conduct, which, among other things, adjured monks to "love fasting" and to eat modestly. He also espoused basically meatless diets. By the fourteenth century, Lenten and weekly fasting were commonplace, especially on Friday, the day of Christ's suffering on the cross. This commitment to fasting and atonement created a huge international fish industry in a devout world where about half the days of the year were deemed holy and thus meatless.[8] Freshwater fish were a luxury for most people, so herring and cod sustained the medieval fish eater.

The Atlantic herring, *Clupea harengus*, migrated in enormous numbers southward close to shore through the North Sea in summer. For centuries, English and Dutch fishers harvested herring from open boats, part of a trade dominated by the Hansa, with catches of up to a staggering 120 million fish annually. By 1600, some five thousand Dutch fishing vessels worked North Sea waters—this apart from smaller boats along the English coast, many of them being "thin-sided [and easily] swallowed by rough seas."[9]

Herring are oily-fleshed and hard to preserve. In contrast, the Atlantic cod, *Gadus morhua*, and its relatives, like hake, have bland, white flesh with little fat.[10] A well-salted, butterflied cod could keep for five years or more if properly cured. The Lofoten Island fisheries, off northern Norway, produced millions of salted cod annually, traded south to Bergen and throughout Northern Europe. The Norse used salt cod as hardtack on their ocean voyages; cod became a staple military ration ashore and afloat. Dried, beheaded cod, known as stockfish, became a dietary fixture throughout Europe for centuries. By the fifteenth century, the Hanse monopoly over the herring and stockfish trade caused English fishers to search out new cod fisheries off southern Iceland, far from their traditional fishing grounds. They shipped out in boats known as doggers, such hard-used working craft that no examples have survived, even as shipwrecks. A mosaic of historical clues gives these fishing boats two masts, an overall length of about 60 feet (18 meters), and a rudder rather than a steering oar.

Cod fishermen fished off Iceland in these semi-open boats with capacious holds through fierce winter gales and only rarely, if ever, went ashore there. Cod fishing is a mind-numbing process with hook and line. A nineteenth-century French naval officer and novelist, Pierre Loti, wrote brilliantly of such fishing. "No sooner had they thrown their lines than they lifted them, heavy with shimmering, steel-gray fish."[11] The crew on this particular boat caught more than a thousand cod in thirty hours. Loti described how the fishermen fell asleep at the rail while their bodies carried on fishing out of muscle memory. The Icelandic fishery was hazardous, with casualty rates in some years as high as 60 percent, many of the deaths occurring when approaching land on the return journey. But these voyages fostered a growing familiarity with the open North Atlantic.

For the most part, sea captains kept their own counsel, quietly passing information to their sons and trusted crew members. They were cautious men who rarely strayed far from established routes. One cannot blame them. To the west lay the vast and terrifying expanses of the Western Ocean, the stuff of bar talk and legend. In their cups, skippers

Figure 15.1 *A hypothetical reconstruction of a North Sea dogger used in the cod fisheries. Drawing by Steve Brown.*

would exchange stories of remote, little-known waters, of sea monsters and mermaids, of fish so plentiful they could be gathered in baskets, of fabled lands dripping with gold lurking over the western horizon. It was said that a mysterious land, the island of Brasil, lay in the vastness of the stormy Western Ocean.

This Brasil was a fictional place—or was it? The ancient legend persisted during a time of restless exploration, of relentless searches for the fabled gold and spices of Asia, which sent ships sailing westward across the Atlantic. The lure of untold wealth fed a deep-seated curiosity about the Western Ocean at a time when both navigational methods and, especially, ship design were changing rapidly, especially with the development of the Portuguese caravel, whose prototypes were deepwater fishing boats. These well-chronicled advances culminated in the voyages of Christopher Columbus to the Caribbean in 1492 and of Sebastian Cabot to Newfoundland in 1497. Perhaps, however, Bristol fishers or others sailed as far west as Newfoundland before Cabot gathered fish there. We will probably never know for sure.

FAR FROM THE front lines of ocean exploration, most of the world's seafarers continued to sail on the ocean as they always had—in working boats, fishing, tramping in fits and starts from landmark to landmark along familiar coasts. For a long time, their lore passed by word of mouth among close-knit communities of sailors and fisherman. Eventually, some of this hard-won knowledge appeared in rutters (from the French word *routier*, route finder) or portolans (from the Italian word *portolano*, meaning related to ports or harbors), which were sets of sailing directions that first covered Mediterranean waters. Such works were rarities, which is hardly surprising, since most mariners were illiterate. It had always been more important to read the tides than to read a book.

By 1400, voyages between Northern Europe and the Mediterranean were relatively commonplace, which is why a Venetian pilot, Michael of Rhodes, covered the Bay of Biscay, the English Channel, and Flanders in his portolan, compiled in 1434. Michael's sailing directions are of unusual interest, based as they are on his firsthand knowledge. Many are little more than courses to steer from one port to the next. Precise language, prominent landmarks: the directions read like a mnemonic passed from one skipper to another for use on the water. He dispenses tidal information, sketchy at best, presumably reminders to amplify verbal instructions. Occasionally, Michael gives more complete instructions, such as those for Santander, on the northern Spanish coast. "If you are coming from the west, you will always see on the coast high mountains, that is, those called Asturias. And when you are at the end of these, you will see some mountains with a few valleys, and these mountains are low and the land appears white like some cliffs. And you will see over a pond a small abbey with three towers. Know that you will be 15 miles from the port of Santander."[12] Like modern-day pilot writers, Michael used mountain ranges, lesser hills, cliff colors, and a conspicuous building.

An early English rutter, dating to about the same time, contains sailing directions for the English coast from the northeast to Land's End, in Cornwall, as well as for the Channel entrance and several crossings and also for Brittany and the Irish Sea. It is remarkable for the extraordinary detail about the seabed: "Upon off Ushant in 50 or 60 fathoms there is red sand and black stones and white shells among . . . Upon Portland there is fair white sand and 24 fathoms with red shells therein. And in 14 or 16 fathoms there is rocky ground and in some place there is fair clay ground." Tides receive careful attention everywhere: "All the havens be full at a west-south-west Moon between the Start [point] and the Lizard." (The Lizard is a major point on the south Cornwall coast.) There are bearings and distances for longer passages. "When ye come out of Spain and ye be at Cape Finisterre, go your course north-north-east. An you guess you 2 parts over the sea and be bound into [the River] Severn, ye must go north by east till ye come into soundings." From there the rutter guides you from 100 fathoms until you reach 72 fathoms and fair gray sand. This takes you west of Land's End on a northerly course until you "come into a sounding of ooze." At this point, you steer northeast until you sight a landmark named Steeplehorde: "He riseth all round, as if it were a capped hill."[13]

Portolans assumed great importance between the sixteenth and eighteenth centuries, when European nations vied with one another over new lands. Pilots became desired captives, pressed into service by their captors. At first, sailing directions were little more than handfuls of bearings and general impressions, like that of Captain John Smith, published in his *Description of New England*, compiled in 1616. He wrote, "I have drawn a Map from Point to Point, Ile to Ile, and Harbor to Harbor, with the Soundings, Sands, Rocks, and Landmarks as I passed close aboard the Shore in a little boat."[14] Much greater precision marked the nineteenth century. Compare Smith's account with the British Admiralty's *Sailing Directions* for an anchorage off Guernsey, in the Channel Islands, written in 1835:

"The Little Road of Guernsey lies to the northward of Castle Cornet, and between it and the rocks called the Blanche and Sarsrette, on both sides of which are placed beacons. This road . . . affords excellent shelter in from 2 to 4 fathoms (fine muddy sand with sea-weed), from almost all winds that blow." Skippers should "drop your starboard-anchor near the Castle, and the other near the Blanche rock, so as to ensure an open hawse to the eastward." No cursory sailing directions here: the author adjures pilots that "gaining sea-room is on all occasions to be preferred in bad weather than anchoring on the coast . . . unless under peculiar circumstances." Strong-running tides are a constant concern in these rocky waters, but "if skillfully managed, will generally enable a vessel, as long as she can carry close-reef top-sails, to hold her own."[15]

The precise instructions in the *Sailing Directions for the English Channel* apply with just as much force today as they did in an engineless era, when anchors, sweeps, and sails carried small boats through tidal channels large and small. Deciphering the minor intricacies of convoluted shorelines and inconspicuous landmarks may have become somewhat easier with electronic navigation, but you can never fight the ocean in a small boat. Portland Bill, a wedge-shaped headland that projects into the English Channel, is notorious for its powerful tidal race. In rough weather it becomes a maelstrom of confused waves powerful enough to buckle the plates of a frigate. But by using the tides and sailing close— very close—inshore, you can slip between the extremity of the Bill and the raging water offshore. The first time I made the passage, I pored anxiously over the sailing directions for hours. We were eastbound, with a moderate southwesterly wind behind us on a beautiful early-summer day. Go east about two hours before local high water, the guide adjured, advising us to make a first-time passage during neap tides, when the streams are weakest. We jilled around offshore, about halfway up the Bill, until the timing was right, then sailed close inshore, the cliffs high above us, then around the very tip, the lighthouse high above us. The calmer water was no wider than a small harbor entrance, but we sailed through effortlessly, tourists gawking at us from the rocks to our left. I've used the inshore passage dozens of times since, for it saves many miles, but your timing has to be exquisitely precise.

Figure 15.2 *The industrial and the traditional: The cruise ship* Ryndam *of the Holland America Line sweeps past small trading vessels from another era. Painting by the German American artist Fred Pansing, c. 1900. The Granger Collection, New York.*

These days, in a world of container ships and supertankers, official sailing directions are much shortened and full of references to radar targets and harbor regulations. The authors now pay little attention to smaller anchorages and ports, for cruising sailors now have their own guides. It is as if the sea has become remote from us again, which is most apparent when you cross the Atlantic on an ocean liner or a cruise ship. The increasingly elephantine vessels of today seem designed to distract their passengers from the waters that surround them on every side.

We've created new leviathans, great ships that effectively ignore the perils of the ocean that have terrified skippers of lesser vessels since seafaring began. Yet the old and the new coexist, even today. Imagine, a century ago, the liner *Mauretania* passing effortlessly off the Cornish coast, bound for New York. She passes a fleet of pilchard-fishing boats a few hundred yards inshore, drifting with wind and tide, motionless as they draw their nets. Their crews still rely on sail and oar, on fishing methods and boats refined over many centuries. They are still fishing and sailing like their medieval ancestors, in the shadow of a product of the Industrial Revolution. Each vessel—the great liner and the tiny fishing boat—has decoded the ocean, but in radically different ways. These various decipherments have been one of the great, quiet currents of human history over the past fifty millennia, testifying to an intimacy with the sea that is receding fast in the face of industrial technology. The now anonymous ocean is no longer the realm of ancestors, gods, or dreaded spiritual forces. But, for all our seeming mastery of its secrets, we ignore its dangers at our peril. We will never completely decode its mysteries.

Acknowledgments

Beyond the Blue Horizon originated in the fertile mind of my editor Peter Ginna a considerable number of years ago. We discussed the idea at intervals, but it is only now that I feel confident enough to write this book. Peter suggested, and he was right, that I should make use of my own broad experience of seagoing in many environments to add color and immediacy to the narrative. The story itself draws on a huge academic and popular literature that is very largely concerned with ships, shipwrecks, and navigation rather than cultural issues. Most of these works cover, often very ably, classical and later seafaring, with a nod to Bronze Age sailors, Egyptians, Minoans, and Phoenicians. *Blue Horizon* goes back to the earliest routes of seafaring, covers a great expanse of little-known maritime ground, and ventures into remote, often unknown seascapes. Above all, it's a book about people and their relationships with the ocean, which developed within much broader cosmological and spiritual horizons. I've attempted to produce a synthesis that is very much my own take on a confusing jigsaw puzzle of archaeology, history, and voyaging. I am, of course, responsible for the conclusions and accuracy of this book and, no doubt, will hear in short order from those kind, often anonymous individuals who delight in pointing out errors large and small. Let me thank them in advance.

The actual writing of this book took three years of research and importuning of many colleagues over many years, many of them far more knowledgeable about maritime history and ancient seafaring than I am. I'm deeply grateful for the input of dozens of archaeologists and historians over the years as this book slowly matured, so many it's impossible to name them. I hope those omitted from the list below will forgive the omission. Thank you, one and all! Special thanks to the late Neville Chittick, Peter Clark, Lynne Gamble, George Bass, Nadia Durrani, Mark Horton, Sven Haakenson, Geoffrey Irwin, John Johnson, the late James Kirkman, Herbert Maschner, George Michaels, Francis Pryor, Patrick Saltonstall, Robert Van der Noort, and Stephanie Wynne-Jones. Finally, a heartfelt thanks to all those who taught me seamanship and the many folk with whom I have cruised in various waters over the years. This book is for them.

The debt I owe my editors, Peter Ginna and Pete Beatty, is enormous. This book is as much theirs as mine. Their perceptive and sometimes fierce insights have made this an immeasurably better story. The least I can do is dedicate the book to them. Shelly Lowenkopf was, as always, a passionate foil and a great source of enlightenment and insights at moments of despair. Steve Brown drew the maps and drawings with his customary skill. Francelle Carapetyan gave invaluable assistance with the photographic research and my obscure requests. Susan Rabiner, the best of agents, stood behind the project all the way.

And, as always, my love and thanks to Lesley and Ana, who provide a wonderful (and sometimes serene) environment for my research. I cannot say the same of our beasts. Have you ever had two kittens (one large and one relatively diminutive) playing games across your computer? Distractions! Distractions! Doubtless, when older, they will fall asleep on the keyboard.

Notes

The references that follow focus mostly on more general and popular works, for obvious reasons. Readers interested in delving further into the complicated literature behind this book should consult the bibliographies in these works.

The literature on maritime history is enormous, but few works explore the complex relationship between humans and the ocean for general audiences. John Mack's *The Sea: A Cultural History* (London: Reaktion Books, 2011) is a notable exception and contains an excellent bibliography. Mack is an anthropologist and art historian with a global perspective—important qualifications for studying humans and the ocean.

Chapter 1: "The Sands and Flats Are Discovered"

1. Alexander Kielland (1849–1906) is one of the greats of Norwegian literature, famous as a "realistic" writer. In his novels, he satirized the hypocrisy of Norway's clergy. Kielland gave up fiction in his thirties and subsequently became a journalist and the mayor of his hometown, Stavanger. Quote from his *Garman og Worse*, trans. William Archer (Oslo: Gyldendal Norges Nasjonal Litteratur II, 1985), p. 3.

2. Knut Kolsrud, "Fishermen and Boats," in Alexander Fenton and Hermann Pálsson, eds., *The Northern and Western Isles in the Viking World* (Edinburgh: John Donald Publishers, 1984), pp. 116–17.

3. Alas, *Admiralty Pilots* are not what they used to be, for much of their traditional content is useless except for supertankers and container ships. You have to consult the editions of a half century ago to appreciate the full richness of their narratives. Quotes from *Baltic Pilot*, vol. 1 (London: Hydrographic Office, 1898), p. 221.

4. Alan Villiers, *Sons of Sinbad* (London: Arabian Publishing, 2006), p. 294.

5. Daniel Defoe, *The Storm* (London: Penguin Classics, 2005), p. 269.

6. John R. Stilgoe, *Alongshore* (New Haven, CT: Yale University Press, 1994), p. 46.

Across the Pacific

1. R. A. Skelton, ed. and trans., *Magellan's Voyage: A Narrative Account of the First Circumnavigation* (New York: Dover Publications, 1969), p. 56.

Chapter 2: Sunda and Sahul

1. Till Hanebuth, Karl Stattegger, and Pieter M. Grootes, "Rapid Flooding of the Sunda Shelf: A Late Glacial Sea-Level Record," *Science* 288 (2000), pp. 1033–35. See also Avijit Gupta, ed., *The Physical Geography of Southeast Asia* (Oxford: Oxford University Press, 2005).

2. J. Peter White and James O'Connell, *A Prehistory of Sunda and Sahul* (Sydney: Academic Press, 1982), offers a general, if somewhat outdated, summary.

3. This discussion is based on Nonie Sharp, *Saltwater People: The Waves of Memory* (Toronto: University of Toronto Press, 2002), chaps. 4 and 5.

4. J. B. Birdsell, "The Recalibration of a Paradigm for the First Peopling of Great Australia," in J. Allen, J. Golson, and Rhys Jones, eds., *Sunda and Sahul: Prehistoric Studies in Southeast Asia, Melanesia and Australia* (Canberra: Australian National University Press, 1977), pp. 113–67; quote from p. 123.

5. Discussion based on Geoffrey Irwin, *The Prehistoric Exploration and Colonization of the Pacific* (Cambridge: Cambridge University Press, 1992), chap. 2.

6. Irwin, *Prehistoric Exploration*, p. 24.

7. The literature on Pacific canoes is enormous. An excellent summary appears in Edwin Doran Jr., *Wangka: Austronesian Canoe Origins* (College Station, TX: Texas A&M University Press, 1981). Doran dedicates his book to James Hornell, who carried out intensive research on the subject before World War II. Hornell's works remain the definitive source. References will be found in Doran's succinct but authoritative work.

8. Extended discussion in Doran, *Wangka*, chap. 5.

9. Summaries of the evidence appear in Ian Glover and Peter Bellwood, eds., *Southeast Asia: From Prehistory to History* (London: Routledge Curzon, 2004). See also Peter Bellwood, *Prehistory of the Indo-Malaysian Archipelago*, rev. ed. (Honolulu: University of Hawai'i Press, 1997).

Chapter 3: "Butterfly Wings Scattered Over the Water"

1. The arbitrary boundary between Near and Remote Oceania passes through the ocean east of the Solomon Islands.

2. Patrick Vinton Kirch, *The Lapita Peoples: Ancestors of the Oceanic World* (Cambridge, MA: Blackwell, 1997), chap. 2, pp. 34–42.

3. Matthew Spriggs, *The Island Melanesians* (Oxford, UK: Blackwell, 1997), p. 29.

4. E. W. Gifford and Dick Schutler Jr., *Archaeological Excavations in New Caledonia*, Anthropological Records vol. 18, part 2 (Berkeley: University of California Press, 1951).

5. Kirch, *The Lapita Peoples*, chap. 3, pp. 52–65.

6. R. Alexander Bentley et al., "Lapita Migrants in the Pacific's Oldest Cemetery: Isotopic Analysis at Teouma, Vanuatu," *American Antiquity* 72(4) (2007): 645–56, offers a summary of this important site.

7. Edwin Doran Jr., *Wangka: Austronesian Canoe Origins* (College Station, TX: Texas A&M Press, 1981).

8. Bronislaw Malinowski, *Argonauts of the Western Pacific* (New York: E. P. Dutton, 1922). Quotes in this paragraph from pp. 107–10.

9. Malinowski, *Argonauts*, p. 225.

10. Malinowski, *Argonauts*, p. 256.

11. Patrick Vinton Kirch, *On the Road of the Winds* (Berkeley: University of California Press, 2002), p. 98.

12. This passage is based on Malinowski, *Argonauts*, chap. 3, the classic description of the Kula. The entire monograph is devoted to aspects of the subject. A huge literature now surrounds the Kula. See J. P. Singh Uberoi, *Politics of the Kula Ring: An Analysis of the Findings of Bronislaw Malinowski* (Manchester, UK: Manchester University Press, 1962). Also Annette B. Weiner, *Women of Value, Men of Renown: New Perspectives on Trobriand Exchange* (Austin: University of Texas Press, 1976).

13. Malinowski, *Argonauts*, p. 89.

14. Kirch, *On the Road*, pp. 219ff.

Chapter 4: A Pattern of Islands

1. Excellent summaries appear in Geoffrey Irwin, *The Prehistoric Exploration and Colonization of the Pacific* (Cambridge: Cambridge University Press, 1992), chaps. 5 and 6, and in the same author's "Voyaging and Settlement," in K. R. Howe,

ed., *Vaka Moana: The Discovery and Settlement of the Pacific* (Honolulu: University of Hawai'i Press, 2006), pp. 54–100. See also Patrick Vinton Kirch, *On the Road of the Winds* (Berkeley: University of California Press, 2002), chaps. 5–7. For recent computer simulations, see Anne Di Piazza et al., "Sailing Virtual Canoes Across Oceania: Revisiting Island Accessibility," *Journal of Archaeological Science* 34(4) (2007): 1219–25; and C. A. Avis et al., "The Discovery of Western Oceania: A New Perspective," *The Journal of Island and Coastal Archaeology* 2(1) (2007): 197–209.

2. Irwin, *Prehistoric Exploration,* chap. 4, analyzes the strategies.

3. Matthew Spriggs and Atholl Anderson, "Late Colonization of East Polynesia," *Antiquity* 67(1) (1993): 200–217.

4. This passage is based on this study: Janet Wilmshurst et al., "High Precision Radiocarbon Dating Shows Recent and Rapid Initial Human Colonization of East Polynesia," *Proceedings of the National Academy of Sciences* 108(5) (2010): 1815–20.

5. David Lewis, *We, the Navigators: The Ancient Art of Landfinding in the Pacific* (Honolulu: University of Hawai'i Press, 1994). Also Ben Finney, with Mary Among, *Voyage of Rediscovery: A Cultural Odyssey Through Polynesia* (Berkeley: University of California Press, 1994), for replica passages.

6. An excellent account: Finney, *Voyage of Rediscovery.*

7. The passage on *etak* is based on Thomas Gladwin, *East Is a Big Bird: Navigation and Logic on Puluwat Atoll* (Cambridge, MA: Harvard University Press, 1970); quote from p. 182. See also Paul Rainbird, *The Archaeology of Micronesia* (Cambridge: Cambridge University Press, 2004).

8. Oral traditions are summarized by Rawiri Taonui, "Polynesian Oral Traditions," in Howe, *Vaka Moana,* pp. 22–53.

9. Cook's journal for February 28, 1778, in J. C. Beaglehole, *The Journals of Captain James Cook on His Voyages of Discovery,* vol. 1: *The Voyage of the Endeavour, 1768–1771* (Cambridge, UK: Hakluyt Society, 1968), p. 81.

10. Johann Forster, *Observations Made During a Voyage Round the World* (London: Robinson, 1778), p. 509.

11. Ben Finney, "Traditional Navigation," in Howe, *Vaka Moana,* p. 162.

12. Douglas Oliver, *Ancient Tahitian Society* (Honolulu: University of Hawai'i Press, 1974), is the definitive account of traditional Tahitian culture.

13. Kirch, *On the Road,* pp. 298–300. The literature is enormous. This is a good starting point.

14. An excellent summary of the controversies surrounding first settlement will be found in Kirch, *On the Road,* pp. 275ff. See also Atholl Anderson, "The Chronology of Colonization in New Zealand," *Antiquity* 65(4) (1991): 767–95.

15. Paul Bahn and John Flenley, *The Enigmas of Easter Island* (New York: Oxford University Press, 2003), offers a general account. For a new and stimulating reappraisal, see Terry Hunt and Carl Lipo, *The Statues That Walked: Unraveling the Mystery of Easter Island* (New York: Free Press, 2011).

16. Geoffrey Irwin, "Voyaging and Settlement," in Howe, *Vaka Moana*, p. 85.

17. A. A. Storey et al., "Pre-Columbian Chickens, Dates, Isotopes and mtDNA," *Proceedings of the National Academy of Sciences of the United States of America* 105(48), E99 (2008), doi: 10.1073/pnas.0807625105.

Poseidon's Waters

1. Homer, *Odyssey*, Book 2, lines 468–71. Quote from Robert Fagles, trans., *The Odyssey* (New York: Viking, 1996), p. 289. All Homeric quotes in this book are from the Fagles translation, whose pagination is used.

Chapter 5: A World of Ceaseless Movement

1. Homer, *Odyssey*, Book 13, lines 93–100, p. 289. Quote from Robert Fagles, trans., *The Odyssey* (New York: Viking, 1996), p. 289. All Homeric quotes in this book are from the Fagles translation, whose pagination is used.

2. Callimachus (310/305–240 B.C.E.) was of Libyan Greek origin. He was a critic, poet, and scholar associated with the Library of Alexandria under the patronage of the Ptolemies. He was known for his hymns, short poems, and epigrams, among them his Hymn 4, "To Delos," from which this quote comes; http:www.theoi.com/Text/CallimachusHymns2.html, 300.

3. Cyprian Broodbank, *An Island Archaeology of the Early Cyclades* (Cambridge: Cambridge University Press, 2000), is a definitive synthesis of seafaring and archaeology in the Aegean. Quote from p. 43.

4. Broodbank, *Island Archaeology*, p. 41.

5. Monemvasia was an important trade and maritime center from the tenth century C.E. under the rule of various powers, including the Venetians and the Turks. An imposing medieval fortress stands on the rock above the small village.

6. Discussed in Broodbank, *Island Archaeology*, chap. 3.

7. Ibid., p. 102.

8. This passage is based on ibid., pp. 76–80.

9. Ibid., pp. 73–74.

10. Sebastian Payne, "Faunal Change at Franchthi Cave from 20,000–3000 BC," in A. T. Clason, ed., *Archaeozoological Studies* (Amsterdam: North-Holland, 1975), pp. 120–31.

11. Described in Broodbank, *Island Archaeology*, chap. 5.
12. Ibid., p. 179.
13. Ibid., p. 131.
14. Ibid., p. 156.
15. Homer, *Odyssey*, Book 13, lines 109–14, p. 289.
16. Ibid., Book 5, lines 297–300, p. 160.

Chapter 6: Timber and Mekku-Stones

1. Homer, *Odyssey*, Book 2, pp. 465–70, p. 106. Quote from Robert Fagles, trans., *The Odyssey* (New York: Viking, 1996), p. 289. All Homeric quotes in this book are from the Fagles translation, whose pagination is used.

2. *Mediterranean Pilot* (London: Hydrographic Office, 1898), p. 131.

3. Fernand Braudel, *The Mediterranean and the Mediterranean World in the Age of Philip II* (Berkeley: University of California Press, 1996).

4. A series of works by Lionel Casson provide admirable syntheses of early Mediterranean seafaring immediately before and after the appearance of Egyptian civilization: *The Ancient Mariners: Seafarers and Sea Fighters of the Mediterranean in Ancient Times*, 2nd ed. (Princeton, NJ: Princeton University Press, 1991); *Travel in the Ancient World* (Baltimore: Johns Hopkins University Press, 1994); and *Ships and Seamanship in the Ancient World* (Baltimore: Johns Hopkins University Press, 1995). Pharaoh Snefru: Peter Clayton, *Chronicle of the Pharaohs* (London: Thames and Hudson, 1994), pp. 42–44.

5. Casson, *Ships*, p. 8.

6. Herodotus, *The Histories*, trans. Robin Waterfield (Oxford: Oxford University Press, 1998), Book 2, line 5, p. 97.

7. Homer, *Odyssey*, Book 19, lines 202–6, p. 396.

8. Eti Bonn-Muller, "First Minoan Shipwreck," *Archaeology* 63(1) (2010): 44–47; archaeology.org/1001/etc/minoan_shipwreck.html.

9. Manfred Bietak, *Avaris: The Capital of the Hyksos* (London: British Museum, 1996).

10. Shirley Wachsmann and George Bass, *Seagoing Ships and Seamanship in the Bronze Age Levant* (College Station, TX: Texas A&M Press, 2008). See also Cemal Pulak, "The Uluburun Shipwreck: An Overview," *International Journal of Nautical Archaeology* 27(3) (1998): 188–224.

11. William L. Moran, *The Amarna Letters* (Baltimore: Johns Hopkins University Press, 1992), p. 163.

12. Richard Steffy, "The Kyrenia Ship: An Interim Report on Its Hull Construction," *American Journal of Archaeology* 38(1) (1985): 71–101.

13. Homer, *Odyssey*, Book 2, lines 472–77, p. 106.

14. Lionel Casson, *Ancient Mariners*, p. 100.

15. Quoted in ibid., pp. 208–209.

The Monsoon World

1. G. R. Tibbetts, *Arab Navigation in the Indian Ocean Before the Coming of the Portuguese* (London: Royal Asiatic Society, 1971), p. 77. Ahmad b. Majid al-Najdi (c. 1432/7–c. 1500) was a dhow skipper from a long line of navigators who sailed mainly in the Red and Arabian seas. A skilled pilot, he is said to have assisted the Portuguese in crossing the Indian Ocean in 1498. His pilotage book, the *Kitab al-Fawa'id*, from which the quotes used in this book come, was probably written in his middle age.

Chapter 7: The Erythraean Sea

1. W. C. Schoff, ed. and trans., *The Periplus of the Erythraean Sea: Trade and Travel in the Indian Ocean by a Merchant of the First Century* (London: Longmans, 1912); quotes from chaps. 40 and 45. (Each chapter is little more than a modern sentence.) The location described is the Gulf of Kutch, in Gujarat, which is notorious for its extreme tides.

2. Felipe Fernández-Armesto, "The Indian Ocean in World History," in Anthony Disney and Emily Booth, eds., *Vasco da Gama and the Linking of Europe and Asia* (New Delhi: Oxford University Press, 2000), p. 16.

3. Michael Pearson, *The Indian Ocean* (London: Routledge, 2003), pp. 19ff.

4. The term *dhow* (probably from the Persian word *dawh*) is a generic term covering numerous forms of Indian Ocean vessel. For simplicity, I have used it here. Alan Villiers, *Sons of Sinbad* (London: Arabian Publishing, 2006), covers his dhow voyage. The book was originally published by Hodder and Stoughton in London in 1940. Quote from p. 40.

5. Pearson, *Indian Ocean*, p. 17.

6. Egyptian boats and ships: Seán McGrail, *Boats of the World from the Stone Age to Medieval Times* (New York: Oxford University Press, 2002). Chapter 2 has a description.

7. William Thesiger, *The Marsh Arabs* (London: Longmans, 1964), is the classic work.

8. Jacques Connan et al., "A Comparative Geochemical Study of Bituminous Boat Remains from H3, As-Sabiyah (Kuwait) and RJ-2, Ra's al-Jinz (Oman)," *Arabian Archaeology and Epigraphy* 16 (2005): 21–66.

9. Maria Graham, *Journal of a Residence in India* (Edinburgh: A. Constable, 1812), p. 124.

10. Pearson, *Indian Ocean*, chap. 3.

11. Jonathan Mark Kenoyer, *Ancient Cities of the Indus Civilization* (Karachi: Oxford University Press, 1998), pp. 96–98.

12. Villiers, *Sons of Sinbad*, pp. 13–17.

13. A. L. Oppenheim, "The Seafaring Merchants of Ur," *Journal of the American Oriental Society* 74(1) (1954): 6–17.

14. S. Luckenbill, *Ancient Records of Assyria and Babylonia* (Chicago: Oriental Institute, 1927), vol. 2, sections 318–21. Discussed in George Fadio Hourani, *Arab Seafaring in the Indian Ocean in Ancient and Early Medieval Times*, rev. ed. (Princeton, NJ: Princeton University Press, 1995), p. 10.

15. Agatharchides was a Greek geographer and historian of the second century B.C.E. His *On the Erythraean Sea* consisted of five volumes, of which only the fifth book survives almost intact, an account of the Red Sea and the coasts of the Horn of Africa. Quote from Hourani, *Arab Seafaring*, p. 22.

16. We know little of Hippalus, a Greek navigator and merchant, who is credited with this discovery by the anonymous author of *The Periplus of the Erythraean Sea*.

17. See Paul Wheatley, *The Golden Khersonese* (Kuala Lumpur: University of Malaya Press, 1961), p. 38, and also Pearson, *Indian Ocean*, pp. 57ff.

18. Hourani, *Arab Seafaring*, chap. 2.

19. The ship descriptions are drawn from Hourani, *Arab Seafaring*, chap. 3, from Villiers, *Sons of Sinbad*, and from my own firsthand observations of modern dhows on the East African coast.

20. Ibn Jubayr (1127–1217) was an Arab geographer from Al-Andalus (Islamic Spain) who traveled widely and made a pilgrimage to Mecca. Quote from Hourani, *Arab Seafaring*, p. 92.

21. These paragraphs are based on Villiers, *Sons of Sinbad*, chaps. 6–17.

22. Quote from Hourani, *Arab Seafaring*, p. 122.

Chapter 8: "A Place of Great Traffic"

1. Ingombe Ilede: Brian Fagan, David Phillipson, and S. G. H. Daniels, *Iron Age Cultures in Zambia*, vol. 2: *Dambwa, Ingombe Ilede, and the Tonga* (London: Chatto and Windus, 1969), chaps. 4–9.

2. W. C. Schoff, ed. and trans., *The Periplus of the Erythraean Sea* (London: Longmans, 1912), section 13.

3. Schoff, *Periplus*, sections 16–18.

4. Al-Masudi (896–956) was a geographer, historian, and traveler who sailed widely around the Indian Ocean and elsewhere. His *The Meadows of Gold and the Mines of Gems*, compiled in 943, is a classic of Islamic travel. See also Pierre Verin, *Les Comoros* (Paris: Karthale, 1994), pp. 86–87.

5. A. LaViolette and J. B. Fleisher, "The Urban History of a Rural Place: Swahili Archaeology on Pemba Island, Tanzania, 700–1500 AD," *International Journal of African Historical Studies* 42(3) (2009): 433–55. See also Stephanie Wynne-Jones, "Remembering and Reworking the Swahili Diwanate: The Role of Objects and Places at Vumba Kuu," *International Journal of African Historical Studies,* 43(3) (2010): 407–27; and J. B. Fleisher, "Rituals of Consumption and the Politics of Feasting on the Eastern African Coast, AD 700–1500," *Journal of World Prehistory* 23(4) (2010): 195–217.

6. Mark Horton, "Early Muslim Trading Settlements on the East African Coast: New Evidence from Shanga," *Antiquaries Journal* 67 (1987): 290–323.

7. G. S. P. Freeman-Grenville, *The East African Coast: Select Documents* (Oxford, UK: Clarendon Press, 1962), p. 20.

8. A genizah (Hebrew: "storage") was a special chamber in a synagogue, a repository for documents containing the name of God, which could not be thrown away. Genizoth contained not only religious books but all kinds of writings that invoked God, even in their opening invocations. Tattered books, public and private letters, legal briefs, accounts, papers both important and mundane filled genizoth. Periodically, the synagogue would remove and dispose of the documents appropriately, often by burying them in a cemetery. By fortunate chance, the Ben Ezra Synagogue, in Fustat, in Old Cairo, never emptied its genizah. Its more than 750,000 documents are a treasure trove of information on Jewish communities and trade in the Mediterranean and the Indian Ocean. S. D. Goitein, *A Mediterranean Society: The Jewish Communities of the Arab World as Portrayed in the Documents of the Cairo Geniza* (Berkeley: University of California Press, 1967–93), is the definitive source.

9. Quoted in Roxani Eleni Margariti, *Aden and the Indian Ocean Trade: 150 Years in the Life of a Medieval Arabian Port* (Chapel Hill: University of North Carolina Press, 2007), offers a brilliant account of early Aden using genizah sources, among others. Quote in this paragraph from p. 1.

10. This passage is based on Mark Horton, "Swahili Corridor," *Scientific American* 257(9): 86–93; and Timothy Insoll, *The Archaeology of Islam in Sub-Saharan Africa* (Cambridge: Cambridge University Press, 2003), pp. 172–77.

11. Roger Summers, *Ancient Mining in Rhodesia and Adjacent Areas* (Salisbury, UK: National Museums of Rhodesia, 1969), p. 218.

12. Paragraphs based on Insoll, *Archaeology of Islam*, chap. 6, and Chapurukha

M. Kusimba, *The Rise and Fall of Swahili States* (Walnut Creek, CA: AltaMira Press, 1999), chap. 8.

13. Mansel Longworth Dames, ed., *The Book of Duarte Barbosa* (London: Hakluyt Society, 1918), vol. 1, pp. 19–20.

Chapter 9: "We Spread Our Cloudlike Sails Aloft"

1. Felipe Fernández-Armesto, *Pathfinders* (New York: W. W. Norton, 2006), summarizes the Zheng He expeditions as part of a more global survey. See also J. J. L. Duyvendak, *China's Discovery of Africa* (London: A. Probsthain, 1949). The quote comes from J. J. A. Duyvendak, "The True Dates of the Chinese Maritime Expeditions in the Early Fifteenth Century," *T'oung Pao* 34 (1938): 399.

2. This chapter draws extensively on Edward L. Dreyer, *Zheng He: China and the Oceans in the Early Ming Dynasty, 1405–1433* (New York: Pearson/Longman, 2006). Dreyer summarizes a complex and often confusing literature and is an admirable source for a short summary.

3. Ibid., p. 3.

4. Fernández-Armesto, *Pathfinders*, p. 116.

5. Quotes in this paragraph from Dreyer, *Zheng He*, p. 116, where an extended discussion of Zheng He's ships will be found.

6. Both Liujiagang quotes are from Ibid., p. 192. Elsewhere in this book, there is a complete translation.

7. Ibid., p. 75.

8. Ibid., p. 78.

9. Quotes from ibid., p. 85.

10. Peter Greste, "Could a Rusty Coin Rewrite Chinese-African History?" BBC News, October 17, 2010: www.bbc.co.uk/news/world-africa-11531398.

11. Dreyer, *Zheng He*, p. 173

12. Quote from ibid., p. 143.

13. Ibid., p. 144.

14. Quoted from ibid., p. 77, which attributes the description to Ma Huan, an interpreter fluent in Arabic who served on three of Zheng He's voyages.

15. Ibid., p. 158.

16. Ibid., p. 163.

17. Quote from ibid., p. 173.

Turbulent Waters in the North

1. Extract from an eight-stanza poem, "Storm at Sea," written in about 700 C.E. by Rumann, son of Colmán, which captures the symbolic power of the waters. Quoted from Simon Winchester, *Atlantic* (New York: Harper, 2010), p. 154.

Chapter 10: Seascapes of Ancestors

1. Based on Paul Mellars and Petra Dark, *Star Carr in Context* (Cambridge, UK: McDonald Institute for Archaeological Research, 1999).

2. Simon Fitch, Vincent Gaffney, and David Smith, *Europe's Lost World: The Rediscovery of Doggerland* (London: Council for British Archaeology, 2009). *Dogge*, as in Dogger Bank, is an old Dutch word for a fishing boat.

3. Seán McGrail, *Ancient Boats in North-West Europe: The Archaeology of Water Transport to AD 1500* (London: Longman, 1987), is a definitive source on early Northern European watercraft, which I relied on here. For dugout canoes, see pp. 85–86.

4. Robert Van de Noort, *North Sea Archaeologies: A Maritime Biography* (New York: Oxford University Press, 2011), chap. 7.

5. The claims are tenuous at best. See D. Ellmers, "Earliest Evidence for Skin Boats in Late Palaeolithic Europe," in Seán McGrail, ed., *Aspects of Maritime Archaeology and Ethnography* (Greenwich, UK: National Maritime Museum, 1984), pp. 41–55.

6. Robert Van de Noort, "Exploring the Ritual of Travel in Prehistoric Europe: The Bronze Age Sewn-Plank Boats in Context," in Peter Clark, ed., *Bronze Age Connections: Cultural Contact in Prehistoric Europe* (Oxford, UK: Oxbow Books, 2009), pp. 159–75.

7. Robert Van de Noort et al., "The 'Kilnsea Boat', and Some Implications from the Discovery of England's Oldest Plank Boat Remains," *Antiquity* 73(1) (279): 131–35. See also Van de Noort, "Exploring."

8. An excellent popular account: Peter Clark, ed., *The Dover Bronze Age Boat* (Swindon, UK: English Heritage, 2004). See also the same author's *The Dover Bronze Age Boat in Context: Society and Water Transport in Prehistoric Europe* (Oxford, UK: Oxbow Books, 2004).

9. These paragraphs draw on Van de Noort, "Exploring," and on Stuart Needham, "Encompassing the Sea: 'Maritories' and Bronze Age Maritime Interactions," in Peter Clark, *Bronze Age Connections*, pp. 12–37.

10. Van de Noort, "Exploring," and the same author's *North Sea Archaeologies: A Maritime Biography (10,000 B.C.–A.D. 1500)* (Oxford: Oxford University Press, 2011).

11. Needham, "Encompassing," pp. 22–23.

12. Barry Cunliffe, *Facing the Ocean: The Atlantic and Its Peoples* (Oxford: Oxford University Press, 2001), is a seminal work. Chapter 3 surveys the evidence for early hide boats. Rufus Festus Avienus was an Etrurian poet of the fourth century C.E., known for his poem *Ora Maritima*, which is roughly based on a periplus of the early sixth century B.C.E. known as the *Massiliote Periplus*. Quote from lines 101–106.

13. Pliny the Elder, *Natural History*, trans. H. Rackham (Cambridge, MA: Harvard University Press, 1907), Book 4, p. 104.

14. Strabo (64/63 B.C.E.–c. 24 C.E.) traveled extensively and wrote his seventeen-volume *Geography* between 7 and 18 C.E., on the basis both of his journeys and others' writings. Quote from vol. 3, chap. 3, line 7.

15. Julius Caesar, *The Civil Wars*, trans. W. A. McDevitte and W. S. Bohn (Internet Classics Archive: classics.mit.edu/Caesar/civil.1.1.html), chap. 54, lines 3–4.

16. Cunliffe, *Facing the Ocean*, p. 67, has a description. Some experts think the hull was of wood.

17. John Millington Synge (1871–1909) was an important contributor to the Irish dramatic movement. In attempts to find his writer's voice, he spent time on the Aran Islands, off the west coast of Ireland. *The Aran Islands* (Dublin: Maunsel, 1907) was the result. Quotes from pp. 97–99.

18. Barry Cunliffe, *The Extraordinary Voyage of Pytheas the Greek* (Harmondsworth, UK: Penguin Books, 2001), is a superb reconstruction of Pytheas's travels that draws on archaeology, classical sources, and other sources. I have followed his interpretation here.

19. See the Venerable Bede, *Lives of the Saints: The Voyage of St. Brendan*, trans. J. F. Webb (Harmondsworth, UK: Pelican Books, 1965). Also see Adomnán, *Life of Columba*, trans. Alan Orr Anderson and Margorie Ogilvie Anderson (London: Thomas Nelson, 1961).

20. Cunliffe, *The Extraordinary Voyage*, p. 69.

Chapter 11: "Storms Fell on the Stern in Icy Feathers"

1. Michael Peter Ancher (1849–1927) is one of Denmark's most popular artists. He is best known for his paintings of fishermen and other scenes in Skagen, in northern Denmark. At the time, Skagen was a major fishing port, as well as a

nascent artists' colony that was to nurture the "Skagen School." You can see his paintings and those of his wife, Anne, at Skagen Museum, in the Anchers' house, set in the museum garden.

2. Psalm 74:13–14.

3. Ezra Pound, trans., "The Seafarer," lines 17–23. www.americanpoems.com/poets/ezrapound/16182.

4. Séan McGrail, *Ancient Boats in North-West Europe: The Archaeology of Water Transport to AD 1500* (New York: Longman, 1987), was the source of this section.

5. Martin Carver, *Sutton Hoo: A Seventh-Century Princely Burial Ground and Its Context* (London: British Museum Press and the Society of Antiquaries, 2005), is the definitive monograph. The same author's *Sutton Hoo: Burial Place of Kings?* (London: British Museum Press, 2000), is a more popular account.

6. The controversy over the sailing qualities (if any) of the Sutton Hoo ship is unresolved. Any resolution will probably have to await the building of a full-size replica. But, as Martin Carver has pointed out in an e-mail to the author, the lack of a keel makes hulls like this one susceptible to capsizing, something he experienced firsthand in a replica of the Oseberg ship. For the sea trials, see E. Gifford and J. Gifford, "The Sailing Performance of Anglo-Saxon Ships as Derived from the Building and Trials of Half-Scale Models of the Sutton Hoo and Graveney Ship Finds," *Mariner's Mirror* 82(2) (1996): 131–53.

7. Seamus Heaney, *Beowulf: A New Verse Translation* (New York: W. W. Norton, 2000), p. 5.

8. These paragraphs draw on Ole Crumlin-Pedersen, *Archaeology and the Sea in Scandinavia and Britain* (Roskilde, Denmark: Viking Ship Museum, 2010), chap. 6.

9. Quoted in ibid., p. 81.

10. Ibid., pp. 83–85, 112.

11. Janet Bately and Anton Englkert, eds., *Ohthere's Voyages* (Roskilde, Denmark: Viking Ship Museum, 2007).

12. Quotes in this paragraph from ibid., pp. 44–45.

13. Quotes in this paragraph from Merja-Liisa Hinkkanen and David Kirby, *The Baltic and North Seas* (London: Routledge, 2000), p. 39.

14. Crumlin-Pederson, *Archaeology*, chap. 4, describes these developments and events.

15. M. O. H. Carver, "Pre-Viking Traffic in the North Sea," in Seán McGrail, *Maritime Celts, Frisians, and Saxons* (Bootham, UK: Council for British Archaeology, 1990), pp. 117–25.

16. This passage based on Leif K. Karlson, *Secrets of the Norse Navigators* (Seattle: One Earth Press, 2003). Quote from p. 59.

17. Guy Ropars et al., "A Depolarizer as a Possible Precise Sunstone for Viking Navigation by Polarized Light," *Proceedings of the Royal Society A.*, published online November 2, 2011, doi: 10.1098/rspa.2011.0369.

18. Quoted in Magnus Magnusson, ed., *The Vinland Sagas: The Norse Discovery of America* (Baltimore: Pelican Books, 1965), p. 15.

The Pacific to the West

1. Quoted from Ivan Veniaminov's notes, in Ales Hrdlicka, *The Aleutian and Commander Islands and Their Inhabitants* (Philadelphia: Wistar Institute, 1945), p. 15.

Chapter 12: The Aleutians:
"The Sea Becomes Very High"

1. Hydrographer of the Navy, *Ocean Passages for the World*, 3rd ed. (Taunton, UK: Ministry of Defense, 1973). Quote from p. 96.

2. Lucien M. Turner, *An Aleutian Ethnography*, ed. Raymond L. Hudson (Anchorage: University of Alaska Press, 2008); quote from p. 53. See also Waldemar Jochelson, *History, Ethnology and Anthropology of the Aleut* (Salt Lake City: University of Utah Press, 2002).

3. George Dyson, *Baidarka* (Seattle: University of Washington Press, 1986), is the definitive source on Aleutian kayaks. Steller quote from pp. 8–9. The controversies surrounding the first settlement of the Americas will never die down. For a recent assessment, see David Meltzer, *First Peoples in a New World* (Berkeley: University of California Press, 2008).

4. See Jon Erlandson et al., "The Kelp Highway Hypothesis: Marine Ecology, the Coastal Migration Theory, and the Peopling of the Americas," *The Journal of Island and Coastal Archaeology* 2(2) (2007): 161–74.

5. Jean Aigner, "The Unifacial, Core, and Blade Site on Anangula Island, Aleutians," *Arctic Anthropology* 7(2) (1970), pp. 59–88.

6. Turner, *Ethnography*, pp. 65–67.

7. Quoted in Dyson, *Baidarka*, pp. 29–30.

8. Quoted in Dyson, *Baidarka*, p. 30.

9. The Aleuts also built double- and triple-cockpit boats. The former may have been used before the arrival of the Russians, but the triple design was a post-

contact innovation that allowed the carrying of a passenger amidships, or even lying full-length inside the hull.

10. Eli L. Higgins, *Kodiak and Afognak Life, 1868–70,* ed. Richard A. Pierce (Kingston, ON: Limestone Press, 1981), p. 24.

11. Herbert D. G. Maschner et al., "Did the Northern Pacific Ecosystem Collapse in AD 1250?" in Herbert Maschner et al., eds., *The Northern World AD 900–1400: The Dynamics of Climate, Economy, and Politics in Hemispheric Perspective* (Salt Lake City: University of Utah Press, 2008), pp. 33–58.

12. Quoted in Dyson, *Baidarka,* pp. 53–54.

13. Quote from ibid., pp. 55–56.

14. Description and quote from ibid., pp. 64–65.

15. Regrettably, Pinart's manuscripts are still unpublished. Description and quote from ibid., p. 72.

16. Letter from Baranov to G. I. Shelikhov, May 20, 1795; quoted in ibid., p. 32.

Chapter 13: Raven Releases the Fish

1. Kenneth M. Ames and Herbert D. G. Maschner, *Peoples of the Northwest Coast: Their Archaeology and Prehistory* (London and New York: Thames and Hudson, 1999), offers an excellent general description of the Northwest Coast.

2. J. C. Beaglehole, *The Journals of Captain James Cook on His Voyage of Discovery,* vol. 2: *The Voyage of the Resolution and Discovery, 1776–1780.* (Cambridge: Cambridge University Press, 1968), p. 274.

3. Ames and Maschner, *Peoples,* chaps. 3 and 4.

4. Julian Raban, *Passage to Juneau: A Sea and Its Meanings* (New York: Pantheon, 1999).

5. Frederica de Laguna, *Under Mount Elias: The History and Culture of the Yukatat Tlingit* (Washington, DC: Smithsonian Institution Press, 1972), p. 794.

6. This passage is based on David Neel, *The Great Canoes* (Seattle: University of Washington Press, 1995), which describes both traditional canoes and the modern revival in Northwest seafaring.

7. De Laguna, *Mount Elias,* pp. 455–56.

8. Hilary Stewart, *Indian Fishing* (Seattle: University of Washington Press, 1977), p. 13. Stewart provides a well-illustrated account of Northwest Coast fishing methods and catches.

9. A popular account of Makah whale hunting and of the spectacular Ozette

archaeological site, which chronicles ancient society along this stretch of coast: Ruth Kirk, *Hunters of the Whale* (New York: William Morrow, 1974).

10. Richard Gould. "Seagoing Canoes Among the Indians of Northwestern California," *Ethnohistory* 15(1) (1968): 11–42.

11. This passage is based on Brian Fagan, *Before California* (Walnut Creek, CA: Altamira Press, 2003), chaps. 10–12.

12. The Smithsonian Institution anthropologist John Peabody Harrington compiled detailed notes on the construction and paddling of the Chumash *tomol*, published in Travis Hudson, Janice Timbrook, and Melissa Rempe, *Tomol: Chumash Watercraft as Described in the Ethnographic Notes of John P. Harrington* (Los Altos and Santa Barbara, CA: Ballena Press and Santa Barbara Museum of Natural History, 1978). Juan Crespi quote: Herbert E. Bolton, ed., *Fray Juan Crespi: Missionary Explorer on the Pacific Coast, 1769–1774* (Berkeley: University of California Press, 1927), p. 38.

13. Hudson et al., *Tomol*, p. 66.

14. Jeanne Arnold, *Origins of a Pacific Chiefdom* (Salt Lake City: University of Utah Press, 2001), describes these complex developments.

Chapter 14: The Fiery Pool and the Spiny Oyster

1. Dennis Tedlock, *Popol Vuh: The Mayan Book of the Dawn of Life* (New York: Touchstone Books, 1996). Quotes from pp. 64–65.

2. Daniel Finamore and Stephen D. Houston, eds., *The Fiery Pool: The Maya and the Mythic Sea* (New Haven, CT: Yale University Press and the Peabody Essex Museum, 2010), defines the Fiery Pool. "To eat men" quote: Ralph L. Roys, trans., *Book of Chilam Balam of Chumayel* (Norman: University of Oklahoma Press, 1967), p. 95.

3. Described by Mary E. Miller and Megan O'Neil, "The World of the Ancient Maya and the Worlds They Made," in Daniel and Houston, *The Fiery Pool*, pp. 24–36.

4. Marc Zender, "The Music of Shells," in Finamore and Houston, *The Fiery Pool*, pp. 83–85.

5. Hernán Cortés, *Letters from Mexico*, trans. Anthony Pagden (New York: Grossman Publishers, 1971), p. 126.

6. Samuel Eliot Morison, ed. and trans., *Journals and Other Documents of the Life and Voyages of Christopher Columbus* (New York: Heritage Press, 1963). Quotes in this paragraph from p. 325.

7. This passage draws on Daniel Finamore, "Navigating the Maya World," in Finamore and Houston, *The Fiery Pool*, pp. 144–59.

8. J. E. S. Thompson, "Canoes and Navigation of the Maya and Their Neighbours," *Journal of the Royal Anthropological Institute* 79(1/2) (1949): 69–78.

9. Robert C. West, "Aboriginal Sea Navigation Between Middle and South America," *American Anthropologist* 63(1) (1961), p. 133.

10. The definitive work on Andean watercraft: Clinton R. Edwards, *Aboriginal Watercraft on the Pacific Coast of South America* (Berkeley: University of California Press, 1965), upon which this passage is based. Quotes in this paragraph from a superb analysis of Andean rafts, upon which my discussion of rafts is based: Lesley Dewan and Dorothy Hosler, "Ancient Maritime Trade on Balsa Rafts: An Engineering Analysis of Balsa Raft Functionality and Design," *Journal of Anthropological Research* 64 (2008): 19–140. Quotes from pp. 59, 70.

11. Dewan and Hosler, "Ancient Maritime Trade," is the basis for this analysis. For a modern-day adventurer's (disastrous) forays, in a book that includes, among other things, a discussion of asphalt coatings: John Haslett, *Voyage of the Manteño* (New York: St. Martin's Press, 2006).

12. Quoted in Edwards, *Aboriginal Watercraft*, p. 71.

13. Allison C. Paulson, "The Thorny Oyster and the Voice of God: *Spondylus* and *Strombus* in Andean Prehistory," *American Antiquity* 39(4) (1974): 597–607. Also see Mary Glowacki, "Food of the Gods or Mere Mortals? Hallucinogenic *Spondylus* and Its Interpretive Implications for Early Andean Society," *Antiquity* 79(1) (2005): 257–68; and Marissa Cevallos, "3,000-year-old Conch Trumpets Play Again," *Wired Science* blog, November 19, 2010, and www.wired.com/wiredscience/2010/11/conch-trumpets-peru.

14. Dorothy Hosler, *The Sounds and Colors of Power: The Metallurgical Technology of Ancient West Mexico* (Cambridge, MA: MIT Press, 1994). See also the same author's "The Metallurgy of West Mexico: Revisited and Revised," *Journal of World Prehistory* 122(1) (2008): 185–212.

Epilogue: Of Fish and Portolans

1. Ernest K. Gann, *Song of the Sirens* (New York: Jove, 1968), p. 3.

2. Joshua Slocum, *Sailing Alone Around the World* (New York: The Century Company, 1900), p. 146.

3. Slocum, *Sailing Alone*, p. 145.

4. Maurice Griffiths, *The First of the Tide* (Greenwich, UK: Conway Maritime Press, 1979), p. 69.

5. Fernand Braudel, *The Mediterranean and the Mediterranean World in the Age of Philip II* (Berkeley: University of California Press, 1996), p. 103.

6. Ibid.

7. David Childs and HRH the Prince of Wales, *The Warship* Mary Rose*: The Life and Times of King Henry VIII's Flagship* (London: Chatham Publishing, 2007).

8. Brian Fagan, *Fish on Friday: Feasting, Fasting and the Discovery of the New World* (New York: Basic Books, 2006), covers the events outlined in these paragraphs.

9. Ibid., p. 163.

10. Mark Kurlansky, *Cod: A Biography of the Fish That Changed the World* (New York: Penguin, 1998).

11. Pierre Loti, *An Icelandic Fisherman* (Alhambra, CA: Braun, 1957), p. 8.

12. Pamela O. Long, David McGee, and Alan M. Stahl, *The Book of Michael of Rhodes: A Fifteenth-Century Maritime Manuscript*, vol. 2: *Transcription and Translation* (Cambridge, MA: MIT Press, 2009), p. 279.

13. E. G. R. Taylor, *The Haven-Finding Art: A History of Navigation from Odysseus to Captain Cook* (New York: American Elsevier, 1971). Quotes in this paragraph from pp. 131–36.

14. John Smith, *A Description of New England* (Boston: W. Veazie, 1865), p. 3.

15. *Sailing Directions for the English Channel* (London: Hydrographic Office, 1835), p. 122.

Index

A Note on the Author

Brian Fagan is emeritus professor of anthropology at the University of California, Santa Barbara. Born in England, he did fieldwork in Africa and has written about North American and world archaeology and many other topics. His books on the interaction of climate and human society have established him as the leading authority on the subject, and he lectures frequently around the world. He is the editor of *The Oxford Companion to Archaeology* and the author of *Elixir*; *Cro-Magnon*; *The Great Warming*; *Fish on Friday: Feasting, Fasting and the Discovery of the New World*; *The Little Age*; and *The Long Summer*; among many other titles.